Architecture of Bali

A sourcebook of traditional and modern forms

Any copy of this book issued by the publisher
as a paperback is sold subject to the condition
that it shall not by way of trade or otherwise be
lent, resold, hired out or otherwise circulated
without the publisher's prior consent in any form
of binding or cover other than that in which
it is published and without a similar condition
including these words being imposed on a
subsequent purchaser.

First published in the United Kingdom in 2003
by Thames & Hudson Ltd, 181A High Holborn,
London WC1V 7QX

© 2002 Editions Didier Millet
Text: © Made Wijaya (Michael White) 2002

All Rights Reserved. No part of this publication
may be reproduced or transmitted in any form
or by any means, electronic or mechanical,
including photocopy, recording or any other
information storage and retrieval system, without
prior permission in writing from the publisher.

British Library Cataloguing-in-Publication Data
A catalogue record for this book is available
from the British Library

ISBN 0-500-34192-3

Printed in Singapore
by Star Standard Industries (Pte) Ltd

*Page 1: A coastal-style low coral gate at
Pura Ratu Agung temple, Suwung Gede.*

*Page 6: Maria Grazzia's beautifully
detailed* petit palais *in Batujimbar, built
in the heyday of the Dream Home
movement. (Designer: Carlo Pessina).*

*Page 7: Statues of the goddess of the
arts, Saraswati—also known as Sang
Hyang Aji, patron saint of architects
and designers—adorn many gardens
and family house shrines in Bali.*

*Page 8: A bird's-eye view of an
idealised Balinese village shows
the traditional layout.*

MADE WIJAYA

Architecture of Bali
*A sourcebook of traditional
and modern forms*

Thames & Hudson

Contents

Preface 7
Acknowledgements 9

1 THE BALINESE VILLAGE 12
1.1 From the Mountains to the Coast 14
1.2 Traditional Public Buildings 18
1.3 Village-style Hotels 20

2 THE COURTYARD 24
2.1 Temple Courtyards 26
2.2 Traditional House Compounds 30
2.3 Palaces 32
2.4 Palace-style Hotels 34
2.5 Modern House Compounds 36
2.6 Courtyard Gardens 38

3 *BALE*: THE PAVILION 44
3.1 Types of Pavilions 46
3.2 Enclosed and Semi-enclosed Pavilions 50
3.3 Pavilion Roof Forms 54
3.4 Shrine Pavilions 56
3.5 Traditional Forms in Modern Houses 58

4 COURTYARD ELEMENTS 62
4.1 Walls 64
4.2 Gates 68
4.3 Terracing, Gate Steps and *Leneng* 74
4.4 Ground Surfaces 78
4.5 Organizing Space in a Courtyard 80

5 PAVILION ELEMENTS 84
5.1 Basic Pavilion Construction 86
5.2 Bases and Foundations 90
5.3 Steps 92
5.4 Post Bases 94
5.5 Columns, Beams and Buttresses 96
5.6 Built-in Platforms 102
5.7 Walls and Screens 106
5.8 Doors 110
5.9 Windows and Air Vents 112
5.10 Roofs and King Posts 114
5.11 Organizing Space in Traditional Pavilions 118
5.12 Storage 120
5.13 Dividing Space in Modern Pavilions 122

6 BUILDING MATERIALS — 132

    6.1   Timber — 134
    6.2   Bamboo — 136
    6.3   Thatch — 140
    6.4   Temporary Architecture — 144
    6.5   Stone — 148
    6.6   *Paras* — 152
    6.7   Coral and Limestone — 156
    6.8   Earth and Brick — 158
    6.9   Terracotta and Terrazzo — 160
    6.10 Cement and Plaster — 162
    6.11 Ceramic — 164

7 ORNAMENTATION — 168

    7.1   *Paras* Carving — 170
    7.2   Brick and *Paras* — 174
    7.3   Stone Air Vents — 176
    7.4   Balustrades and Railings — 178
    7.5   Woven Elements and Cloth — 180
    7.6   Carved Wood — 182
    7.7   Colour — 188
    7.8   Statuary — 190
    7.9   Boma and Sai — 194

8 ARCHITECTURAL HYBRIDS — 200

    8.1   Early Modern Hybrids — 202
    8.2   Chinese Influence — 206
    8.3   Javanese Influence — 208
    8.4   Late Modern Hybrids — 210

Map of Bali — 216
Glossary of Terms — 218
Picture Credits — 220
References — 221
Index — 222

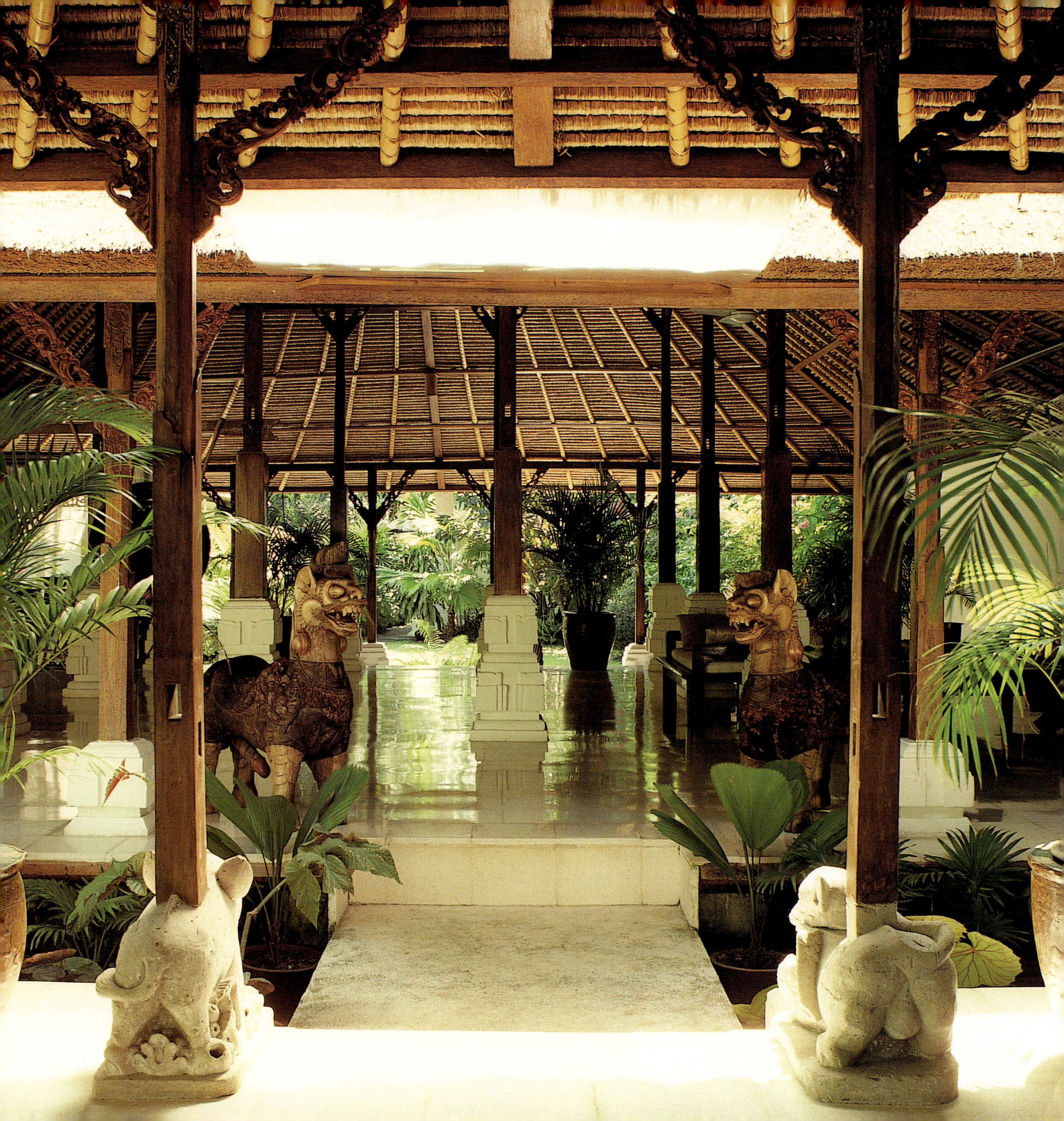

Preface

This book is for lovers of Bali Style and for lovers of Balinese courtyard architecture, that play of roofs and pavilions within a walled garden court.

Classic Balinese architecture is one of the world's great art forms, surviving within a culture keen on adopting the latest trends from overseas. And so it has been ever since the influence of Buddhist priests from eastern Java and traders from southern China turned the humble Balinese *bale*, a pan-Pacific native, into an exotic Indochinese hybrid.

But this book is not about history; it is about built form, an architecture the great ethnographer Miguel Covarrubias called "a masterpiece of simplicity, ingenuity and good taste". A Balinese temple carver once told me: "If it's worth doing, it's worth doing beautifully." This is apparent in the island's more than 60,000 temples, 500,000 shrines and other sacred structures. It has also been the guiding principle of many tropical architectural greats who did some of their best work in Bali before moving on: top international architects such as Geoffrey Bawa, Peter Muller and Kerry Hill, and interior designers such as Jaya Ibrahim, Ed Tuttle and Terry Fripp, to name a few.

Bali is now home to a full complement of furniture designers, lighting consultants, bamboo queens, landscape designers, industrial designers, ceramic artists and painting specialists who, together with the local artisans, complete a constellation of design talent that few Southeast Asian capitals can match. And Bali is by no means your typical Asian hub. It is still a thriving medieval culture (complete with god-kings and feisty feudalism) which annually absorbs the effects of two million tourists.

The word Bali is synonymous with beauty—of culture, of spirit and of form. The term Bali Style is synonymous with a trend in modern tropical architecture for an open and natural pavilion style. For that reason, I've included many references to exciting developments in modern Balinese architecture. Many have failed in this area: the streets of Kuta-Legian-Seminyak-Ubud-Sanur are littered with the corpses of bad architectural ideas appallingly rehashed. Mannerism now reigns supreme where once an almost Japanese sense of restraint held court.

Modern Balinese architecture started after the full establishment of the Dutch colonial administration in the early 20th century, when architectonic Art Deco became synonymous with nationalism. Not all modern trends have been hard-edged, though: this book also documents contemporary trends in the gorgeous Rustic Charm, Palazzo Splendido and Expatriate Dream Home movements.

It is mostly the classic golden oldies, however, that are documented in this book. Many have disappeared in the 25 years since I first started recording the island's architecture.

To students of Balinese architecture everywhere I say, gaze upon these lost marvels of a golden civilization devoted to architectural merit. I hope that this book will help remind some, and inform many, of the wonder that is traditional Balinese architecture. It is arguably the most perfect architectural language, in terms of scale, beauty and functionality, that ever evolved in the tropical world.

Bali modernists, this book is for you, too: dig deeper into the Balinese treasure-trove of built form and pure proportions, that Lego box of the luscious, for pared down and seamless solutions.

Most of all, I hope this book inspires the nascent Baliophile or tepid tropical architect to be as bold as the Balinese of old were, with their full integration of architecture, landscape and way of life.

Made Wijaya

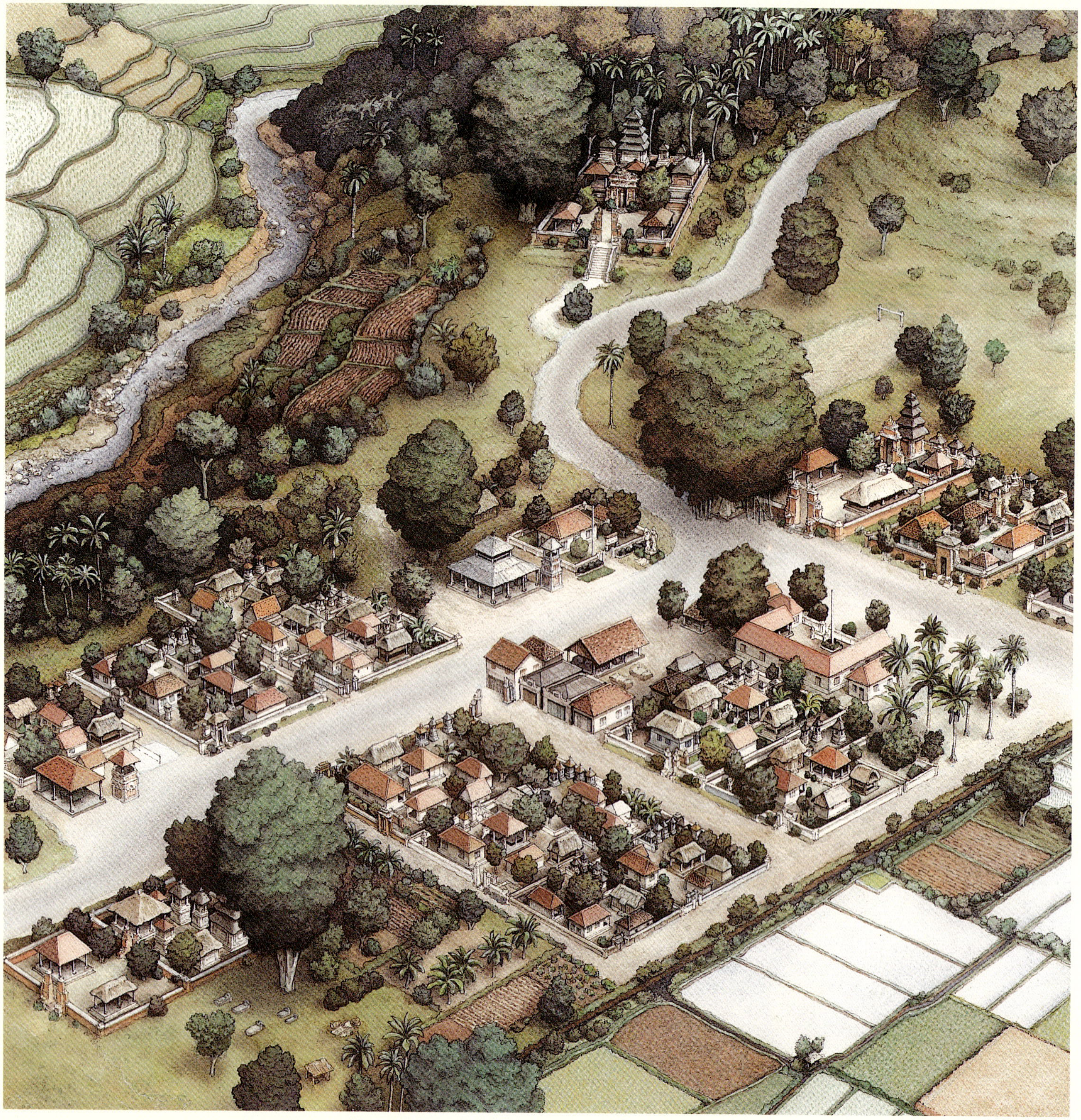

Acknowledgements

Over 20 years in the making, this book has been through numerous incarnations. The first was an article in the *Sunday Bali Post* entitled "Gems of Modern Balinese Architecture today—a lament" which was typed on the *Bali Post*'s old Remington Rand by Sarita Newson and let through by the then editor, Rio "Bali Style" Helmi.

As a colonial administrator with a passion for traditional architecture, I have often had the occasion to press people into service. In 1982, for example, a band of architecture students from Sydney University were fed chips in exchange for a quite comprehensive survey of the island's architecture which became the nucleus for this book. The glint of official recognition afforded by this tutorial programme helped me, a year later, in securing the services of Kristina Melcher, then U.S. Consular agent, to do more typing and pasting.

This book's immediate predecessor, *Balinese Architecture: towards an Encyclopedia—the photocopy*, first published by Super Express photocopy house of Jakarta in 1983, was thus created. A companion volume, *Statues of Bali*, inspired by writer-photographer Tim Street-Porter's book *Interiors* (1969), was published simultaneously. To this day P.D. Super Express is still churning out fat photocopies, which are lovingly bound by Sarita Newson's merry widows at Saritaksu, in Sanur. God bless you all.

During the 1980s, various publishing czars—Paul Hamlyn, Kevin Weldon, Hans Hoefer, to name a few—passed on the opportunity to publish, properly, my collection of essays and photographs, but encouraged me to continue my one-man rogue publishing efforts. Over the years the encyclopedia in embryo was enriched by images from photographer Tim Street-Porter and artists Peter Kingston and Stephen Little. Annual sorties into the Balinese countryside with Annie Kelly and Tim Street-Porter during the years 1983 to 1997 provided many photographs for this book: their enthusiasm for my project over the years has been unstinting. Thank you. To Soedarmadji Damais, my mentor in all Indonesian cultural matters, and to John Darling, my role model for redhead survival in Bali, a big *terima kasih* for your decades of encouragement.

In 1997, friends Maggie and James Dallmeyer led me to Editions Didier Millet where I found comfort from decades on the battlefield of the Southeast Asian properties sector. A book, *Tropical Garden Design*, and an option to co-publish this book, ensued. Finding Didier and Marie Claude Millet and their wonderful team at EDM was a gift from Bali's gods.

This book would not have been possible without the assistance of three angels: this book's consulting editor, Diana Darling; Carole Muller, who was consulted on all matters architectural, historical and ethnographic; and Shan Wolody, the book's managing editor, who, despite having never been to Bali, displayed great understanding. Thank you.

To Chang Huai-Yan, who acted as project co-ordinator and artist, together with Deni Chung in Bali, I am deeply indebted. Likewise, to my long-suffering staff in Bali: Sri Sudewi, Agus Ferry Setiawan, Putu Semiade, Kadek Wirawan, Nuraji, Agung Chandra, Yudi and Made Kader, my driver and collaborator since 1979. Tjok Oka from Guwang was very helpful during my research in that village. Drs. I Gusti Ngurah Oka Supartha and Wayan Surpha must be thanked for their learned advice. Mark Keating of P.T. Bale Gede was most helpful with research on building terminology. To Ms Yang Tong Wah at the Dorothy Pritzler Collection (ISEAS, Singapore) I extend gratitude for giving my research slides a safe home.

Special thanks to Fairuz bin Salleh for support services and cash advances in Singapore, and to Tim Street-Porter, Rio Helmi, Caroline Younger, Claude Vanheye, Luc Bouchage, Luca Invernizzi Tettoni, Tan Hock Beng and Bali Photo Studio for permission to reproduce their beautiful photographs. Thanks also to the trustees of the Arnott Estate for permission to reproduce the paintings by Donald Friend, to Christie's Singapore for the Adrien Jean Le Mayeur de Merprès painting, to Yu-Chee Chong for the Thilly Weissenborn photographs, and to Albert Beaucourt for the Ida Bagus Nyoman Rai painting.

To regional architects Peter Muller, Kerry Hill, Cheong Yew Kuan, Anak Agung Yokasara, Hendro Hadiprana, Grounds Kent Architects, Palmer and Turner, Ernesto Bedmar, Atelier 6, Terry Fripp and Chan Soo Khian, I offer my gratitude for permission to use images of your inspiring work. Legions of Balinese architects and artisans, responsible for most of the work in this book, must be acknowledged too. I will start with thanks to my associates, Ir. Gusti Sarjana and Drs. Nyoman Miyoga, who have been unflinching in their devotion to the conservation of Balinese architecture and landscape design, as have my earlier collaborators, I Wayan Lagawa, Dewa Putu Sedana and Dewa Made Mudita. All are still working to uphold Bali's tradition of design excellence. Special thanks to local hero and environmental activist Drs. Putu Suasta who protected me from predators during the 1990s and to Akhmad Yani, my anchor.

Special, special thanks to EDM's Singapore team, especially designer Annie Teo, who were a joy to work with, as ever.

"The village is a unified organism in which every individual is a corpuscle and every institution an organ. The heart of the village is the central square, invariably located in the centre of the village, the intersection of the two main avenues … the crossroads are a magic spot of great importance."

Miguel Covarrubias, artist and anthropologist, on the Balinese village in *Island of Bali*, 1937.

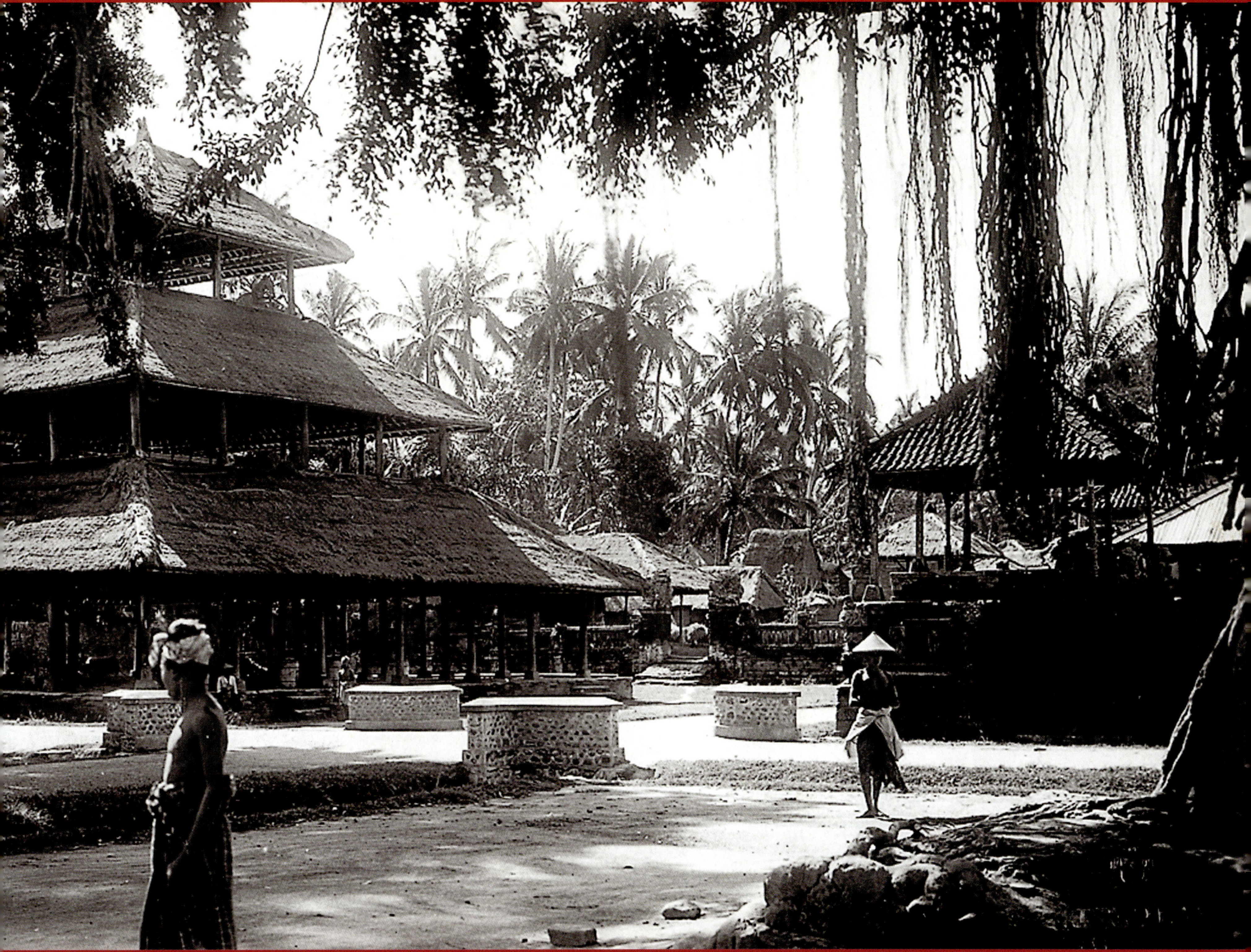

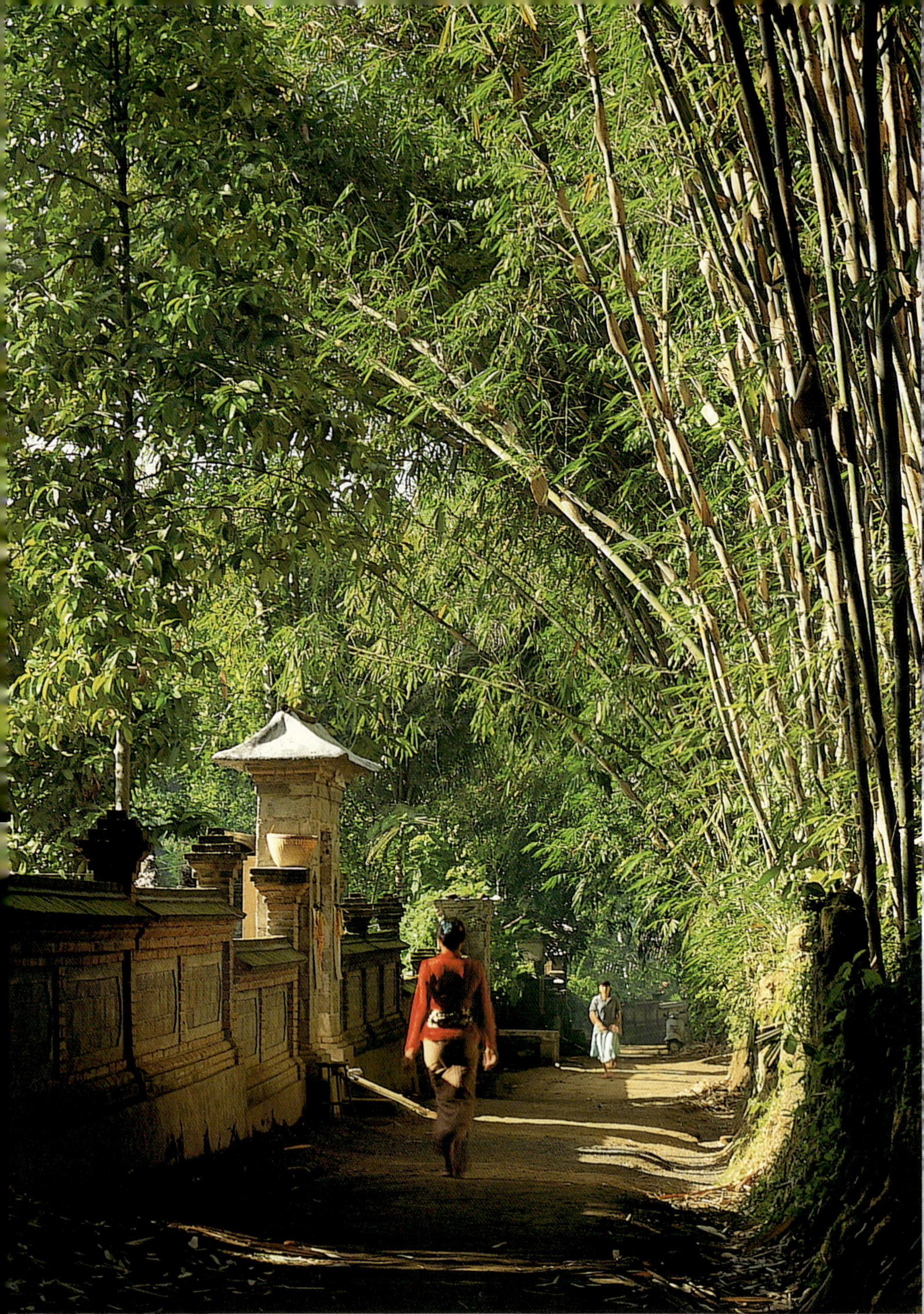
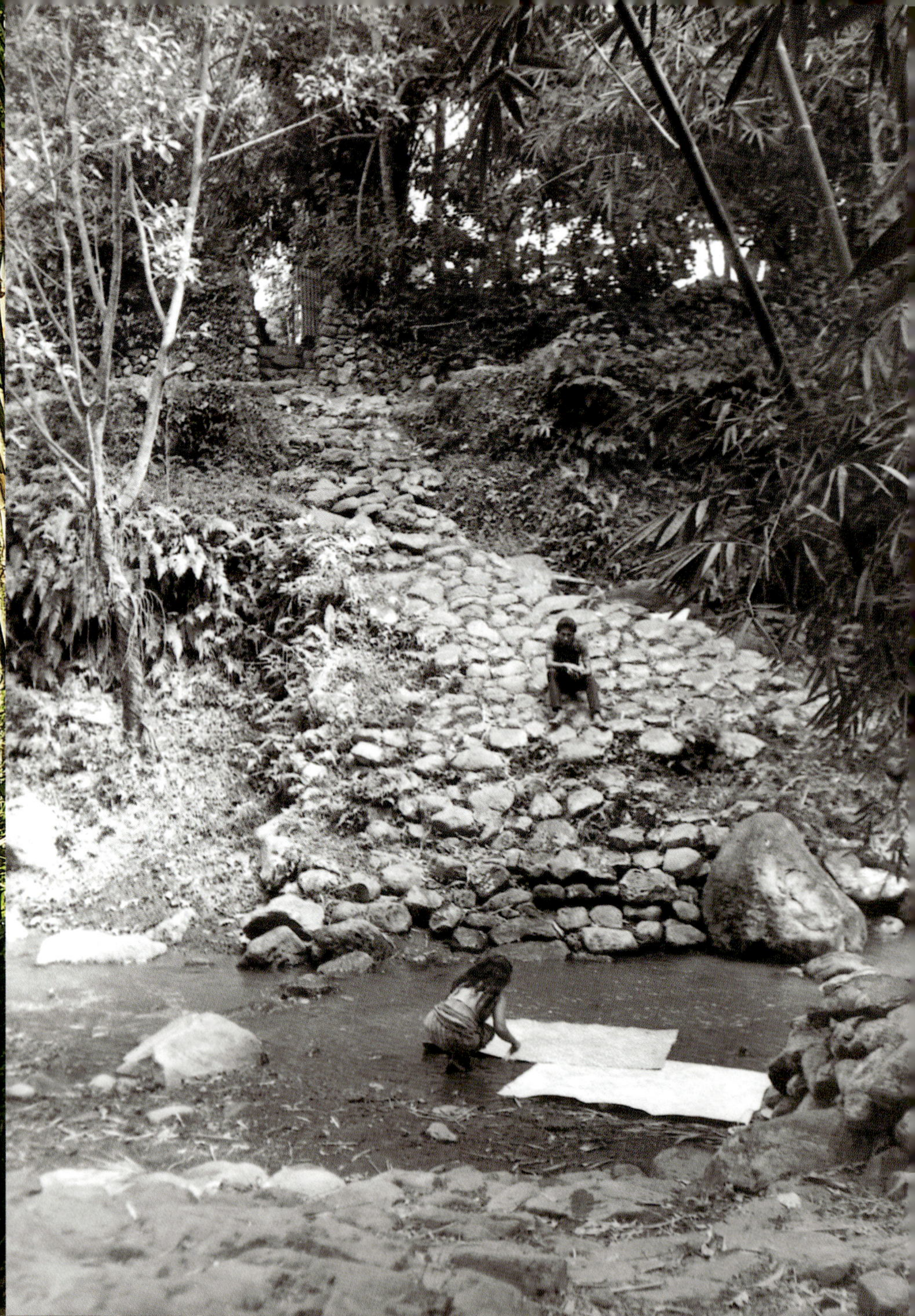
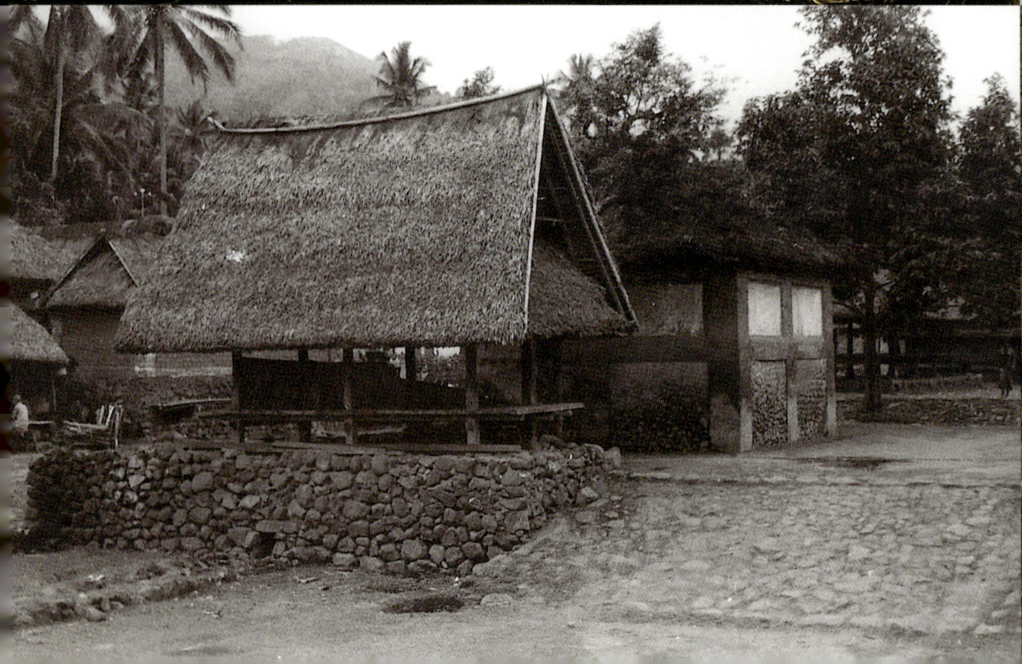
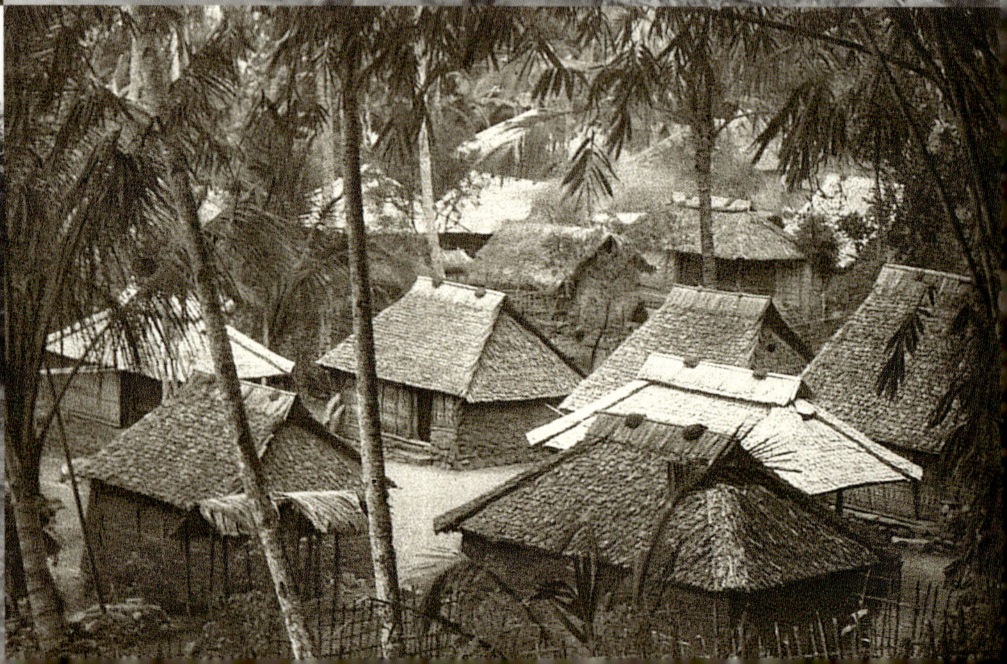

CHAPTER 1

THE BALINESE VILLAGE

1.1	From the Mountains to the Coast	14
1.2	Traditional Public Buildings	18
1.3	Village-style Hotels	20

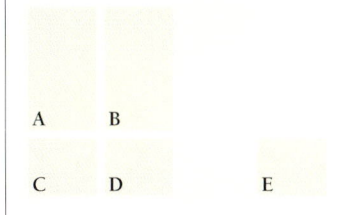

The Balinese Village

Old mountain villages are aligned with their heads (holy springs, temples of origin, chief's house) towards the holy mountain and their legs (graveyard, temples of death) towards the sea. They are generally linear in form: many have spine-like ceremonial long-houses running down their central axes.

On the fertile plains and on the coast the ancient linear Bali Aga (the aboriginal Balinese) style has, particularly since the Majapahit era (15th century), grown into a matrix of walled compounds, with the market at the crossroads or on a common-like village square, called *bancingah*. Starting in the 10th century, when the Javanese classic Hindu culture first appeared in Balinese history, larger villages grew palaces and a trinity of temples to the gods Brahma, Shiva and Wisnu. The traditional Balinese village today is one cohesive unit where temple, people and palace are linked, as they were in medieval Europe.

All villages have sub-village units called *banjar*. Each *banjar* has a community hall (*wantilan*), traditionally a timber building used for village meetings, communal offering-making and preparations for cremations. *Wantilan*, often with their attendant banyan trees, were until recently the most imposing traditional structures on the island. Sadly, few are still constructed in traditional materials except as part of hotels: since the 1970s, Balinese have demanded more permanent concrete structures. Each *wantilan* has a slit-drum tower, called a *kul-kul* tower, for summoning village members. Village graveyards or cremation grounds—open fields between stands of giant trees—are located near the "temple of the dead", the *pura prajapati*, which generally signals the seaward (*kelod*) end of a village proper.

Some mountain villages—and one thinks here of Bayunggede and Belantih—are mainly rows of steep-pitched cabins with bamboo-shingled roofs. Clan temples, usually small and unobtrusive, are found in the cul-de-sacs that branch off the main axes.

There are many picturesque landscape elements that complete the traditional Balinese village scene: giant banyan trees in the village squares at the crossroads; plumeria and coconut trees along the roadsides, flanking handsome house gates; and, occasionally, communal baths in romantic locations.

Most traditional villages are surrounded by rice fields or, above the padi line, by orchards and pastures.

Preceding pages: 1920 photograph of Gianyar's main palace square with attendant wantilan agung *hall and palace belvedere.*

A. *A village lane in a rural community near Ubud.*

B. *The village laundry in the river that bisects Padangkerta village in the hills near Tirtagangga, eastern Bali.*

C. *Two of the most handsome buildings in Bali—one a communal rice loft and the other a temple to the founding spirits—in the village common in Tenganan, a Bali Aga village in eastern Bali.*

D. *An early 20th-century photograph of a typical highland village in early courtyard configuration i.e. with few compound walls. Note the bamboo-shingled roofs.*

E. *A Vietnamese artist's painting of a tribal village on a lake near Dong S'on in North Vietnam, regarded by some as the cultural homeland of many Balinese customs. The similarity to Bali's ancient villages is striking: compare this image with the photograph of Trunyan village on page 15.*

1.1 From the Mountains to the Coast

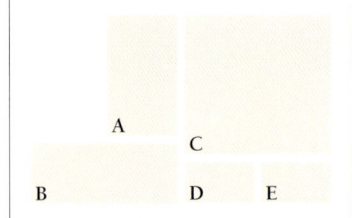

A. Songan village on Lake Batur.
B. Tourist villages of ubiquitous rice lofts converted to boudoirs encroach on the rice fields of Legian-Seminyak.
C. Trunyan village, on Lake Batur.
D. A fairly typical village square off a *pura puseh* temple with attendant roadside kiosk—which is probably a food stall in the morning—in a village near Ubud untouched by main roads.
E. The unique rows of courtyards in Bayunggede village, near Kintamani, Mt Batur.

As one moves from the volcanic highlands of Bali down to the coast, regional variations in village architecture are very pronounced.

The spacious stark villages of the mountain Bali Aga culture, with their rows of timber huts, terraced communal spaces and axial long-houses, are radically different from the cruciform settlement patterns of most coastal villages, with their walled family compounds and imposing public buildings. The lifestyle is more communal in the mountains, and the scale is more human—eaves get closer to the ground as one moves up the volcanic peaks, as do the mountain folk—compared with the more labyrinthine villagescapes and compounds of gentrified pavilions on the coast.

Unfortunately, in coastal Bali the concept of the village lane as the communal living room has disappeared with the encroachment of highways.

In the mountain villages one finds striking simplicity—a more "ethnic" or aboriginal style—in temples and worshipping grounds. On the coast the temple gates are almost gothic, and the temple gardens Indochinese (Oriental-ornamental). Public buildings have become more ornate and less handsome, as more and more villagers leave the rice fields for a suburban lifestyle. Traditional proportions survive, for the most part, in ceremonial buildings, but they are often hard to discern under the veneer of decorative excess.

THE BALINESE VILLAGE → **FROM THE MOUNTAINS TO THE COAST 1.1**

15

16

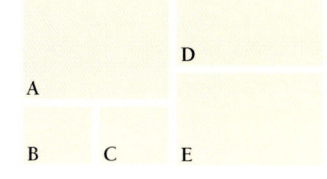

THE BALINESE VILLAGE → **FROM THE MOUNTAINS TO THE COAST 1.1**

	D
A	
B C	E

A. A typical Balinese village surrounded by rice fields. A large subak temple—probably dedicated to the rice goddess Dewi Sri—sits in the middle of the inter-village padi fields. They are called subak temples because they are maintained by agricultural organizations called subak, which regulate the distribution of irrigation waters.

B. Padangkerta village in eastern Bali has many lanes and small plazas that act as communal sitting rooms. In this typical rural village scene, fighting cocks in their distinctive cages are being aired by their masters.

C. Bugbug village, a Bali Aga village in eastern Bali, has a unique tight-packed architectural style: the lava rock house compound walls are often cut into for warung food stalls and other village activity pavilions.

D. A 1918 drawing by Dutch artist W.O.J. Nieuwenkamp of the Bali Aga (mountain Bali) village of Songan, near present day Kintamani.

E. A 1937 drawing by W.O.J. Nieuwenkamp of a typical market scene in a village square in early-20th-century Bali. One can still find such scenes in many villages in Bali today, more or less unchanged.

17

1.2 Traditional Public Buildings

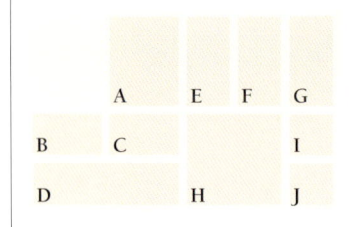

A		E F	G
B	C		I
D		H	J

A. *Interior of a* wantilan *hall outside Tampaksiring temple with unusual bamboo truss work (1989 photo).*

B. *The venerable central communal long pavilion of Tenganan village, eastern Bali.*

C. *The* bale agung *(assembly hall for the gods) in Singapadu village.*

D. *A cross-section and a side elevation of a classic* wantilan. *This type of* wantilan *was often used as a cockfighting hall.*

E. *An ancient form of the village drum tower found throughout the Pacific—a wooden slit-drum in a tree.*

F. *A kul-kul tower in the pagoda style typical of mountain temples.*

G. Kul-kul *towers of this architectural type are common on the corners of many of the island's temples and* banjar *complexes. This tower, built in 1926 in a thoroughly modern style, is near Kerobokan, southern Bali.*

H. *The* bale lantang *(long communal pavilion) at Pura Batu Karo temple in Tabanan Regency (1987 photo).*

I. *The* wantilan *of Sayan (1979 photo).*

J. *In the modern era,* kul-kul *warning drum towers perform their traditional functions with modern systems.*

Traditionally a village centre was "announced" by a large two-tiered pavilion, called a *wantilan*, standing next to a giant banyan tree on the *alun-alun* village square. These handsome big-boned structures with their octagonal or round coconut-wood columns are also found in the palaces and mosques of post-Hindu Java and Madura. They are probably descended from the audience halls, found in exactly the same village hierarchical position, in Sri Lanka and Myanmar. Today they are harder to discern amidst the billboards and art shops.

Temples and palaces are still easily spotted, however, by the drum towers, called *bale kul-kul*, on their village-side corners.

The other imposing secular buildings, the long-houses, are most often found running up the spine of mountain villages. Called *bale lantang,* and used as community halls for village feasts and rites of passage, these are quite distinct from the eight- or 10-post *bale agung*. All these buildings, very much a part of the Balinese village landscape, perform vital functions within both the social (*adat*) and the religious communities.

THE BALINESE VILLAGE → **TRADITIONAL PUBLIC BUILDINGS 1.2**

19

1.3 Village-style Hotels

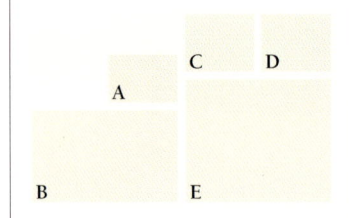

A	C	D
B	E	

A. *Master site plan of the seminal Amandari hotel (Architect: Peter Muller) in Kedewatan, Ubud. The architect's laying out of the village lanes deferred to the existing site topography, and to typical Balinese village streetscapes.*

B. *Canggu Puri Mertha, built in Canggu village in 1997, was inspired by classic 19th-century Balinese villages.*

C. *The village lanes in the Amandari hotel were a collaboration between Carole Muller—who found the camel-hair-coloured paras taro stone—and PT Wijaya Tribwana, which softened Peter Muller's signature Teutonic style.*

D. *A typical villa in the Bali Oberoi hotel. Architect Peter Muller's stylized Balinese house compound was an early trendsetter in the ethnic chic stakes. The corner bale, called a bale patok, is parked in the corner of the compound wall: it was a great success as a dining-cum-lounging pavilion. The swimming pools were added in 1995.*

E. *A guest wing of the Serai hotel in eastern Bali, Kerry Hill Architects' 1995 take on a classic bale agung pavilion. The clever siesta sofas slung over the verandah edges create a friendly, communal feel to the otherwise regimented lines of the building.*

Following pages: In 1994 Hong Kong-based entrepreneur Bradley Gardener had a dream to create a village of Balinese architectural excellence. Architect Cheong Yew Kuan, formerly of Kerry Hill Architects, was chosen to create a series of seven compounds, all different, over a five-year period. The sensational Begawan Giri stretched the envelope of Balinese hotel pavilion design in a most innovative way.

Bali's best traditional-modern hotel architecture—Geoffrey Bawa's Batujimbar Estates buildings; Peter Muller's Bali Oberoi and Amandari hotels; Grounds Kent Architects' Four Seasons Resort, Jimbaran; Kerry Hill's Serai hotel; and Anak Agung Yokasara's Bali Sani Suites—have been inspired by traditional village layouts and structures. These hotels have *wantilan*-like reception halls, village lanes and Balinese gates leading to each villa compound.

Muller wove his love of courtyards into his Bali work: the Bali Oberoi and the Amandari remain, despite many copies, the most elegant of Balinese village-style hotels. Muller also reworked the Balinese house compound, with its individual pavilions, into hotel villas, without losing the flavour of the original.

Above all, these guest artists, with the passion of converts, set their interpretations and stylings into villagescapes that ooze charm. Religious structures were always included in their mixes, as even hotels need temples and villas need spirit houses.

THE BALINESE VILLAGE → **VILLAGE-STYLE HOTELS 1.3**

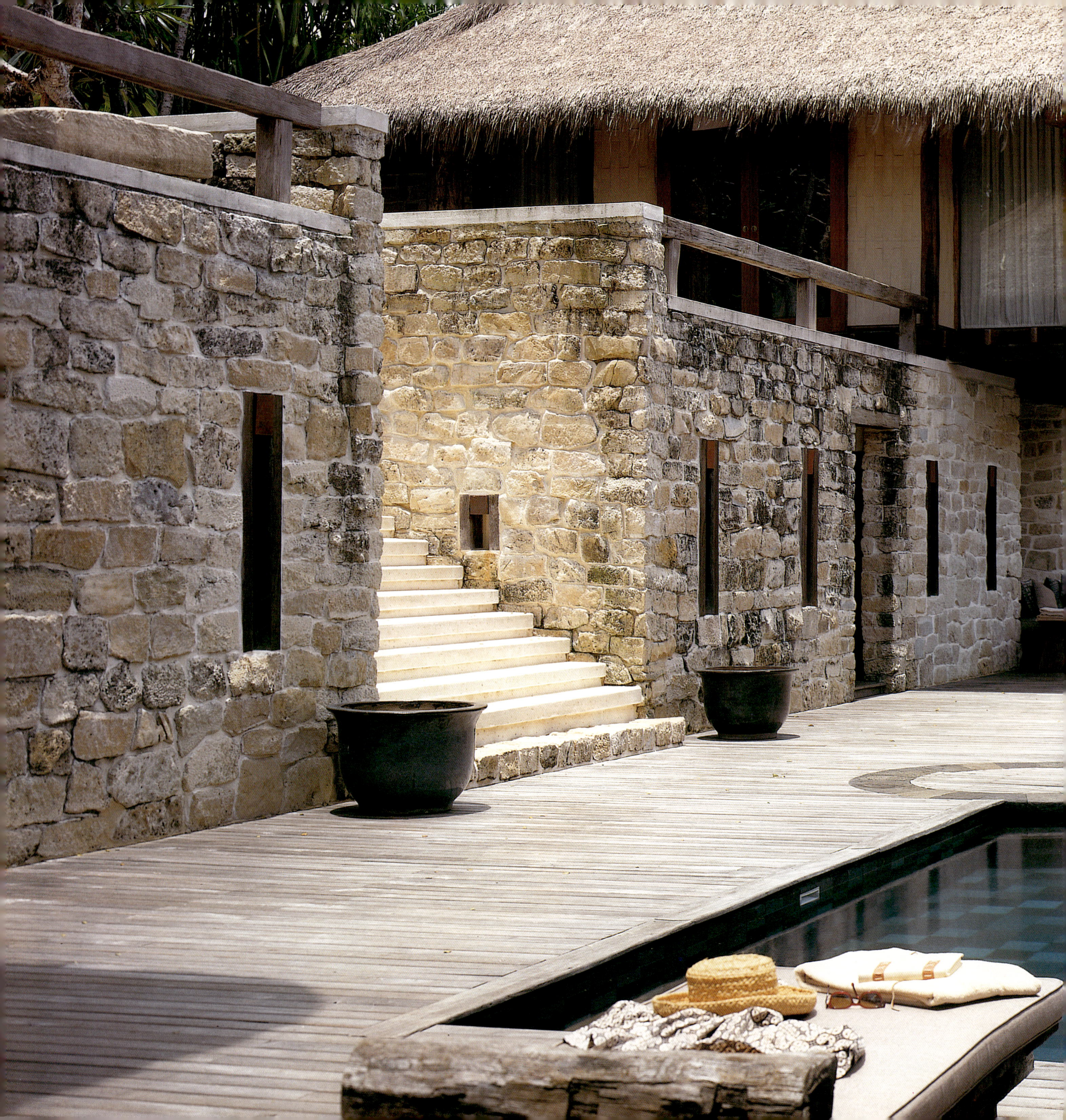

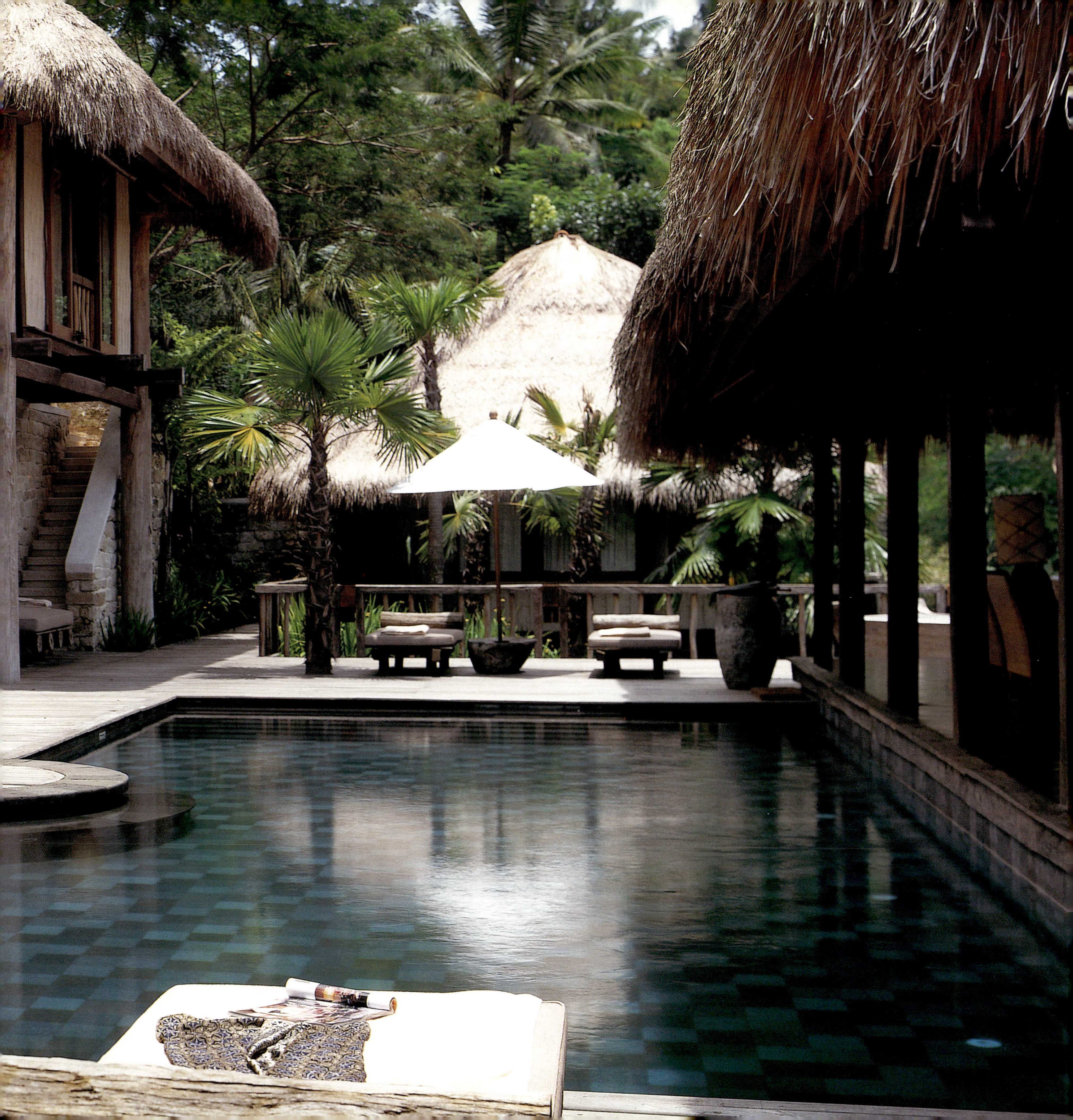

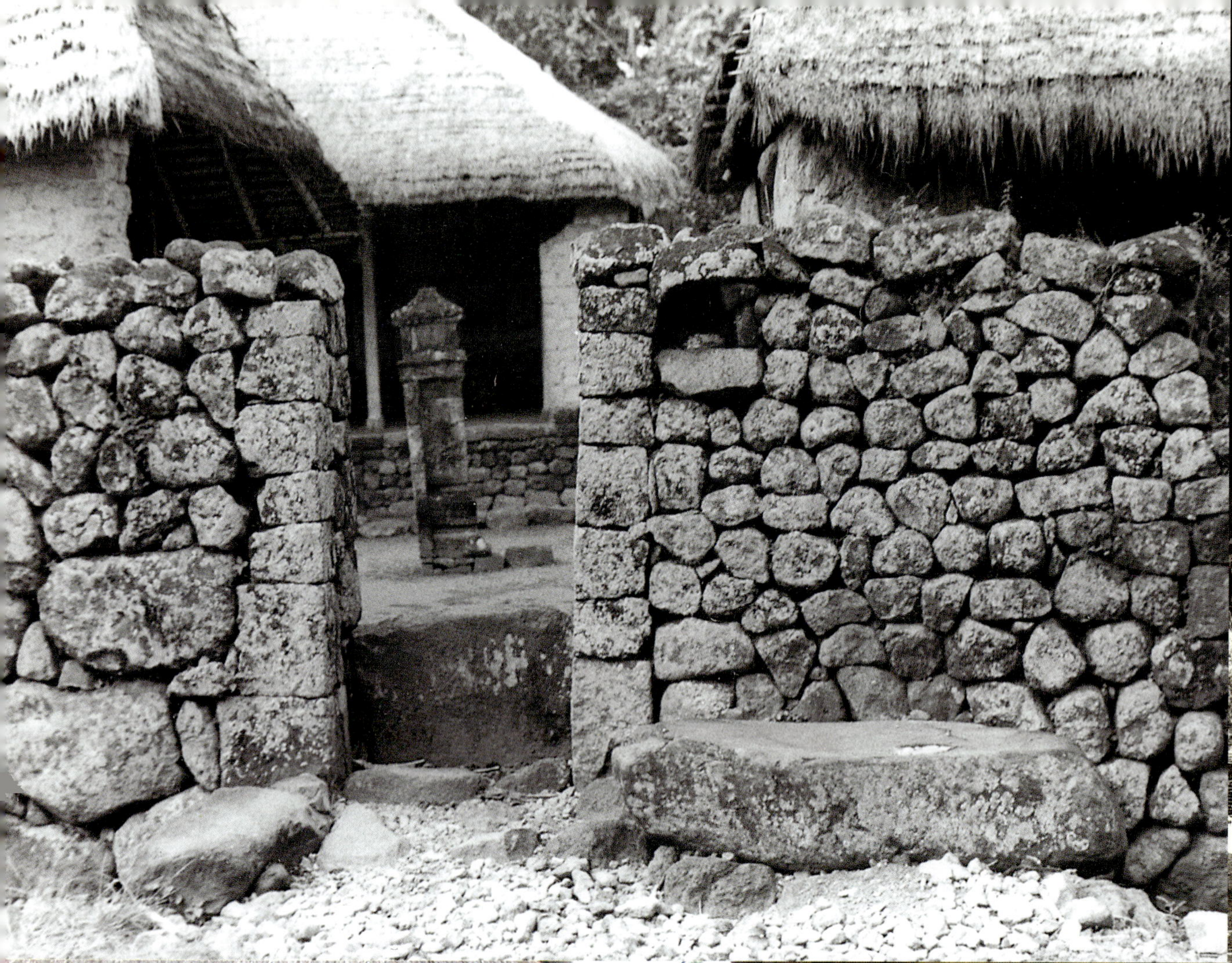

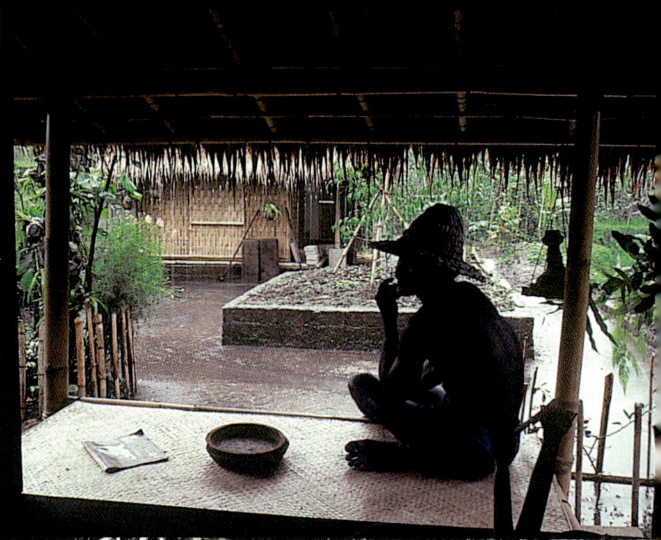

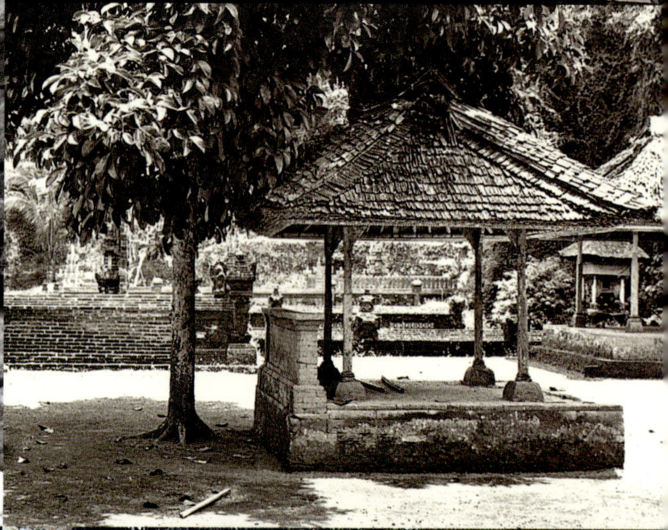

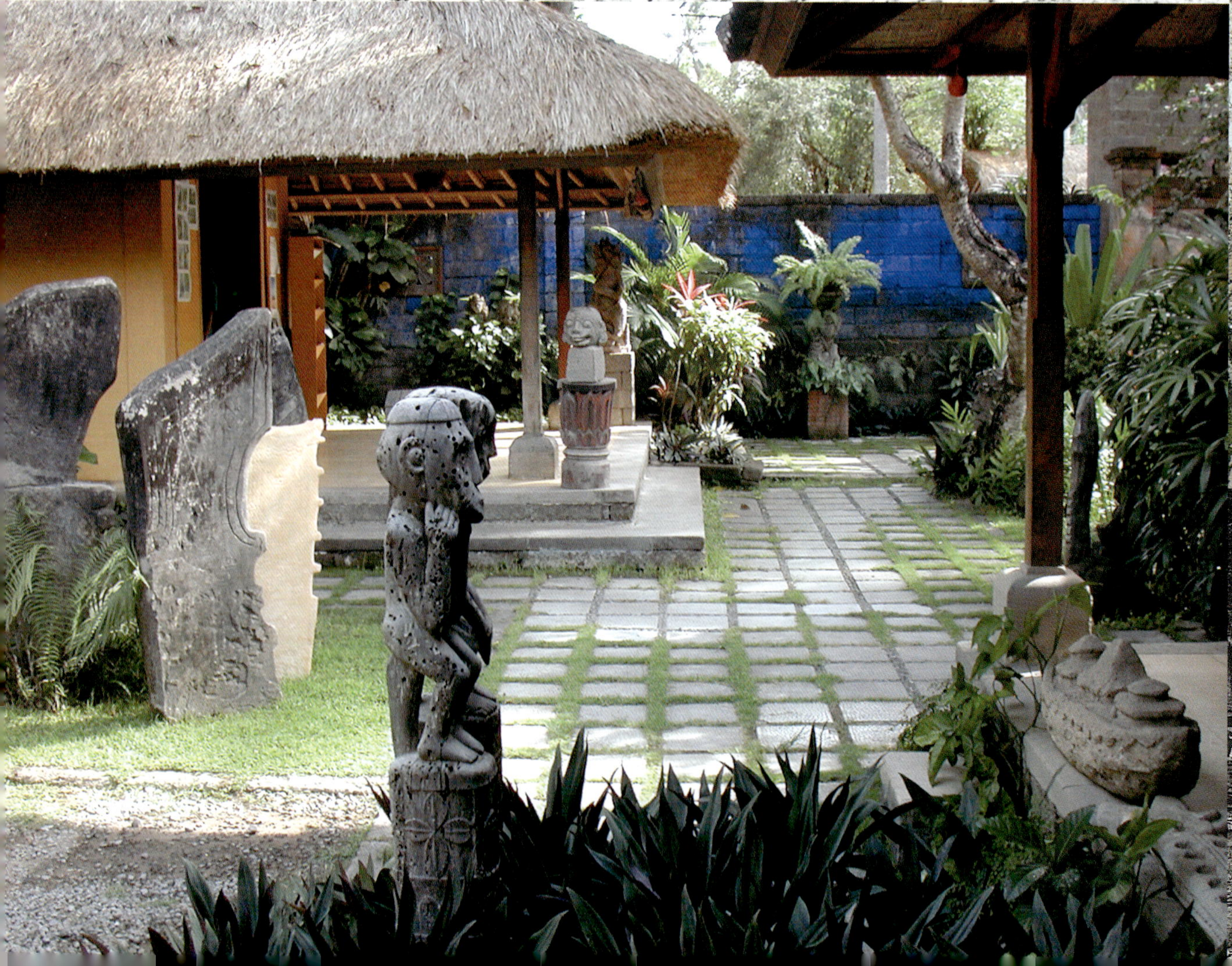

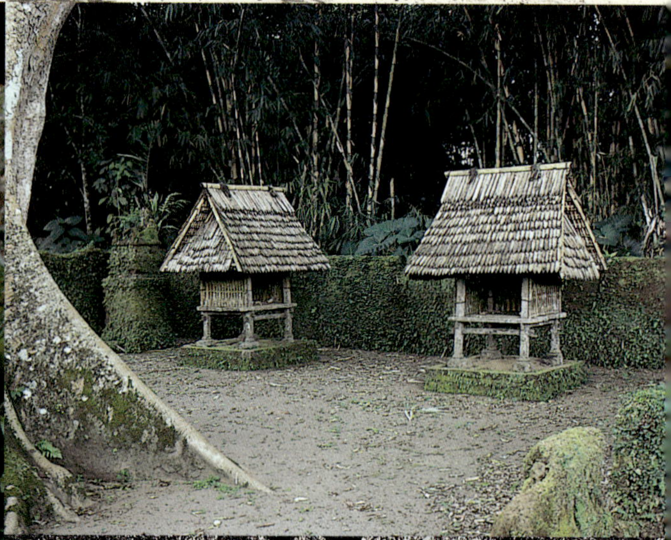

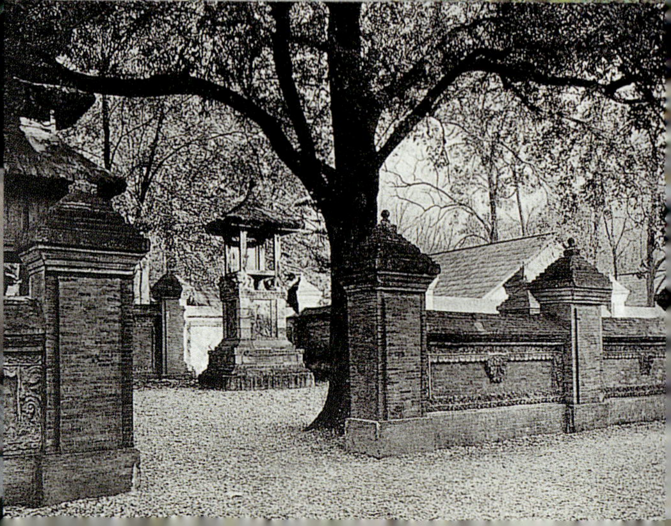

CHAPTER 2

THE COURTYARD

The Courtyard

2.1	Temple Courtyards	26
2.2	Traditional House Compounds	30
2.3	Palaces	32
2.4	Palace-style Hotels	34
2.5	Modern House Compounds	36
2.6	Courtyard Gardens	38

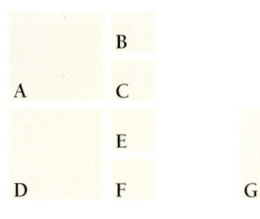

```
      B
A  C
      E
D  F     G
```

Balinese architecture, be it ceremonial or secular, is an architecture of courtyards. The courtyards consist of freestanding pavilions and garden elements—open spaces, gates, walls and shade trees. Temple complexes (*pura*) and palaces (*puri*), two prime examples of courtyard architecture, often have many interlocking courts to accommodate mass rituals. Courtyards vary in level, higher or lower depending on their occupants' status or the courtyards' use, and are connected by ramps or steps through gates.

Even in modern suburbia the basic orientation of the house—kitchen in the south, house temple in the northeast, bed-heads facing north or east—is respected. In a Balinese house compound—and even modern houses are compound-like—the house temple is almost invariably a walled courtyard within a courtyard or at the very least a cluster of shrines occupying an entire roof garden. Whatever the architectural style, there is fairly strict adherence to these cardinal principles. Determining the size and proportions of pavilions, walls, shrines and gates was traditionally the job of an *undagi* or priest-architect. These proportions were based on the body measurements of the homeowner or, in the case of a temple, the priest.

The three main village temples—the *pura puseh*, *pura dalem* and *pura desa*, or *bale agung*, of the Balinese *kahyangan tiga* trinity of temples—are often imposing compounds replete with tiered-roof pagodas (to the mountain gods) and towering gates. In front of the temples large formal open spaces, called *jaba*, are used for cockfights, temple festival fairgrounds and dance performances. There are often one or two large open pavilions within the open courtyard—space to house gamelan orchestras or for seating dignitaries.

Balinese house compounds—called *umah, jero, puri* or *puri agung*, depending on the caste of the occupants—are divided into house forecourt, house proper, house temple and a back yard.

Structures in both temple and house courtyards face into the centre of the court. The clever organization of landscape is vital to the proper functioning of these courtyards: in temples and houses, much activity goes on in these inter-pavilion spaces. A thorough understanding of the organization of space in a Balinese courtyard leads to a good understanding of the Balinese culture and lifestyle.

A. A farmer's compound wall made of lava rocks in Padangkerta village, eastern Bali.

B. Poet-filmmaker John Darling's courtyard home in the rice fields north of Ubud (1983 photo).

C. A classic 19th-century temple courtyard—ornate walls enclose a courtyard dotted with pavilions and shrine buildings—in the Pura Tirta Gunung Kawi, Sebatu village.

D. The Villa Bebek in Sanur is a studio-home built in Balinese courtyard architectural style: garden areas are mostly paved as they are also outdoor work or circulation zones.

E. An austere temple compound near Bukian, in the mountains.

F. A classic red brick temple compound in Sanur.

G. The village square of ancient Dali village on the Erhai Lake in Yunnan province, southern China. The walled courtyard is made up of interlocking rectangular spaces, just like a Balinese traditional courtyard.

2.1 Temple Courtyards

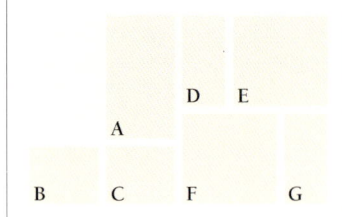

	D	E	
A			
B	C	F	G

A. Temple courtyards are spatially organized to accommodate quite complex circulation patterns and pavilion usage. This photo of the handsome Pura Desa, Guwang shows a fairly typical southern Bali temple layout.

B. This Young Artist-style painting depicts a hypothetical village courtyard scene that is full of the religious and rural activities of Balinese daily life. Note how most of the activities are taking place in the courtyard, not just in the covered pavilions.

C. Aerial view (1960 photo) of Pura Tirta Empul, in Tampaksiring, showing both bathing and temple courts.

D. A drawing by W.O.J. Nieuwenkamp illustrating a typical double courtyard temple in north Bali at the beginning of the 20th century. Note the three different styles of gate, the long-house (bale lantang) in the outer jeroan court and the meru (pagoda) to the god of holy Mt Agung in the inner dalem court.

E. An elegant shrine on an island in a koi-filled, spring-fed pond is the ultimate temple garden: this shrine garden is at the Pura Gunung Kawi bathing springs, near Sebatu.

F. The dalem court of the Pura Beji, Sangsit: the flamboyant "Balinese-Baroque" architecture, ancient frangipani trees and clean grass courtyard floor make for a striking garden.

G. The most beautiful temple in the outrageously ornamental style is on the south coast: the Pura Jagatnata, Peyogan Agung, Ketewel, near Sanur, where the shrine buildings themselves are incredible artworks, accented by ancient plumeria trees and giant stands of lady palms. An ornate gate and attendant ancient frangipani tree are staples of classic temple garden design.

Balinese temples are homes for the gods, holy ground demarcated by walls and pavilions. Offerings are made to, and festivals held for, these gods regularly. The temples are maintained by palace families in many villages and by *adat* (customary) communities in others. Architecturally they are descended from both southern Chinese and Indian temples, both of whose classic models feature walled compounds comprising open and enclosed pavilions.

The classic Balinese temple is divided into a forecourt *(jaba)* for fairground activities and dance performances; a middle court *(jaba tengah)* for audience halls and auxiliary buildings; and an inner sanctum *(jeroan)* where the gods dwell and prayers are offered. One enters the middle court through a split gate *(candi bentar)* and into the inner sanctum through a roofed gate *(paduraksa* or *kori agung).*

The walls of a temple are higher and grander than those of a house compound, often featuring elaborately carved ornamentation on the temple gates and wall pillars, also called *paduraksa*. In the 19th century many temple walls had a semi-transparent treatment—timber fretwork, groupings of glazed ceramic air vents or just slats of soapstone—between the *paduraksa* pillars.

As one moves deeper into a temple, the courtyard floor levels get higher. In northern coast temples, the shrines in the *jeroan* are perched on elaborate raised terraces, like the terraced sanctuaries of pre-Hindu times.

THE COURTYARD → **TEMPLE COURTYARDS 2.1**

28

THE COURTYARD → **TEMPLE COURTYARDS 2.1**

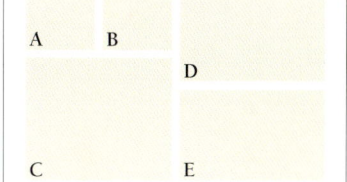

A	B	
		D
C		E

A. *Pre-Majapahit temples were often just terraced sanctuaries, like the Hawaiian* heiau. *This* pura puseh *temple outside the walls of Tenganan village, eastern Bali, shows a central shrine pavilion, pengapit lawang, and "outrider" audience halls that were probably added over time.*

B. *Temple forecourts, called* jaba, *are ideal for photo opportunities (1955 photo). They are also used for ceremonies directed towards the underworld and for human entertainment activities such as gambling and food stalls.*

C. *The mossy main court, called the* dalem *court, of the important Pura Batu Karo mountain temple in Tabanan.*

D. *A 1930 photograph of a major temple's inner sanctum (called* dalem*). Note the tiered* paduraksa *gate, the* aling-aling *screen wall, the giant pagoda shrine called* meru *and the packed-earth courtyard floor.*

E. *The inner sanctum of the Pura Luhur, Uluwatu, during a temple anniversary festival called* odalan.

2.2 Traditional House Compounds

The traditional Balinese house is a walled compound with several courtyard elements: a *jaba* forecourt in front of a main entrance gate; a kitchen *(paon)* in the southern quarter; a ceremonial pavilion, the *bale bali* (for tooth-filing ceremonies, weddings, lyings-in-state) in the eastern quarter; a procreation building, the *bale meten*, in the northern quarter; the family house temple, called a *sanggah* or *merajan* depending on one's caste, in the northeast; and a backyard *(teba)* for refuse. All pavilions face inwards, onto the central court. Often there is also a workhouse pavilion in the western quarter of the compound; rice lofts *(lumbung)* and other auxiliary pavilions (typically a *warung* food stall hung off the front wall and run by an unmarried daughter, or, these days, an art shop facing the road that eats into one of the court's corners). The central courtyard is a communal living room which can fill up at night with card tables or offering-making platforms. In the wet season nocturnal courtyard activities retreat into the open pavilions that dot the tree-shaded court.

A. Shrines to Surya, the sun god, or to the spirit of the land, are a major decorative element in a traditional house compound. A traditional Balinese garden always has a shrine to the spirit of the land, similar to a Japanese garden, even if it's just a special rock or a statue on which offerings are laid.

B. Bird's-eye view (artist's impression) of a typical rural domestic compound.
(1) Central courtyard
(2) Family shrine (sanggah)
(3) Principal sleeping pavilion (meten)
(4) Ceremonial pavilion (bale bali)
(5) Guest pavilion, to the west
(6) Bale sakenam
(7) Kitchen, or paon, in the south
(8) Rice barn (lumbung)
(9) Pigsty
(10) Compound entrance
(11) Small screening wall (aling-aling)

C. A spartan courtyard in Sayan, Ubud, shows how the pavilion bases are a strong part of Balinese courtyard definition. Note how the family house temple (seen in background, top right-hand corner) is on a raised podium, but not walled.

D. A 1906 drawing by Dutch artist W.O.J. Nieuwenkamp of a typical house compound, perhaps of a nobleman, in Singaraja.

E. The Villa Bebek in Sanur is an art factory, an office, a training camp for aesthetic warriors and a barracks. The courtyard style and scale are modelled on 1960s Sanur homes.

THE COURTYARD → **TRADITIONAL HOUSE COMPOUNDS 2.2**

2.3 Palaces

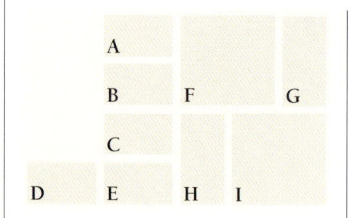

A		
B	F	G
C		
D	E	H	I

A. The ruins of the fabulous Taman Ujung water palace in Karangasem, a pleasure garden built—along with Tirtagangga water palace—by the last raja of Karangasem, Anak Agung Anglurah Ketut Karangasem.

B. For scale and proportion Puri Gede Karangasem is the grandest in the land. In this 1995 photograph only a few gates and audience halls remain to demonstrate full-blown puri style.

C. The most regal treatment in palace architecture is reserved for the prince's verandah, a space where visiting dignitaries are parked to witness family ceremonies, and where important family summits are held. This 1982 photograph was taken in the Puri Anyar, Gianyar.

D. A Balinese palace often consists of numerous interlocking courtyards. This artist's impression from 1975 is modelled on the old Puri Agung Klungkung.

E. Aerial view of the Puri Kanginan palace, Amlapura, in eastern Bali, showing the bale kambang (floating pavilion) in the prince's pleasure gardens.

F. The lotus lake and temple gate at the Puri Saraswati palace temple, designed by the great I Gusti Nyoman Lempad (1862–1978).

G. The entrance to the main court of the Puri Kanginan, Amlapura, Karangasem, eastern Bali, inspired perhaps by the palace architecture of Surakarta in central Java.

H. A gate of the Jero Kubutambahan palace, northern Bali, built in a unique neo-colonial pesisir style.

I. A beautiful bale bandung, with late Bali Rococo detailing, in the Puri Saren palace, Ubud.

Bali was once an island of feudal fiefdoms and native chieftains. During the era of King Udayana in the 10th century Bali's first imperial palace was built near present day Goa Gajah, the Elephant Cave, in Bedulu. From the 11th century onwards much of the populace converted to a classic Hindu Javanese god-king worship system.

Over the centuries vassal princes from the eastern Javanese kingdoms of Kediri, Daha and Majapahit and priest-architects called *undagi* imported the idea of grander multi-courtyard compounds, inspired by classical Hindu-Javanese models, and introduced these into the local architectural language.

This 500-year period of Javanization/Hindufication begat princelings who eventually became real estate developers and bought up most of the coastline. The Balinese palace architecture that survives today is essentially Javanese-Majapahit architecture.

During Bali's golden age in the 16th-19th centuries, Bali's rajas built pleasure gardens which were actually walled courts, like the Moroccan *riyads*, and Mogul-Indian fragrant gardens, where princes entertained guests. Belvederes, called *bale patok*, were situated at corners of these courtyards, from which palace wives surveyed the world outside. In the royal palaces *(puri agung)*, and in many temples, *kul-kul* drum towers can be found in the corners of "marshalling ground" forecourts, called *jeroan* or *ancak saji*.

At last count there were some 5,000 *jero* "mini palaces" in Bali but only nine *puri agung* palaces, where the royal families, descended from Bali's former regents, live. Of these, only Puri Gianyar, Puri Kesiman (the *merajan agung* moated house temple), Puri Agung Jero Kuta and some pavilions in Puri Gede Karangasem exhibit classic *puri* architecture.

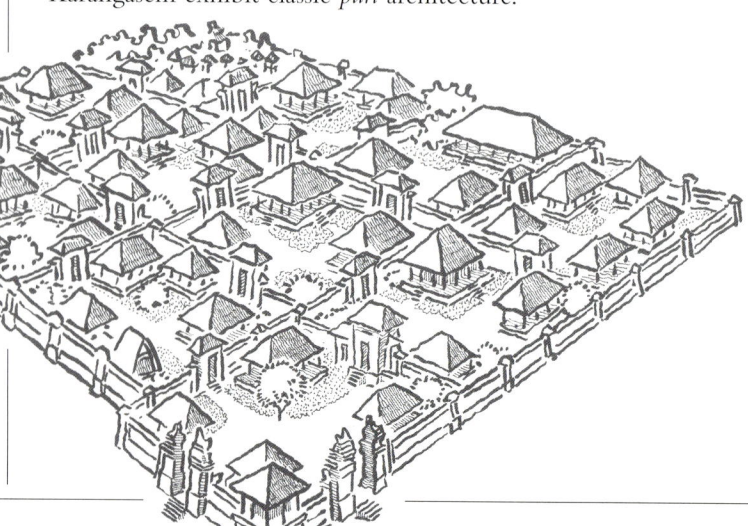

THE COURTYARD → **PALACES** 2.3

2.4 Palace-style Hotels

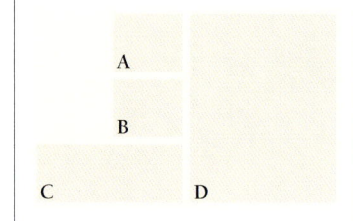

A	
B	
C	D

A. *The lobby of the seminal Tanjung Sari hotel in Sanur underwent many transformations in the period 1970–90. Today the lobby remains as a palace-style meten bandung space, with recycled Balinese palace columns and recycled carved timber panels from a nobleman's home in eastern Java.*

B. *Canggu Puri Mertha hotel in Canggu village, southern Bali, was modelled on the formal water gardens of the raja's water palaces of Karangasem, eastern Bali.*

C. *The upper lobby lounge of the Bali Oberoi was first designed as a palatial private residence. The door in the background led to the master bedroom: it is an exact copy of an important door in the Puri Agung Gianyar palace.*

D. *The lobby of the Amanusa hotel in southern Bali is traditional Balinese architecture realized on a palatial scale (Kerry Hill Architects, 1997).*

Judith and Wija Waworuntu's charming collection of beach-side cottages, the Tanjung Sari hotel, was completed at Sanur in 1968. It was arguably Asia's first tropical boutique hotel. An ambitious upgrade in 1971 added palace-style structures. A Javanese pavilion was reworked as the hotel's lobby (photo A, right); the dining room was styled as a museum of traditional Balinese decorative arts; and a small raised *bale* was put on the beach, like the *bale patok*, or belvederes, found in most royal palaces on the island. The rooms were also redesigned to reflect the rich brick coursing and gilt windows and doors that are a feature of post-Majapahit palace architecture.

Global gentrification, such a force in the second half of the 20th century, found fertile ground indeed in Bali. Swiss hotel managers were becoming raja-like just as rajas were building palace-style hotels. No wonder the populace was confused. The movement reached its apotheosis with the completion of the mega-glitzy Nusa Dua Beach hotel in 1980, Garuda Airlines' answer to Versailles.

As Bali's royal palaces have slipped into suburbia (physically but not culturally) five-star hotels—the new temples to style—have become the island's palaces.

By the 1990s visionary developer Adrian Zecha had three palace-style properties in Bali: the Amandari, the Amankila and the Amanusa. All were incredibly deluxe in a stylishly elegant way. Many developers followed suit; there are now over 100 Amanwannabes on the island.

THE COURTYARD → **PALACE-STYLE HOTELS 2.4**

2.5 Modern House Compounds

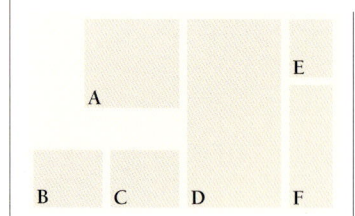

Pioneers of the Bali Style movement—Walter Spies, Adrien Jean Le Mayeur de Merprès, Judith and Wija Waworuntu, Peter and Carole Muller—took elements of the traditional Balinese house and worked them into new hybrid forms. In the 1930s, Ubud-based artist and architectural pioneer Walter Spies retooled the *wantilan* and other traditional forms to achieve more spacious interiors. The Waworuntus reworked the traditional *meten* and *paon* forms into idyllic beach bungalows at their Tanjung Sari hotel and, later, with Geoffrey Bawa and Donald Friend, the Batujimbar Estates. Peter Muller took the traditional communal Balinese *mandi* (open-air bathing place) and re-fashioned it in his classic Bali Style bathrooms for the legendary Kayu Aya villas (now the Bali Oberoi).

In the 1990s the Bali Style house movement really took off as the Southeast Asian region's top architects—Kerry Hill and Ernesto Bedmar of Singapore; Cheong Yew Kuan and Chan Soo Chian of Malaysia; a host of young Philippine architects, and half of Queensland—tried the movement on for size on their home turf.

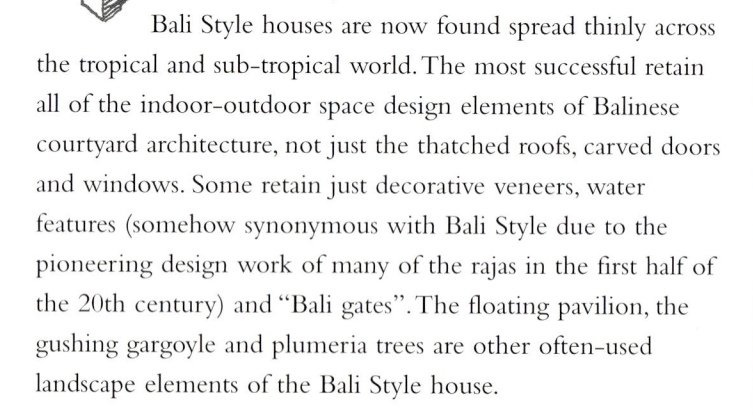

Bali Style houses are now found spread thinly across the tropical and sub-tropical world. The most successful retain all of the indoor-outdoor space design elements of Balinese courtyard architecture, not just the thatched roofs, carved doors and windows. Some retain just decorative veneers, water features (somehow synonymous with Bali Style due to the pioneering design work of many of the rajas in the first half of the 20th century) and "Bali gates". The floating pavilion, the gushing gargoyle and plumeria trees are other often-used landscape elements of the Bali Style house.

A. The Warung Mie restaurant at the Four Seasons Resort, Jimbaran is a modern adaptation of a traditional house compound for hotel use.

B. Belgian painter Adrien Jean Le Mayeur de Merprès immortalized his Sanur beachside compound garden in a series of impressionist paintings from 1940-57.

C. Donald Friend's painting (1973) of Batujimbar Estates shows the eclectic mix of courtyard architectural elements in these estates, including the museum and kul-kul tower by Geoffrey Bawa.

D. The Villa Kirana in Sayan, completed in 2001, features individual pavilions wrapped around cascading ponds. The pavilions can all be opened up to allow the sort of courtyard transparency and indoor-outdoor lifestyle associated with Bali Style houses.

E. The Villa Bebek in Sanur has many tightly interlocking courts, like the traditional Balinese jero houses of the lesser nobility. Courtyard walls have been "punched out", however, to afford inter-courtyard views.

F. Three loosely connected pavilions of the Villa Kirana in Sayan, near Ubud.

THE COURTYARD → **MODERN HOUSE COMPOUNDS 2.5**

2.6 Courtyard Gardens

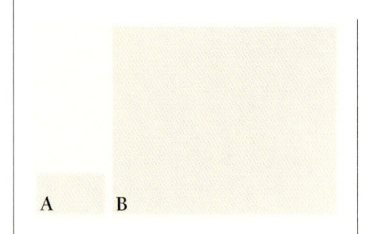

A. *The ethnic chic look—otherwise known as Rustic Charm or as Zen, but once just Village Balinese—has become popular since the start of the Bali Style boom. This large* paras vat, *from the Canggu area, was once a water-holding vessel in someone's kitchen.*

B. *Balinese designer Putu Suarsa's Big Bamboo Villas in Sidakarya feature many charming courtyard spaces.*

In Bali one can still find the type of vibrantly colourful gardens that inspired the Dutch artist, W.O.J. Nieuwenkamp, when he arrived in 1904 and which he depicted in his early paintings. The Balinese love bright colours and shapeliness in their gardens: even the Zen-like gardens of mountain temples, with their simple dirt courtyards, handsome adobe walls and striking ancient pagoda forms, have bold splashes of screaming red cordyline plants flanking austerely handsome shrines and rich adobe walls.

Restless artists feel an overpowering sense of joy and tranquillity when presented with a Balinese temple courtyard in full ceremonial flush, its decorations so stunning and its inhabitants so beautiful. Likewise a well-composed Balinese garden, with a balance of the fecund and the spacious, allows its admirer a sense of joy and well-being. Even bankers and developers have gone weak at the knees when led into a fully flourishing Balinese garden such as the fern court of the Bali Hyatt at Sanur or the Pura Jagatnata at Ketewel village, with its tortured plumeria and ancient pagodas.

Most Balinese gardens exhibit a mixture of artful naturalism and ornamentation—the "peopling" of a space with sensual silhouettes, shrines, accent plants or statues, or pots nuzzling up to trees. In some ways, the Balinese garden is descended from the formal, asymmetrical courtyard gardens of Java with their spacious courts, water elements and shapely trees. Yet the Balinese courtyard is more tightly packed with pavilions and loveliness than perhaps Hindu Java ever was. One also senses the pervading influence of Chinese ornamental gardens in many of the more ornate palace gardens of Bali.

While the true Balinese garden is rarely found outside Bali, some modern Bali Style gardens manage to be minimal yet inspired.

THE COURTYARD → **COURTYARD GARDENS** 2.6

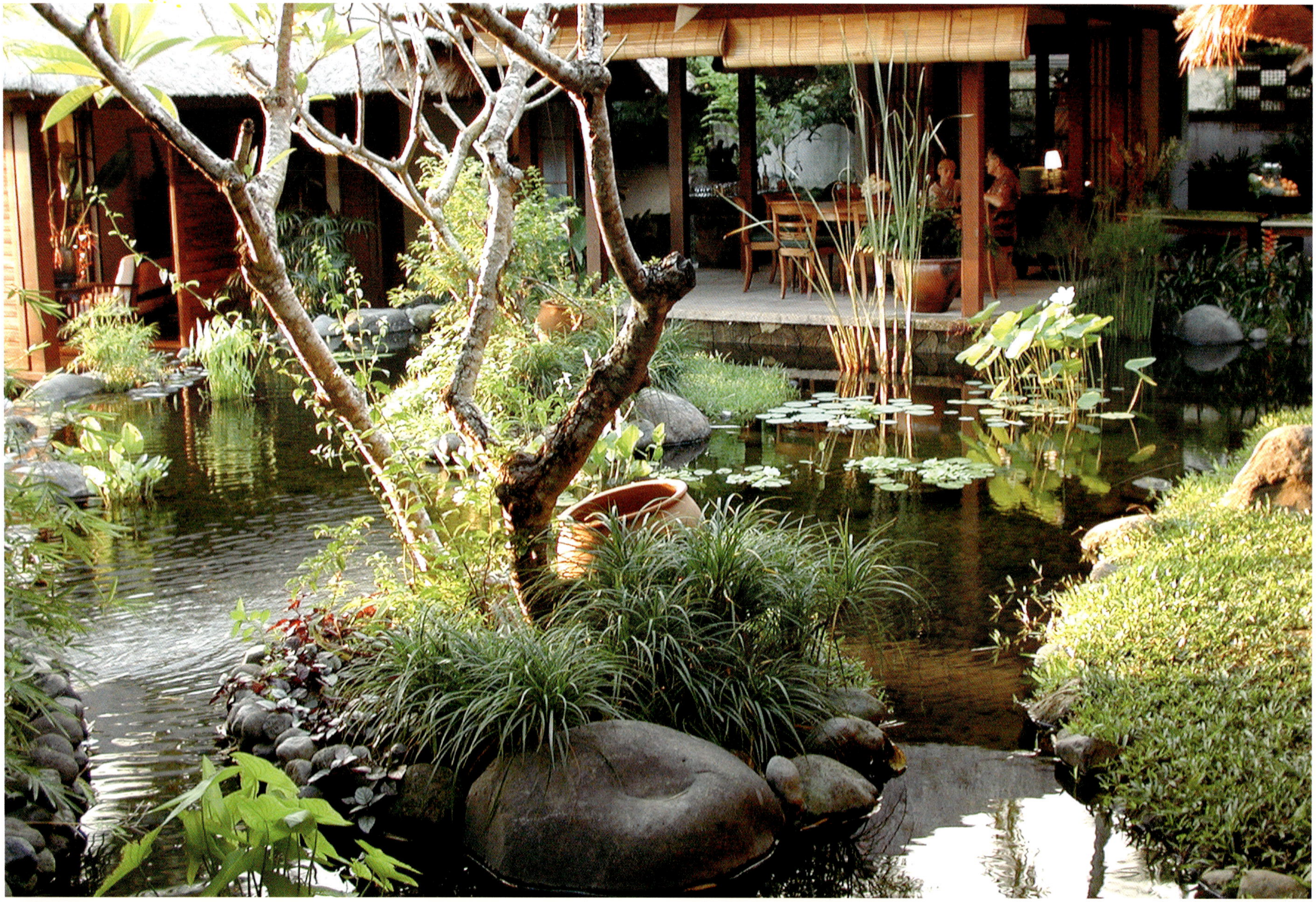

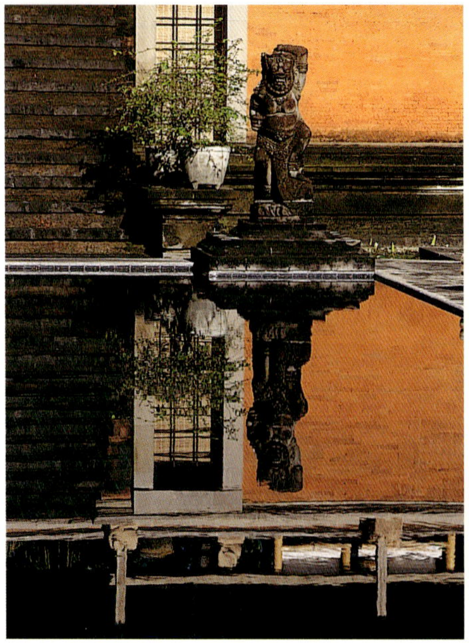

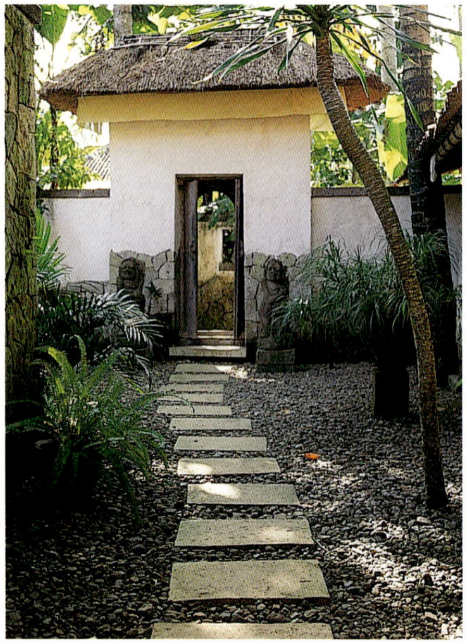

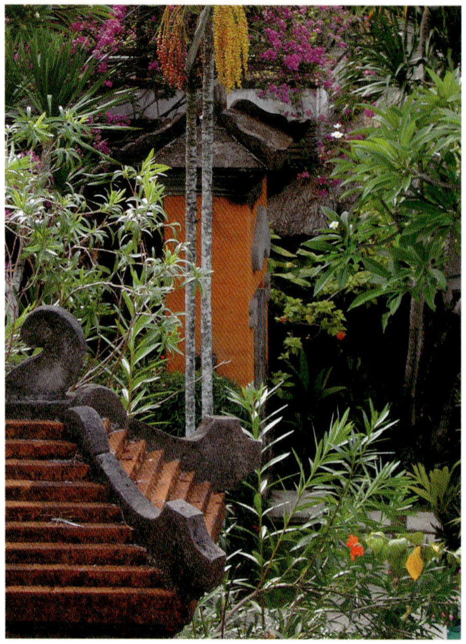

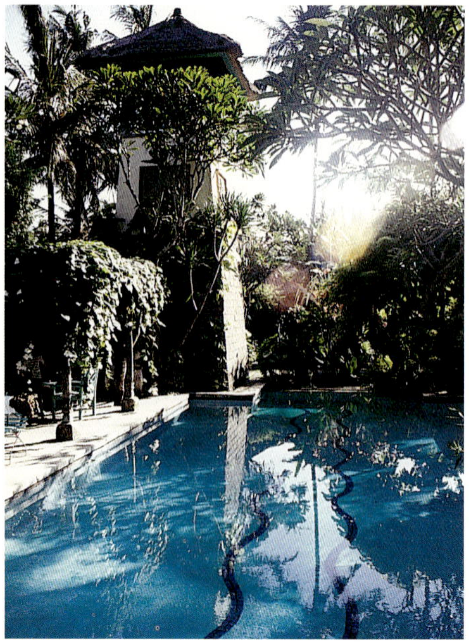

THE COURTYARD → **COURTYARD GARDENS** 2.6

A. *Central garden court at the Villa Kirana, Sayan, Ubud. The water garden acts as a passive cooling system for all the open pavilion entertainment spaces. The planting style is "courtyard Balinese poetic", a mixture of romantic natural and ornamental Oriental styles.*

B. *The reflecting pond, or moat, around architect Geoffrey Bawa's museum for Donald Friend (1974).*

C. *Entrance garden at Nyoman Miyoga's villa in Sayan.*

D. *Detail of the mature central gardens at the Villa Bebek: Balinese gardens should exhibit an energetic play of natural and man-made elements.*

E. *Swimming pool as reflecting pond: the joy of a tropical poolscape is often in the appreciation of its surrounding plants and architectural accents.*

F. *Ed Tuttle designed this temple garden for the Adrian Zecha renovation of Donald Friend's old house in Batujimbar.*

Following pages: A single-storey wantilan *pavilion in Bedugul on Lake Bratan.*

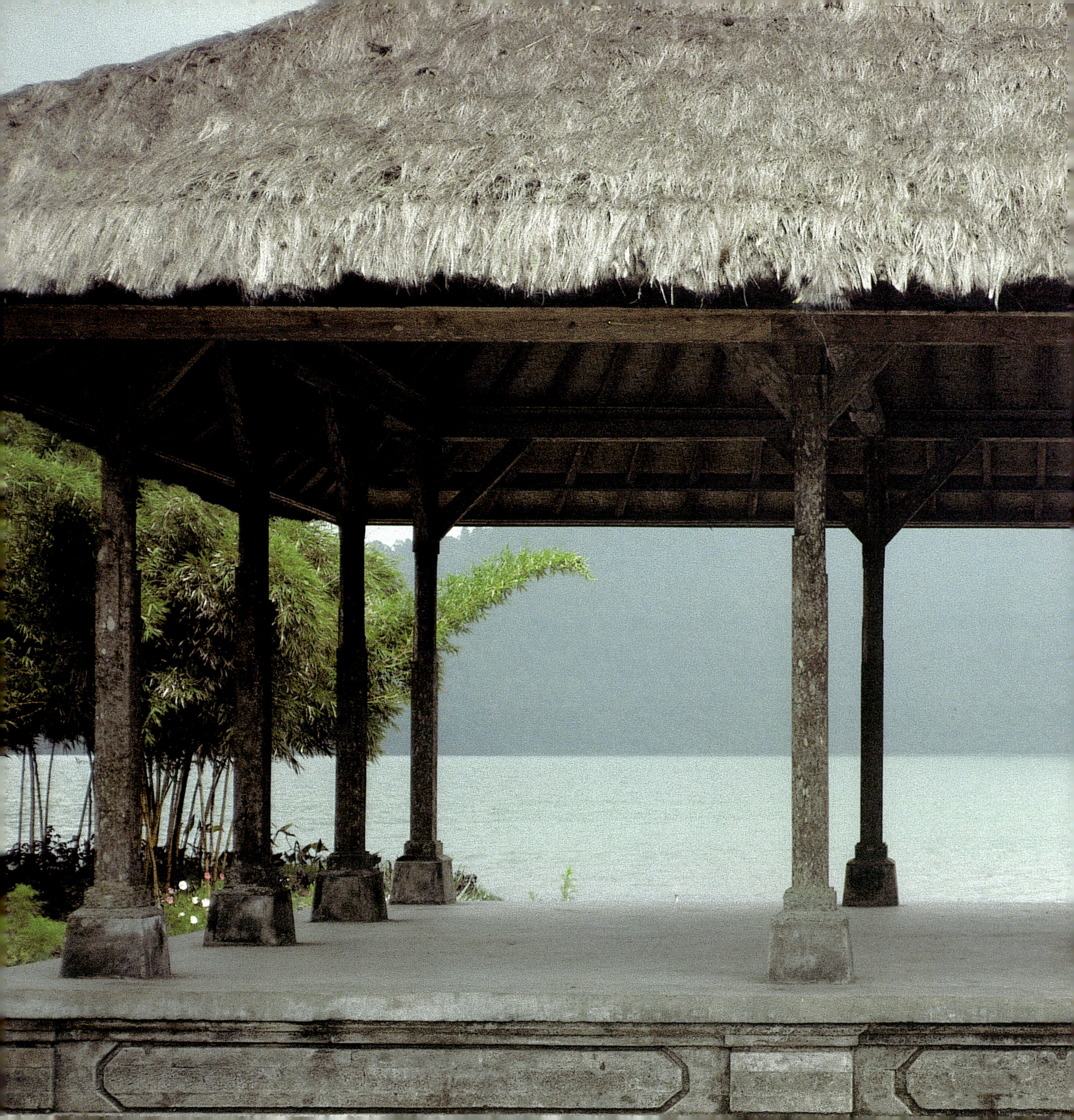

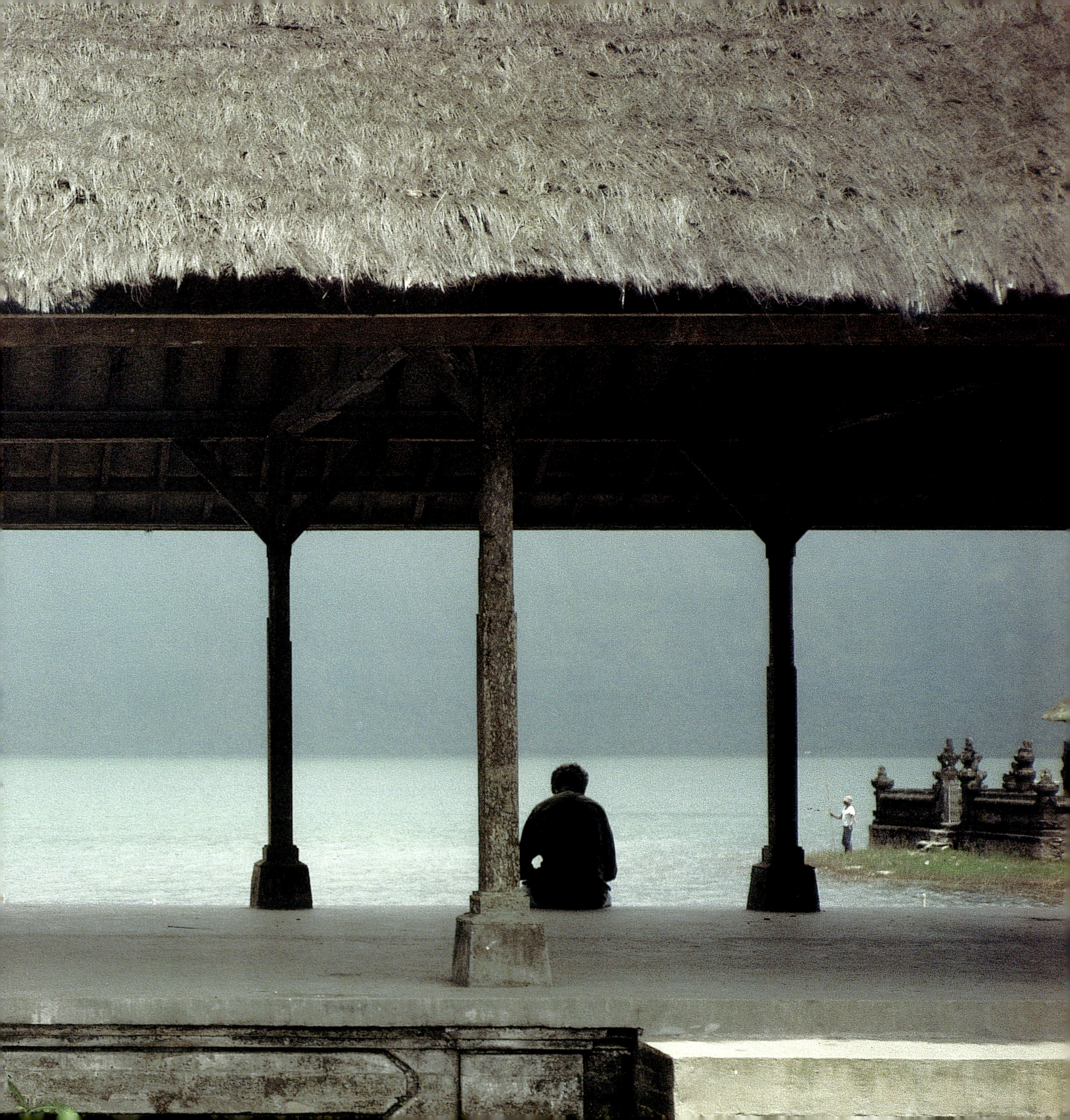

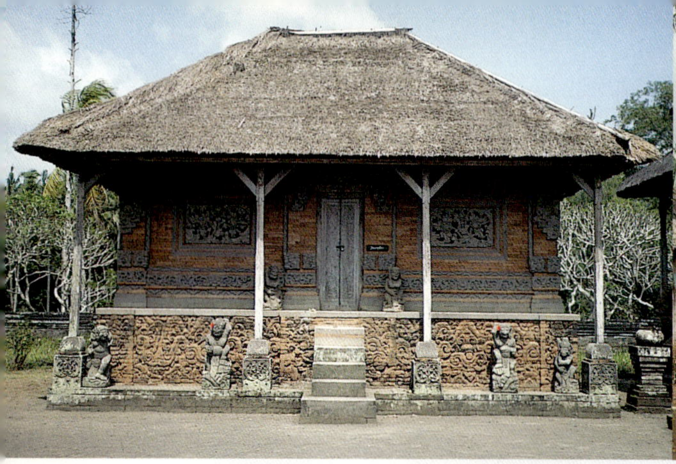
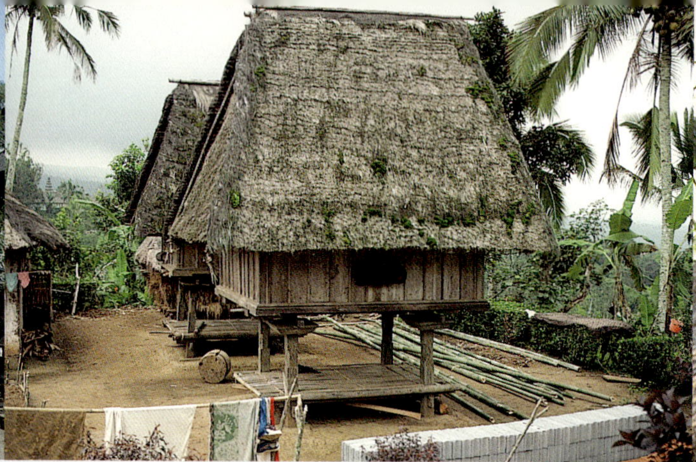
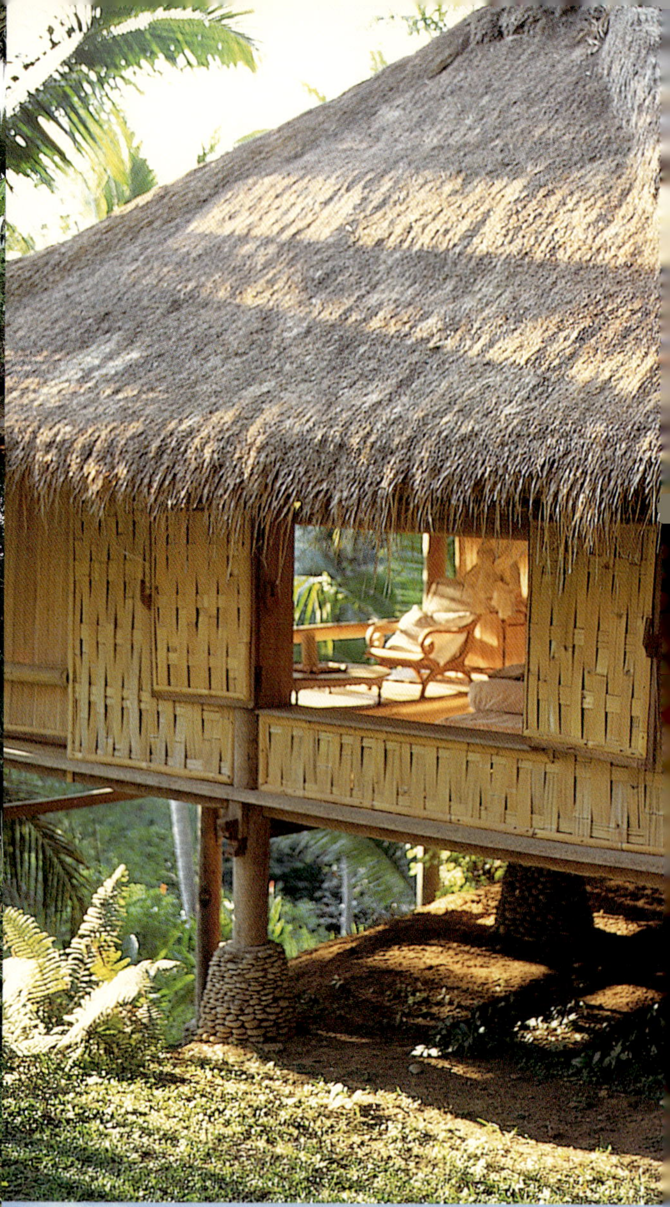
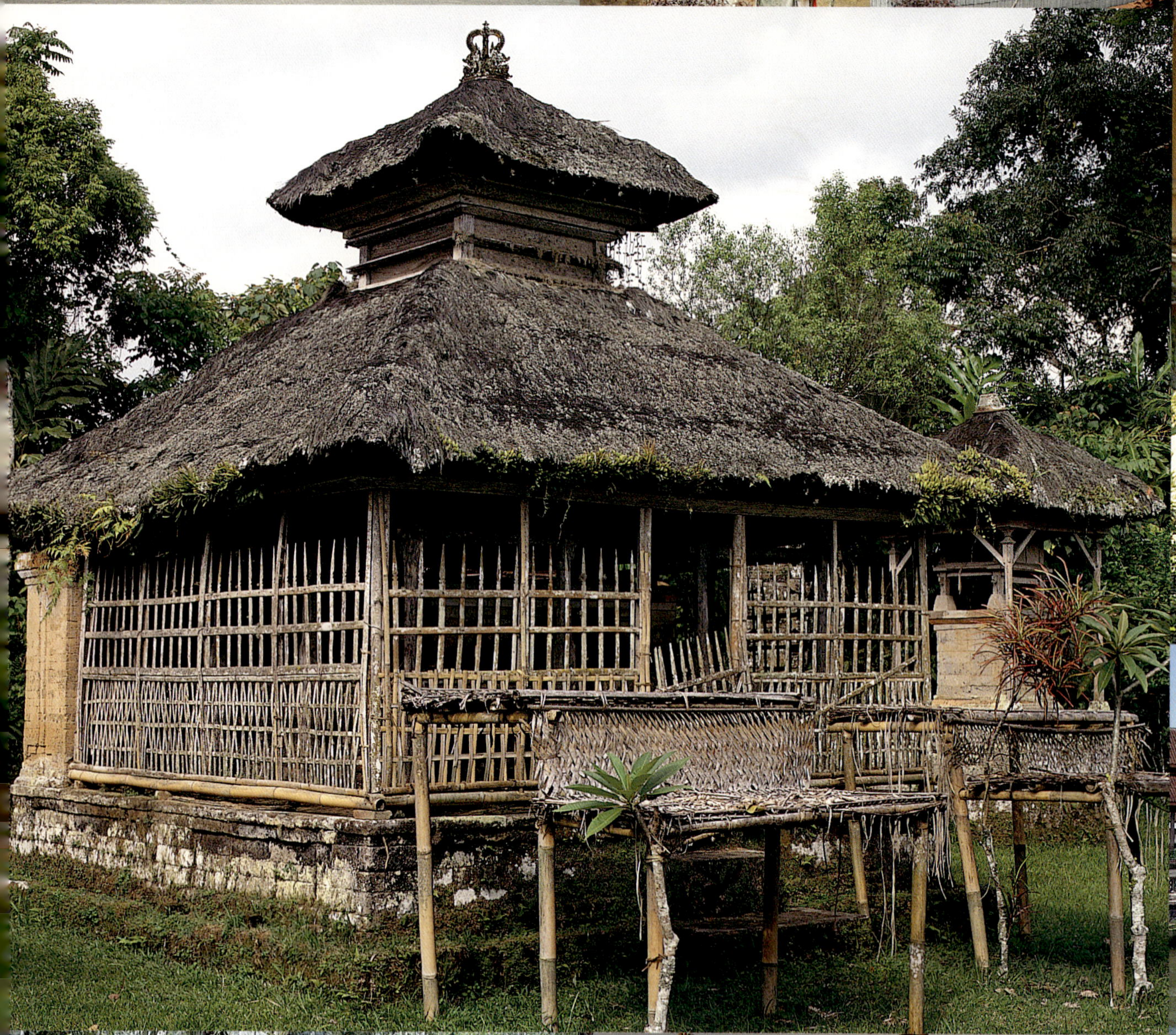
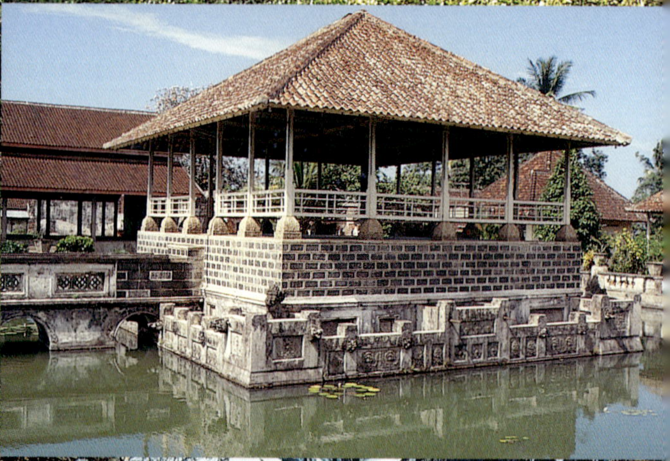
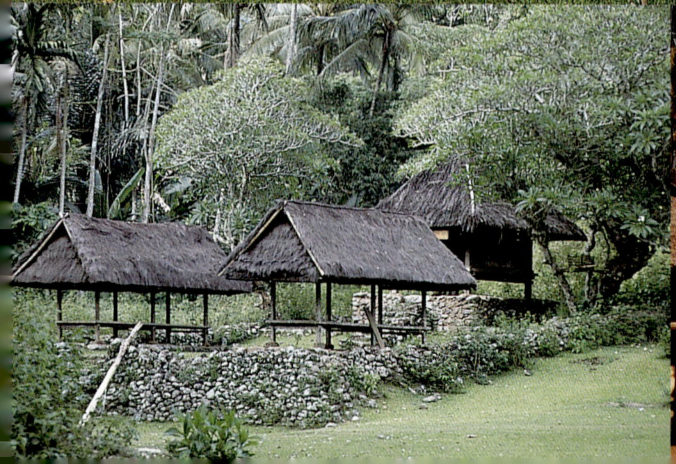
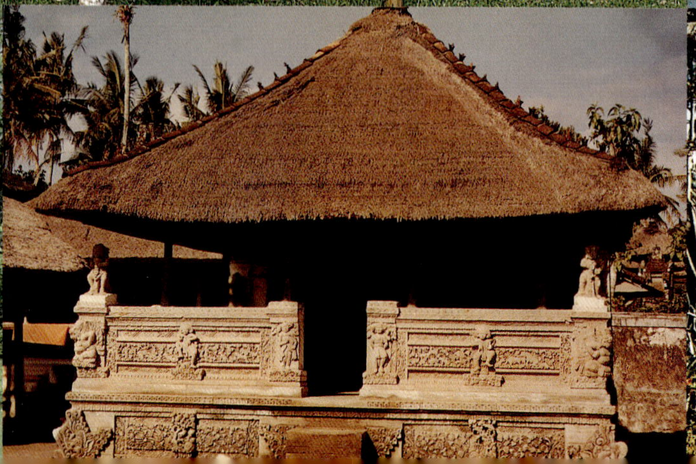
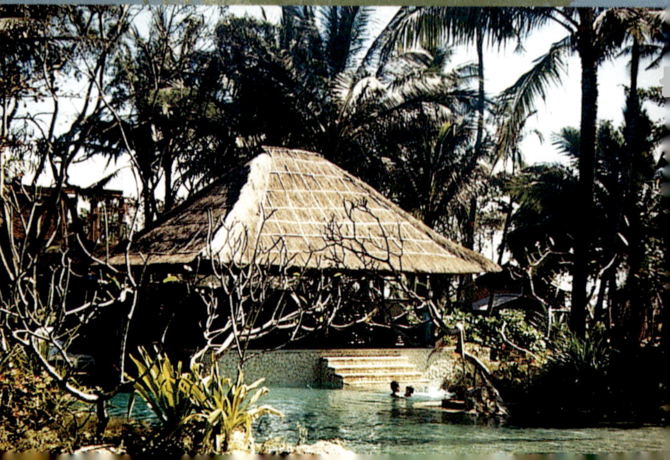

CHAPTER 3

BALE: THE PAVILION

3.1	Types of Pavilions	46
3.2	Enclosed and Semi-enclosed Pavilions	50
3.3	Pavilion Roof Forms	54
3.4	Shrine Pavilions	56
3.5	Traditional Forms in Modern Houses	58

Bale: The Pavilion

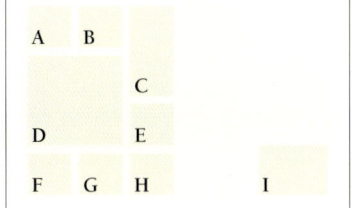

Many houses along Bali's northwest coast have charming multi-purpose roadside kiosks: they act as sitting rooms, siesta platforms, gambling dens, watchtowers (during periods of strife) and love nests. In times of economic woe, they are often converted into *warung* food stalls or even newsstands.

This pavilion form, called *bale* in Bali, *balai* in the Spice Islands, *hale* in Hawaii or *faré* in Tahiti, is a pan-Pacific classic. Over the centuries, the *bale* has evolved from its humble beginnings on the archipelago's foreshore into a whole architectural language with complex geomantic rules and regulations. The proportions of the Balinese *bale* are guarded by equations of scale that set out lengths, breadths and widths relative to the body measurements of the *bale* owner.

These proportions are dying fast in domestic architecture, due to the propensity of many modern architects to put decoration ahead of proportion. In most of the island's sacred architecture, however, the rules of classic proportions are observed.

It is not just a matter of aesthetics, however. In well-designed tropical shelters, eaves are low to keep out the sun and rain. Bases are high to stop splash-back on the floors as gutters are traditionally not used. There is an ideal length for a sleeping platform wrapped between four posts, as there is for the distance between posts in public buildings—such as the *wantilan* and the *bale bundar* gamelan pavilion—to allow for group activities.

Roofs traditionally follow a pitch of between 42° and 45° to allow for the efficient disposal of water from tropical down-pours and thus prevent rot from setting into the thatch.

The equations of scale that dictate the proportions of a *bale* are, to an extent, sliding scales: reduce a *kulkul* tower's *bale* by 400%, for example, and one has a spirit house; enlarge a typical cockfighting *wantilan* by 50% and one has a large hotel lobby. The enclosed or walled pavilions which house votive figurines (*arca*) in the island's temples re-appear in family compounds as sleeping pavilions. It is not an open-ended scale—there is a maximum size before the truss work required becomes messy and un-Balinese—but some tourism industry architects have managed to stretch the envelope, as it were, without deserting traditional pavilion materials and proportions. The Amandari and the Four Seasons Resort in Jimbaran are the best examples on the island.

A. Shrine pavilion in a mountain temple.
B. Rice lofts, called jineng or lumbung, are pavilion hybrids.
C. The expatriate building boom has led to a new breed of pavilion hybrids.
D. Semi-enclosed shrine pavilion in a mountain temple.
E. "Floating" pavilions are often found in Balinese palaces.
F. Shrine pavilions at the Pura Puseh, Tenganan, where many of the island's most beautiful pavilion structures are found.
G. My favourite pavilion in all of Bali, the bale bali in the inner sanctum of the fabulous Pura Peyogan Agung Ketewel.
H. A poolside pavilion at the Nusa Dua Beach hotel.
I. A temple courtyard is depicted on a 15th-century Javanese temple, Candi Sukuh. The reliefs show a Javanese pavilion similar in form to today's Balinese architecture.

3.1 Types of Pavilions

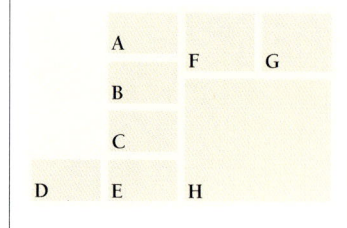

Pavilion forms come in all shapes and sizes for a variety of functions: think of building blocks consisting of pavilion bases, posts (*saka*) and pitched roofs of varying shapes. Pavilions are most commonly denoted by the number of posts:

PAVILION (*BALE*) NAME	DESCRIPTION	COMMON USAGE
sakepat	4-post	Shrine, belvedere, ancient gate form
sakenam	6-post	Kitchen, or ceremonial pavilion in small houses
sakutus	8-post	Auxiliary pavilion in temples
meten	Enclosed 8-post	Bedroom, procreation pavilion (for head of house)
bandung	8-post with a front porch	Northern or western pavilion for ceremonial use. A large *meten*
bale agung	8- or 10-post with raised base	Assembly hall for the gods, or *arca* votive statues
sakesia bunder	9-post (one taban)	Workhouse pavilion
bale bunder	8-post, or 12-post when in a palace or temple	Gamelan pavilion
bale bali	12-post (two or more taban)	Ceremonial pavilion in large houses
bale lantang	Long (12, 14, 16 or 20-post) with raised base	Community hall (Balinese long-house) for village feasts or rites of passage
wantilan	2-tiered pavilion with 4- or 8-post core, and 12- or 16-column apron. Can be square or rectangular	Cockfights, *banjar* hall, dance hall
bale kul-kul	4-post on very high base	Drum tower or watchtower

A. A simple six-post lumbung *rice barn.*

B. *A* bale agung *with eight posts and a high ornate base.*

C. *A six-post* sakenam *kitchen building.*

D. *The classic two-tiered* wantilan *pavilion.*

E. *An eight-post mountain* meten *pavilion.*

F. *A fully enclosed shrine pavilion, called a* gedong, *at Samuan Tiga temple.*

G. *A 12-post* bale bundar *in a mountain village.*

H. *Twelve-posted pavilions, called* bale bali, *are often found in the* dalem *courts of major temples. This ceremonial pavilion has a high stylobate with a fence around its perimeter, to keep dogs away from the offerings.*

LUMBUNG

BALE AGUNG

SAKENAM

METEN

BALE: THE PAVILION → **TYPES OF PAVILIONS 3.1**

48

BALE: THE PAVILION → **TYPES OF PAVILIONS 3.1**

A	B	H
C	D	
E F G	I	

A. A very grand *bale bali*-style ceremonial pavilion, called Garuda Makaam, at Samuan Tiga temple in the 12th-century capital, Bedulu, Gianyar, in central Bali.

B. The eight-posted *bale bundar* as a gamelan pavilion in Peliatan village, central Bali.

C. During the 1960s many government buildings in Denpasar experimented with oversized Balinese pavilion style, using reinforced concrete building frames.

D. A pavilion in the Kesepuhan Palace in Cirebon, western Java, built in the Majapahit style which has also been popular in Bali since the 16th century.

E. This beachside hut at the Puri Ganesha in Pemuteran is, in fact, a *jineng* rice loft bought from a neighbouring village.

F. An unusual single-post pavilion in a temple courtyard. Note the concrete roof.

G. Walls, where they exist, are rarely load-bearing in traditional pavilions, as seen in this house temple in a Kubutambahan village home.

H. Australian architect Peter Muller designed this "floating" pavilion for the Amandari hotel's pool in 1989.

I. In 1990 I built a series of Samoan-style pavilions in the foreshore parklands of the Four Seasons Resort, Jimbaran. The columns were living santen trees; the roofs were woven coconut-leaf thatch.

3.2 Enclosed and Semi-enclosed Pavilions

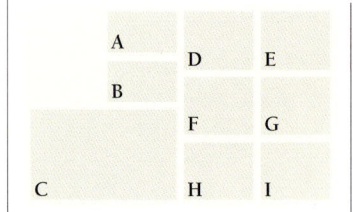

A		D	E
B			
		F	G
C		H	I

A. *Ruins of the main gedong naga, dragon shrine, at the 14th-century Candi Penataran in central Java. The internal timber pavilion and roof, originally inside the enclosing wall, has rotted away over the centuries. Many Balinese temples have the same proportions (see also photo G and photo A, page 208).*

B. *A beautifully proportioned meten pavilion in a family compound in Guwang, Ketewel, an ancient village once renowned for its neat, compact domestic architecture. Note the sexy canopy over the pavilion steps.*

C. *This mountain gedong (fully-enclosed pavilion) is a classic temple building form.*

D. *The fountain-of-youth pavilion at Taman Narmada gardens in Balinese western Lombok features a partially transparent enclosing half-wall.*

E. *An early entrant in the Expatriate Dream Home stakes.*

F. *In the more remote mountainous regions there are single pavilion dwellings which incorporate kitchen, sleeping quarters and attic storage under the one roof.*

G. *A rare form of pavilion-temple in Tenganan village.*

H. *A meten in a mountain village with shocking blue colour highlights. Blue decorative accents are popular with early mountain cultures in many Asian countries.*

I. *Sri Lankan architect and trad-mod enthusiast Geoffrey Bawa ingeniously adapted the bale agung assembly hall of the gods for Australian artist Donald Friend's museum. Bawa raised the stylobate and vastly enlarged it, so it could become an air-conditioned museum, with a spacious open-air pavilion on top.*

Most buildings in Bali are pavilion style, of one type or another, whether built of timber or reinforced concrete. Pavilions are either open and leggy, or enclosed and walled off to create "rooms". In enclosed house pavilions, the columns are generally inside the wall, as they are in all *meten* procreation pavilions, which sit at the north end of a family court. In larger, enclosed temple buildings the columns are often outside the walls (see diagrams page 53).

The "garage" for the *barong*, the village's giant protector puppet, for example, is an enclosed building, called a *gedong*. Other vault-like pavilions, called *gedong persimpanan*, are used for storing the temple's statues.

Enclosed pavilions may have small fretwork windows and carved doors as in the example of the *meten*, or faux windows and carved panels as is the case in most temple *gedong*. In modern Bali Style houses, a clever working of open and closed pavilion space is required to create a fully functional, fully tropical, Balinese house.

BALE: THE PAVILION → **ENCLOSED AND SEMI-ENCLOSED PAVILIONS 3.2**

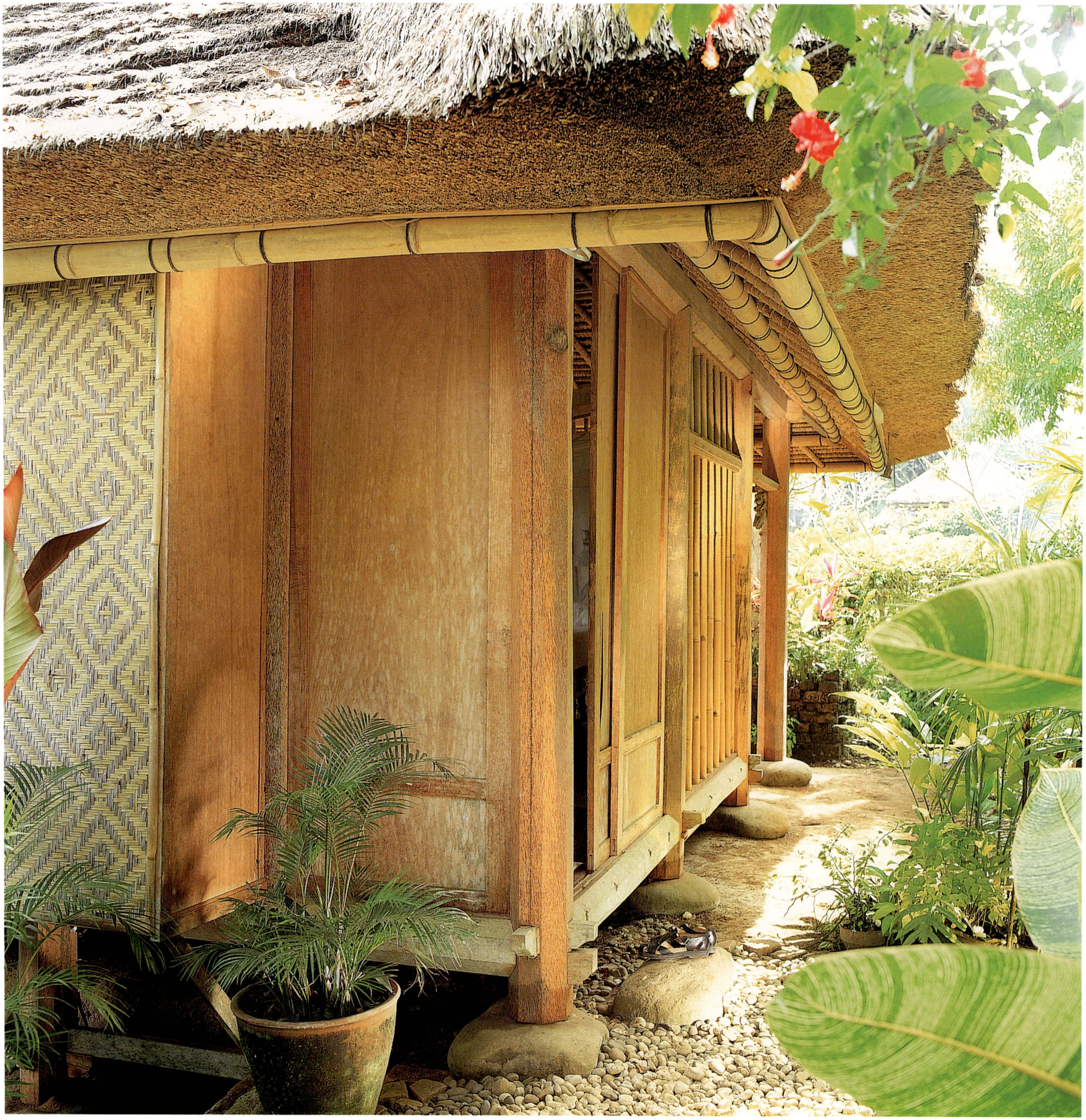

BALE: THE PAVILION → **ENCLOSED AND SEMI-ENCLOSED PAVILIONS 3.2**

DOMESTIC ARCHITECTURE

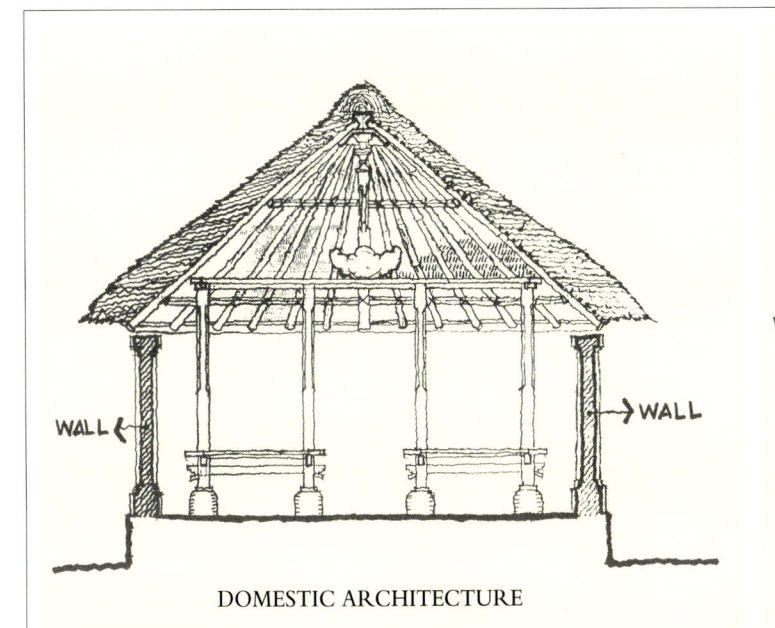

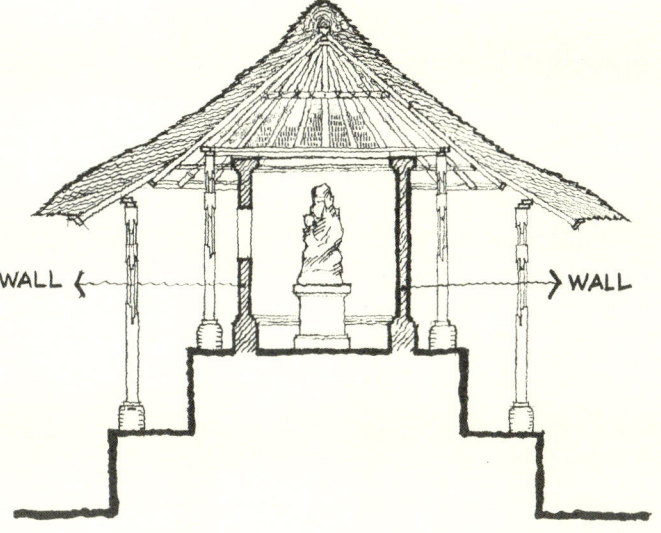

TEMPLE ARCHITECTURE

A. This mountain-style pavilion at the Taman Bebek hotel in Sayan has sliding screen doors between the coconut wood columns. Note the handsome big bamboo eave plates (kolong tiying) and natural river-stone column plinths (sendi). The pavilion was modelled on the cabin-like dwellings in Belantih village, a Bali Aga village near Kintamani, but inspired by Peter Muller's 1972 reworking of Dutch artist Rudolf Bonnet's old studio (1950-1965) in Campuhan, Ubud.

B. In domestic architecture walls sit on the edge of the stylobate outside the columns.

C. In many ceremonial structures, walls are placed inside the columns.

D. The kitchen pavilion at PJ's restaurant, the Four Seasons Resort, Jimbaran.

53

3.3 Pavilion Roof Forms

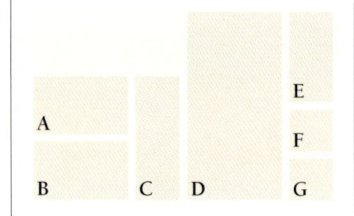

A. Traditional roof shapes.

B. Traditional roofs with porches or awnings (emper) added or roof sections removed.

C. Non-traditional roof shapes, suitable for tiled roof pavilions.

D. The magnificent meru to the god of Mt Agung on the top terrace of the Pura Jagatnata temple in Ketewel.

E. A pagoda-like meru in an austere temple in the ancient lakeside village of Songan.

F. The central gedong shrine pavilion of the pura puseh in Bayunggede has a striking ijuk roof and an unusual carved treefern-trunk ridge cover.

G. A bamboo-shingled lumbung roof.

Roofs on Balinese pavilions are either pure rectangular prism forms—called *malimas*, from the Javanese *limasan* (fused at the ridges)—or gabled, like the six-poster *bale sakenam* most often used for kitchens. Porch-like verandah attachments are called *emper*. Traditionally one should never have more than two, sheet-like *emper* off a pure roof form (see diagrams below) or the building becomes "hot" (unlucky).

Roofs also come piled one on top of the other, as in *meru* pagodas, *wantilan* halls, or *bale bali* in mountain temples.

The humble *lumbung* (rice loft) roof form has lately been used with limited success in many expatriate homes and hotels in Bali and Lombok and the broad Bali Style diaspora. The shape traps hot air and can shed bamboo dust (*bubuk*) on the human occupants. Restraint needs to be exercised in using this roof form if one hopes to escape criminal offences against geometry and theology.

Since the advent of the Dream Home movement in the 1970s, amateur architects have been fusing and cramming together different roof forms. One should take care not to create ungainly mishmashes: the beauty of the best Balinese architecture is in its elegant roof lines and the simple "play of roofs" in a courtyard.

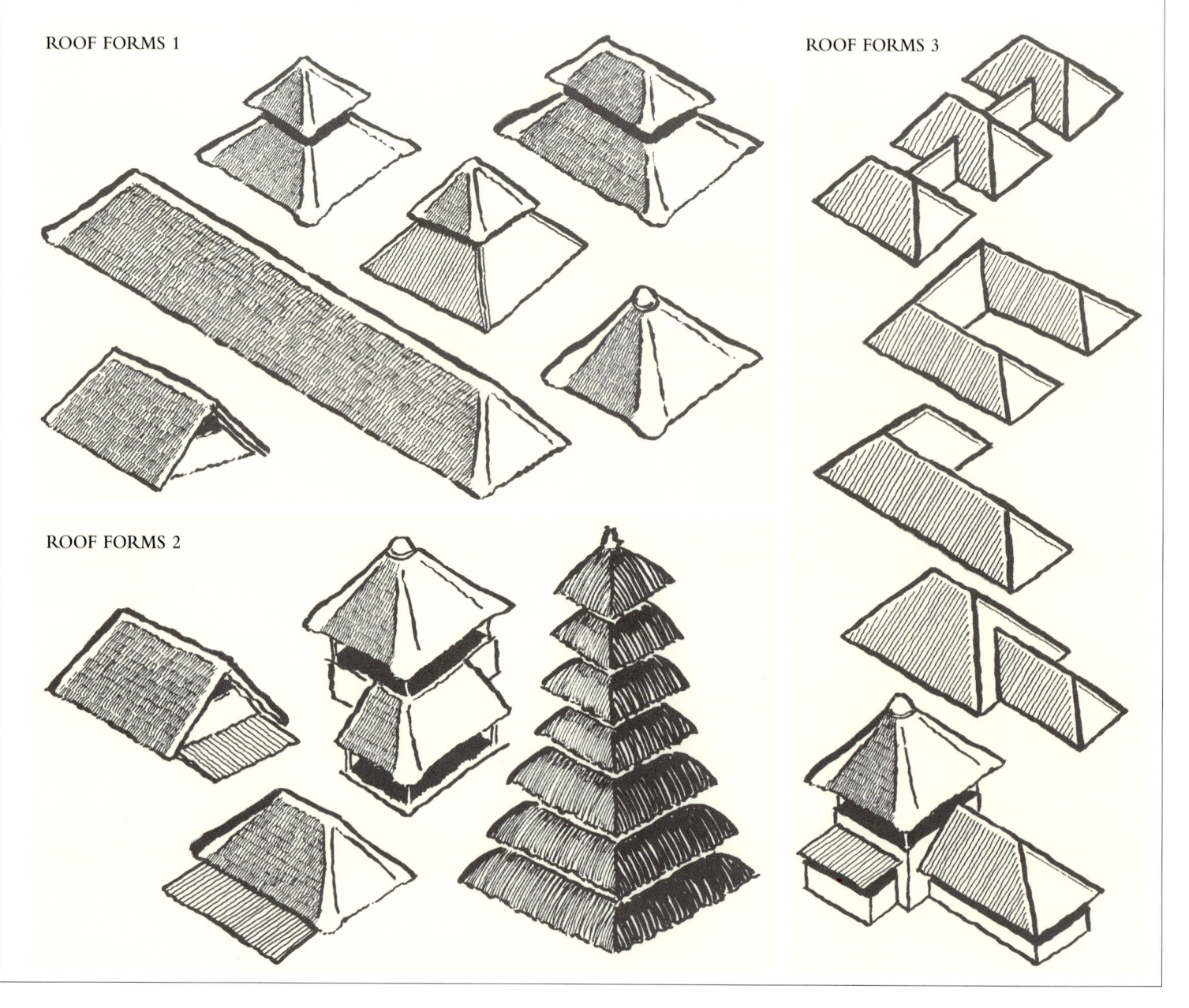

ROOF FORMS 1

ROOF FORMS 2

ROOF FORMS 3

BALE: THE PAVILION → **PAVILION ROOF FORMS 3.3**

55

3.4 Shrine Pavilions

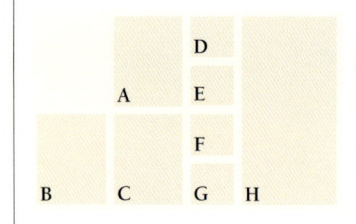

	D		
A	E		
	F		
B	C	G	H

A. *A bale pepelik pavilion for the gods. Note the double row of posts called Adegan Mabanjah.*

B. *This shrine in the Javanese Majapahit style in the old Majapahit Museum in Trowulan, east Java was built by famed Dutch architect-archaeologist Henri Maclaine Pont in the 1930s.*

C. *Mountain, Bali Aga and north coast temples often have shrine pavilions with multiple altars. This example is in Padangkerta village. Note the simple, ancient Bali ornamentation.*

D. *A typical shrine pavilion spirit house, mountain style, sketched by Stephen Little.*

E. *In many mountain villages shrines are just miniature spirit boxes modelled on special bale pavilion proportions, placed on low stone plinths.*

F. *Pelinggih shrine in a holy, spring-fed lake at Pura Gunung Kawi, Sebatu.*

G. *In Munduk village, high on the Bedugul-Seririt mountain pass, rows of altars gathered inside one low-slung pavilion can be found in family house shrines.*

H. *Shrines to Dewi Sri, the rice goddess, and to mountain deities often have pointy roofs—in this case, ijuk fibre roof thatch—over simple timber altars.*

Shrines, called *pelinggih*, have three portions: the base, usually fashioned out of stone; the *praba* (meaning "head"), usually made from timber; and the roof which may be *ijuk* sugar palm fibre (as this is the tallest of the island's palms), corrugated iron or, in the mountains, bamboo shingles.

The *praba* takes its dimensions from the golden proportions of Balinese pavilion architecture; in fact, *praba* are miniature pavilions. The auxiliary shrine buildings—the *paruman*, *payadnyan*, *payogan* and *pewedan*—are also variations on pure pavilion form. The *padmasari* style of shrine is more an open altar and has neither *praba* nor roof.

In ancient Bali Aga villages, one finds temples that are really just elegant four-poster pavilions, as in the stunningly located Pura Puseh at Tenganan. One also finds shrine buildings in these ancient villages that are *bale bali* 12-poster ceremonial pavilions with handsome walls, and even miniature *candi bentar* gates wrapped tightly around reduced pilasters, on the edge of the stylobate (*bataran*).

BALE: THE PAVILION → **SHRINE PAVILIONS 3.4**

3.5 Traditional Forms in Modern Houses

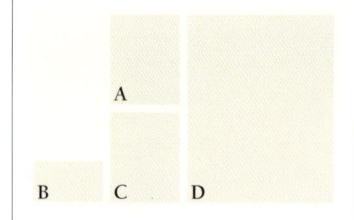

A. A high-based staff house building at Villa Kirana, Sayan is quasi-traditional in the sense that a timber pavilion structure has been placed on top of an exaggerated stylobate, like a ceremonial *bale agung*.

B. The Cheadle House, Canggu mixed mountain pavilion style with more Mexican and Moroccan influences.

C. Amir Rabik's three-tiered *wantilan*-style guesthouse in his Sanggingan, Ubud, home (1995 photo).

D. A guesthouse on the Linda Garland estate is made entirely of bamboo, coconut wood and thatch.

Following pages: An unusual brace of meru pagoda and pelinggih shrines in the dalem (inner sanctum) of the vast Pura Desa, Batuan. The carved treatment of the beautiful brick and paras shrine bases is typical of the Gianyar Regency.

The use of traditional architecture in contemporary western-style houses has been the preoccupation of progressive architects since Dutch colonial times. The studio-homes of Rudolf Bonnet and Walter Spies in Ubud in the 1920s and '30s exhibited a deft reworking of Balinese traditional forms for western needs, such as en suite bathrooms and spacious reception rooms. One can find early colonial-era examples in the island's churches, the retirement villas in hill stations such as Bedugul, and in Singaraja on the northern coast where oversized *meten*-like mansions were built from mud balls.

In the late 1950s, local architects built government buildings that were essentially oversized traditional buildings made of concrete. They were often faced with a veneer of red brick and soapstone—sometimes handsome, often gaudy. From the 1970s, expatriate architects, in their designs for contemporary houses, have worked with and around traditional architecture. Following the example of early settlers, such as artists Bonnet and Spies, the architects of the Expatriate Dream Home movement and the tourism boom have bent, borrowed and contorted traditional forms to accommodate modern needs.

The lobby of the Bali Hyatt and its main restaurant, for example, were the first mega-*wantilan* used in hotel design. Peter Muller also fused traditional form and modern need with considerable success in the public areas of his ground-breaking Kayu Aya (now the Bali Oberoi) and, 15 years later, in the handsome public areas of the Amandari.

The challenge has always been to keep the roof forms traditional while minimizing the rows of tightly packed pavilion posts that clutter open areas.

BALE: THE PAVILION → **TRADITIONAL FORMS IN MODERN HOUSES 3.5**

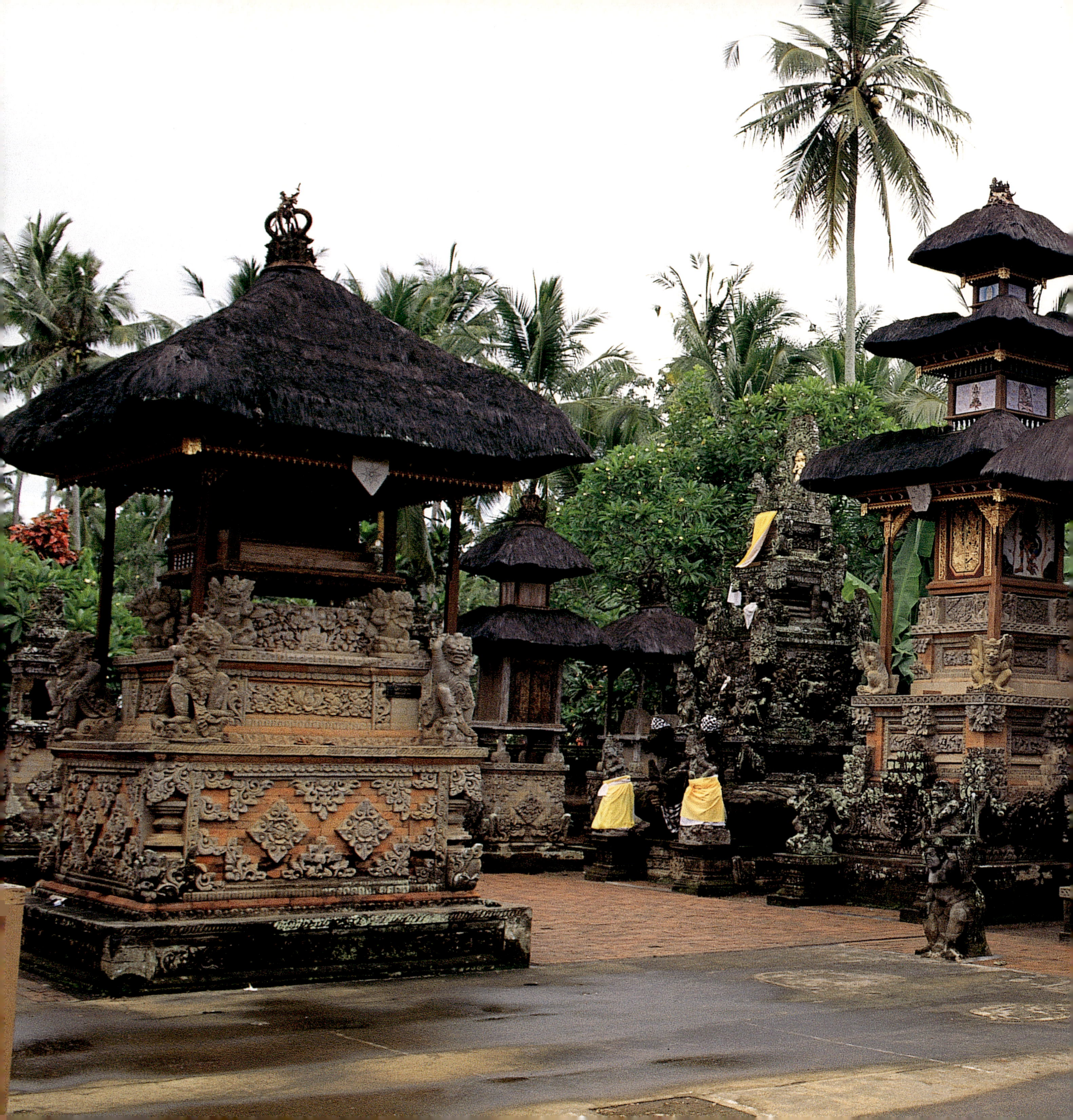

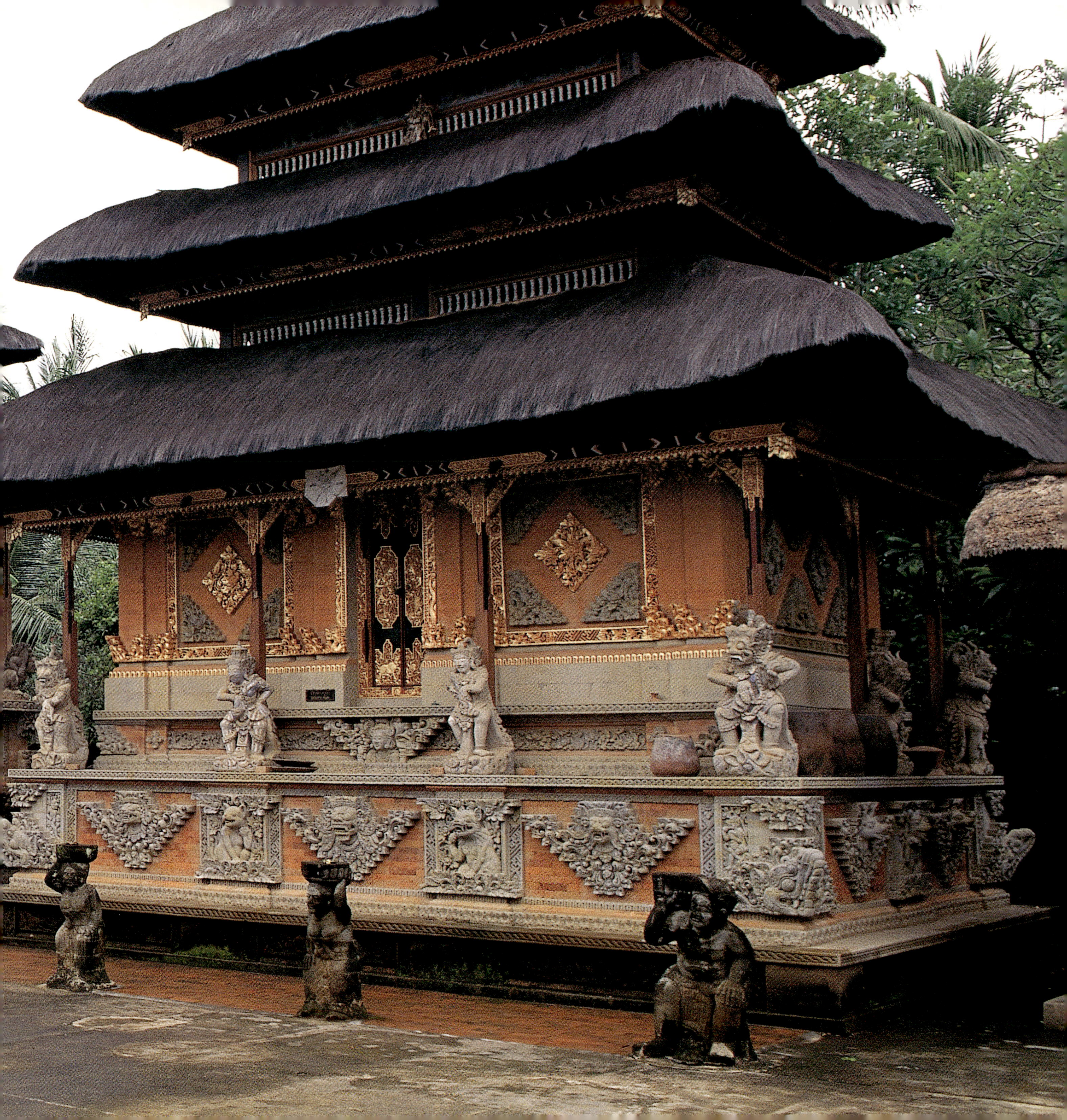

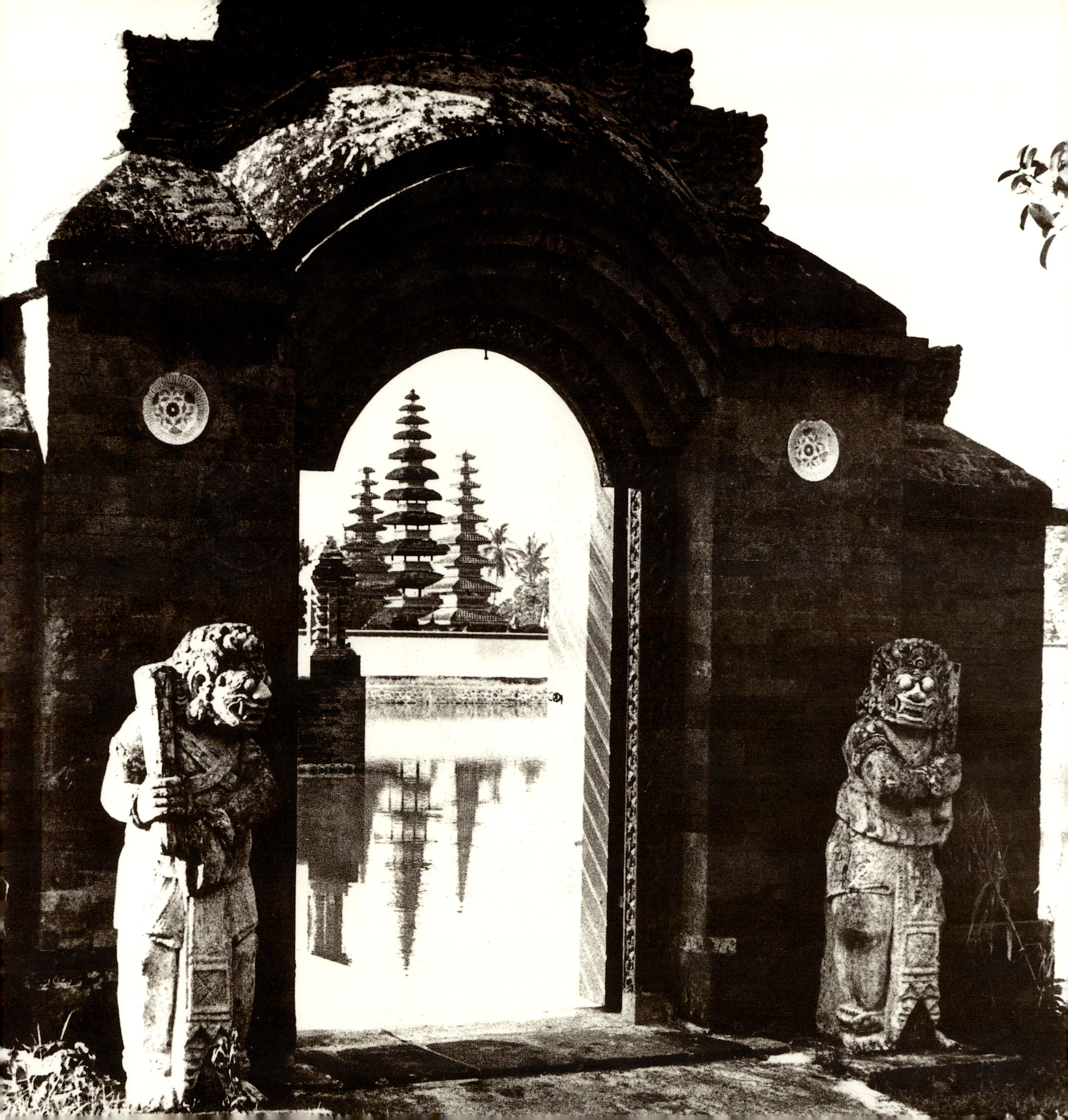

Chapter 4

Courtyard Elements

4.1	Walls	64
4.2	Gates	68
4.3	Terracing, Gate Steps and *Leneng*	74
4.4	Ground Surfaces	78
4.5	Organizing Space in a Courtyard	80

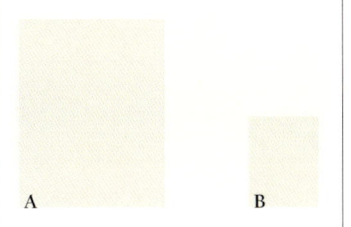

A   B

A. The pleasure gardens of the Puri Mayura palace in Cakranegara, the Balinese quarter of western Lombok. The complex is surrounded by thick red brick walls.

B. The steps and gate of Pura Pengerebongan in Kesiman, Denpasar become a stage during the biannual odalan *festival*.

The Balinese courtyard is much more than just pavilions within a walled compound: the organization of the space between pavilions into zones of activity is as important as the placement of the pavilions themselves. The type of gate is a function of the courtyard's usage too. Family compounds are announced by imposing gates, while temples have giant carved split gates called *candi bentar*. Gates lead from one realm into another through a succession of walled courts. They are as significant to the courtyard's spatial and spiritual functioning as are the changes of level that denote the status—temporal to spiritual—of different zones of activity.

Most courtyards have numerous sacred spots: there are shrines to the spirit of the land, often outside the main gate; an ancestor shrine on an elevated portion in the mountainward sector of the compound; and, since Majapahit times, altars to Shiva in the centre of the main temple court. In palaces, central audience halls and music pavilions sit among paved courts and paths.

In modern times the *jaba* forecourts of old have become car parks or art shops and the *teba* backyards have sprouted homestays for tourists. The paved spaces between buildings, however, no matter how small, are still work and entertainment areas.

Architects on both sides of the equator have long been aware of the power of courtyard architecture. Since the 1980s, more and more have opted for Balinese courtyard-style homes, particularly in Southeast Asia. A good example of successfully borrowing from traditional courtyard elements is the rotunda-like *bale bengong*, or corner pavilion, which is today found in many of the island's hybrid homes, either poolside or in a quiet garden corner.

"Less is more" has become "too much is not enough" in many modern courtyard homes, palaces, hotels and art museums. Restraint is needed in the selection of courtyard elements used to emulate successfully the elegance and organization of the traditional Bali courtyard.

4.1 Walls

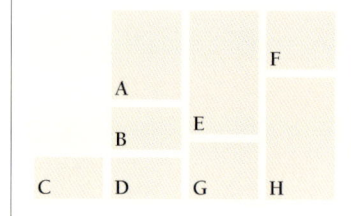

		F	
A			
B	E		
C	D	G	H

A. *A handsome river-stone wall surrounds a farmer's compound in Padangkerta, eastern Bali. The little alcoves are for daily offerings.*

B. *Capped walls and pillars are typical on courtyard walls across the island. They help disperse the tropical rain.*

C. *Temple and palace walls often have elaborate panels of rich decoration or, as became popular during the 19th century, ceramic air vents.*

D. *In the temples and palaces of old, walls were often perforated with see-through panels of timber or stone.*

E. *A woven bamboo fence, elevated to protect it from rising damp, in Pemuteran, northern Bali.*

F. *In villages high in the mountains the popolan (adobe) walls are sometimes built without coping elements. The night cold hardens the adobe mix and makes it more impervious to the detrimental effects of rain.*

G. *Ornate paras stone temple wall, viewed from inside a temple pavilion, at the Pura Puseh temple, Guwang, Sukawati. The capitals on the pillars are of the gunung penanggungan form.*

H. *In mountain villages bamboo shingle cappings protect the tops of adobe courtyard walls.*

The main compound wall differentiates the realm of the humans from the *jaba*, the zone of the netherworld. It also keeps out stray dogs, chickens, pigs and thieves. In palaces, main family branches are often enclosed in separated walled courts. In the case of temple compounds and house temple courtyards, walls differentiate the spiritual world from the temporal.

The proportions and treatment of courtyard walls say a lot about the status of the inhabitants, or the deities, housed within. Palace walls are tall and imposing, using a grander scale (as do palace pavilions). Temple walls are ornate, lovingly fashioned from masoned blocks of soapstone or outsized bricks. Pillars, called *paduraksa*, are capped with pyramidal forms. In temples these cappings are highly decorative, often symbolizing the sacred mountain form of Gunung Penanggungan with its four surrounding peaks, from the Majapahit-era architecture in Java.

The style and type of courtyard walls, while often uniform within a village, vary widely across the island. In northern Bali, rich Bali Baroque cement work creates a spun-sugar sweetness of decorative form in the walls and pillars of the palaces and temples. In the simple mud architecture of mountain villages, pillars are often non-existent. In eastern Bali, compound walls are often low and quite squat. In the Gianyar Regency, walls are slender and shapely.

Low walls (*leneng*) often flank Balinese gates: they are neighbourhood sitting rooms, neutral spaces where neighbours stop to chat or feuding family members, stroking bipartisan roosters, may sit together without it counting as an official house call.

COURTYARD ELEMENTS → **WALLS 4.1**

65

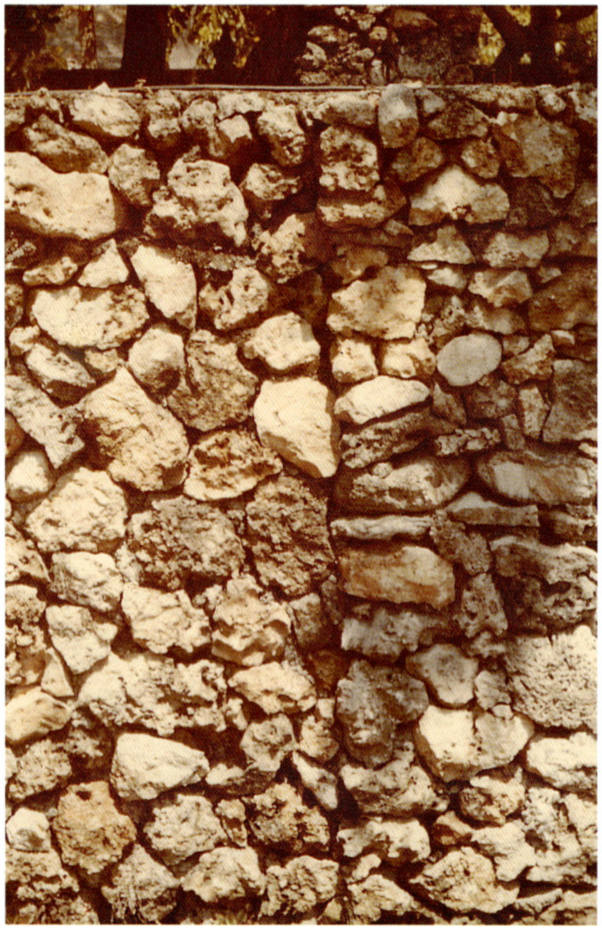

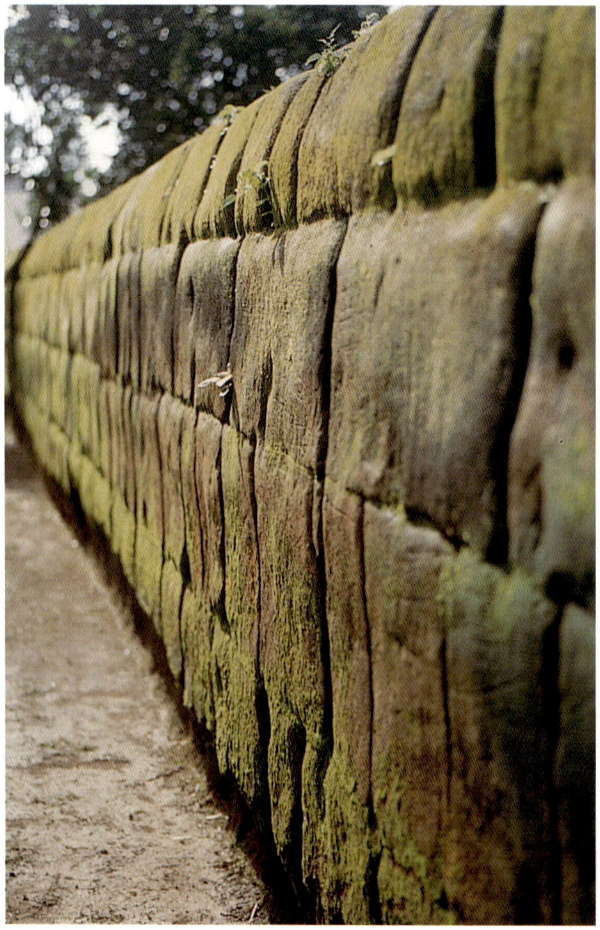

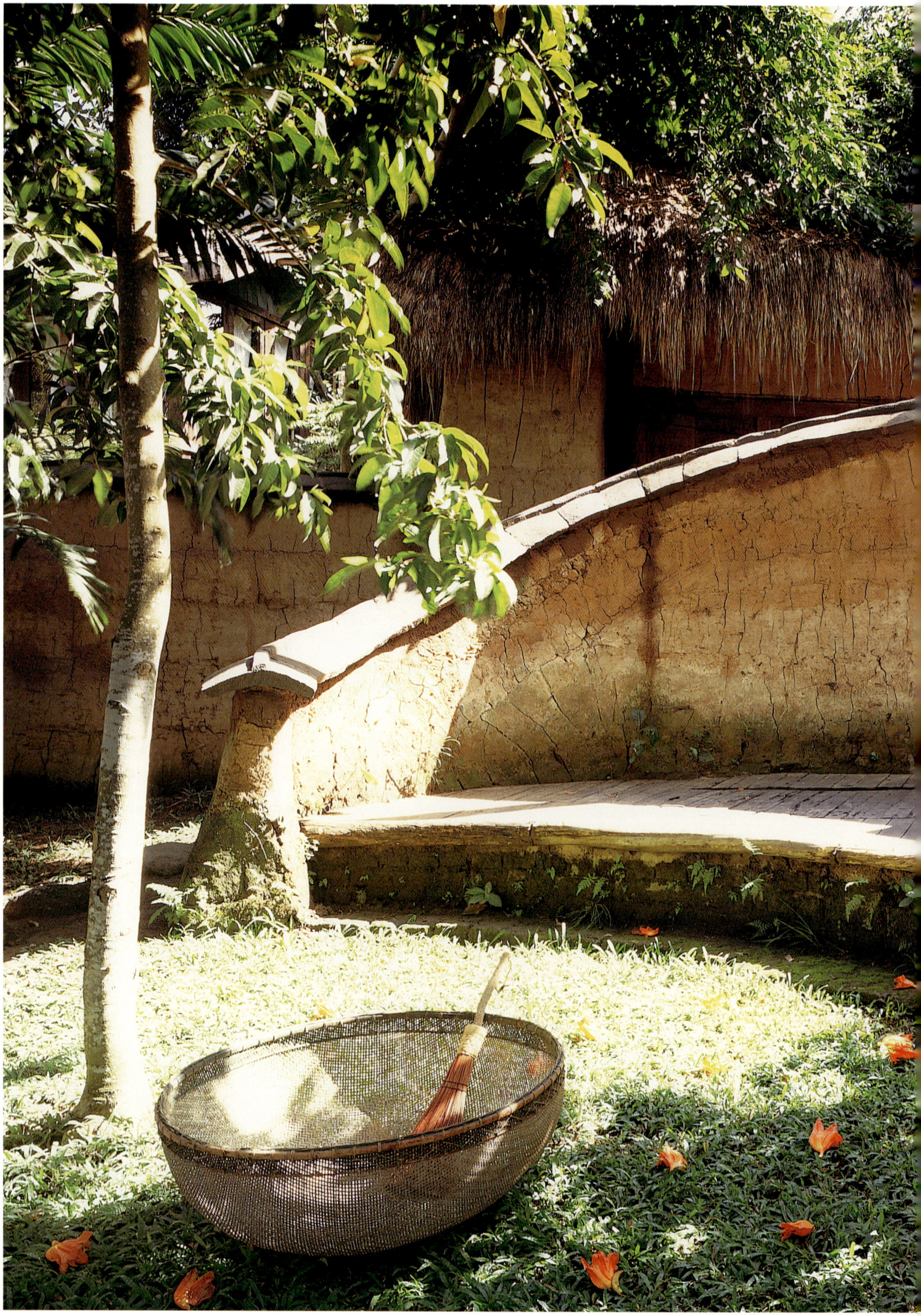

COURTYARD ELEMENTS → **WALLS 4.1**

A. *The limestone courtyard walls popularized by Geoffrey Bawa in his work at Batujimbar in Sanur (1972) and Peter Muller in his Bali Oberoi (1972) were much used in the Bali coastal architecture of the 1980s and '90s.*

B. *Popolan (adobe) walls are constructed in stages. "Stretch marks" often appear during the 3-10-day drying period.*

C. *The Hardy house in Sayan exhibits many interesting adobe and bamboo fencing elements.*

4.2 Gates

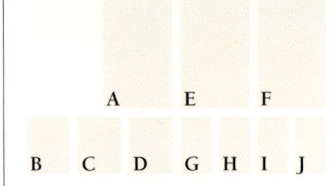

A	E	F

| B | C | D | G | H | I | J |

A. *The* kori agung *gate (with Boma guardian face realized in neo-art nouveau style) on the Pura Puseh, Gaji, Kerobokan.*

B. *A striking but simple* paduraksa *form gate, built of paras ukir stone, Geria Guang, Guwang, Gianyar. Note the Majapahit-style two-leafed door decorated with bold, contrasting, ancient Bali colours.*

C. *The entrance gate to the old* pura puseh *in Bayunggede, Kintamani, has side platforms, called* taban, *wrapped around its pavilion columns.*

D. *Brick or stone screen walls, called* aling-aling, *are often set just inside the gate, to deflect malign influences. Gates lead from one realm to another and are important to the spatial and spiritual functioning of the courtyard, as are the changes in level.*

E. *Ancient Bali gates are sometimes found in mountain temples: these are just pavilions with a timber partition wall, and with a door in the centre of the pavilion.*

F. *This* angkul-angkul popolan *gate,* sumi-*thatch courtyard wall and village lane streetscape on the Sanur road at Batujimbar, my home during 1980-88, is no more. It is now a video rental emporium.*

G. *The brick main gate of the Pura Lingsar in western Lombok (a Balinese colony since the 17th century) has flanking walls, called* gandengan.

H. *Italianate palace gate at the Puri Batubulan.*

I. *A village lad, bearing offerings, on the steps of the main gate to Geria Guang, a Brahman house in Gianyar Regency.*

J. *A beautiful temple gate with an ancient pavilion roof form appearing to be squeezed off the top, Kuda village, Bali.*

The courtyard gate is a welcoming element, not a barrier. Left open in the daytime, it is bolted shut at night, when the last person goes to sleep.

Gates are also the "processing portals" of Balinese courtyard psychology: they can lead one from one state of mind to another, from the dreamily indifferent to the guarded, as experienced in a Balinese multi-courtyard home, with all its sibling rivalries.

One ancient form of the temple gate was a four-posted pavilion bisected by a wall (see photos C and E) which evolved into the *paduraksa*, or roofed gate, form. Interestingly this Hindu form is also found in the gate of Mesjid Agung, the 18th-century mosque on the palace square in Yogyakarta, central Java.

Today, temple gates are either split gates, called *candi bentar*, or large *paduraksa* roofed gates. House gates and *paduraksa*-type temple gates often have attendant screen walls just inside the courtyard. Called *aling-aling*, these are usually built of brick or stone and are said to block the entry of malevolent spirits, which, we are told, only travel in straight lines.

Traditionally, one could read a person's social rank, and even his aesthetic senses, from his gate. With creeping gentrification, gates are now indicators of a family's aspirations.

COURTYARD ELEMENTS → **GATES 4.2**

69

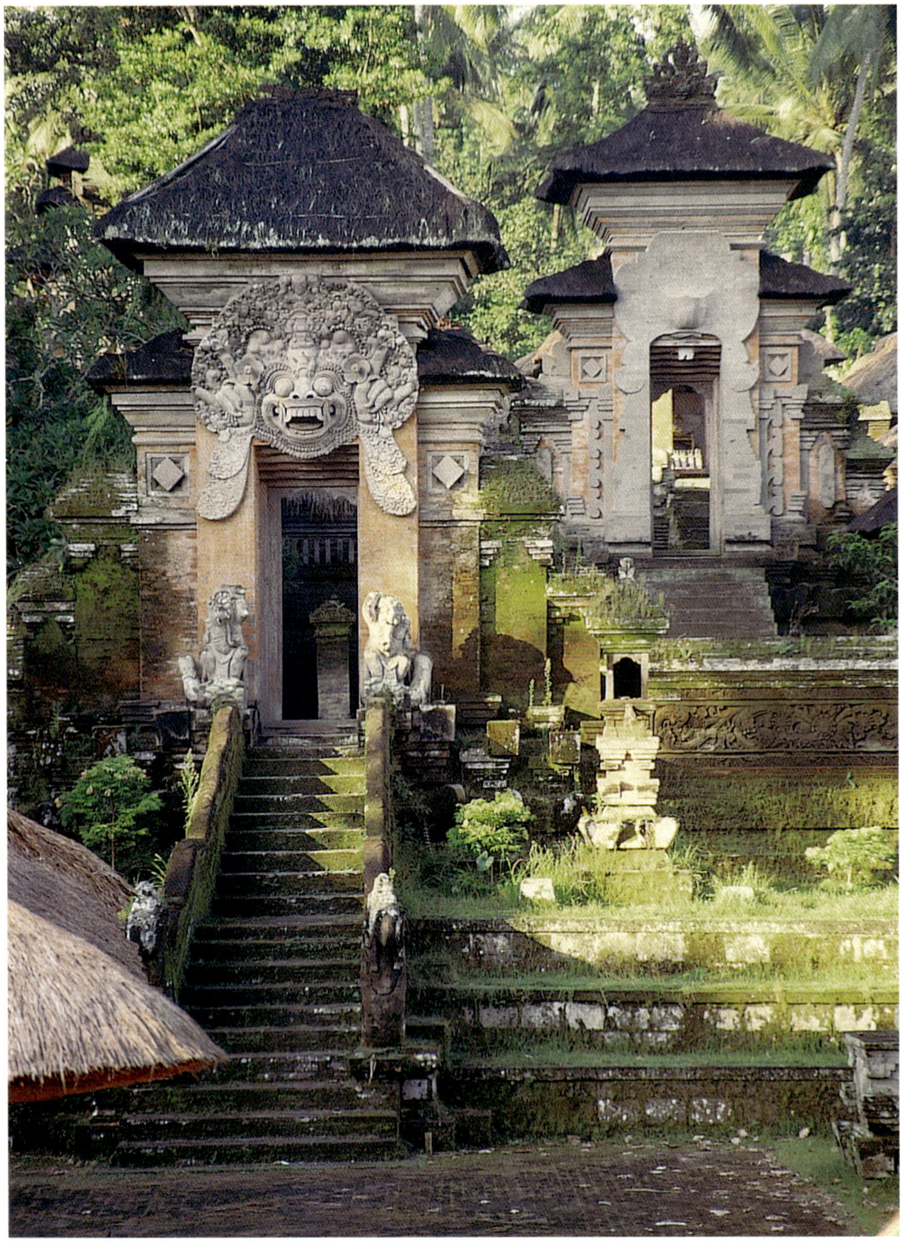
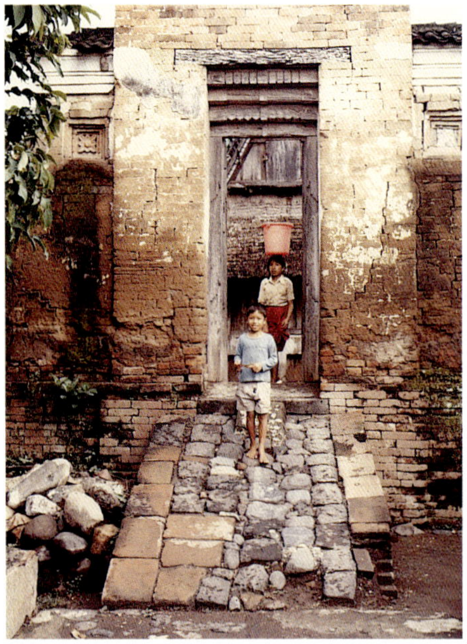
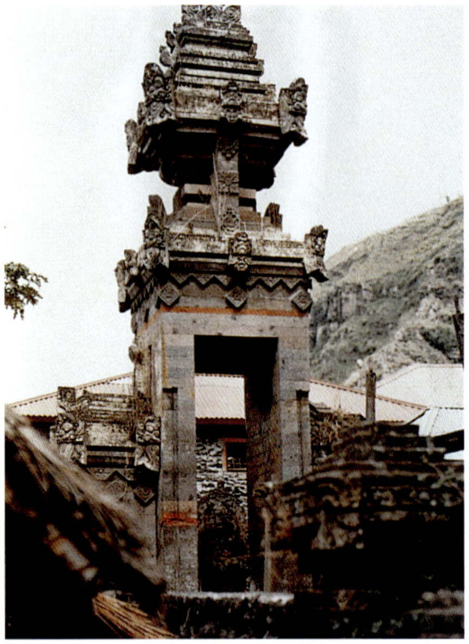
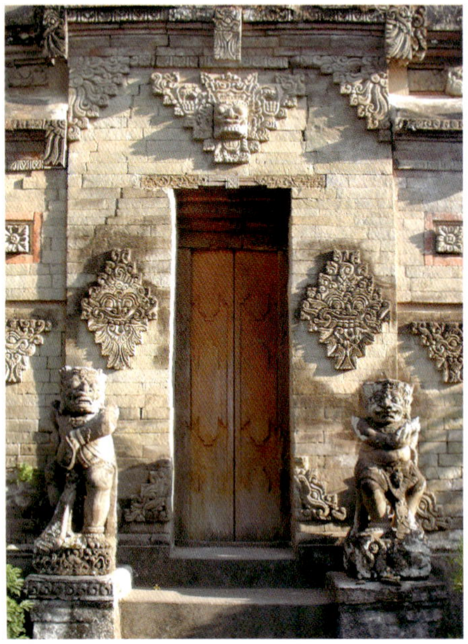
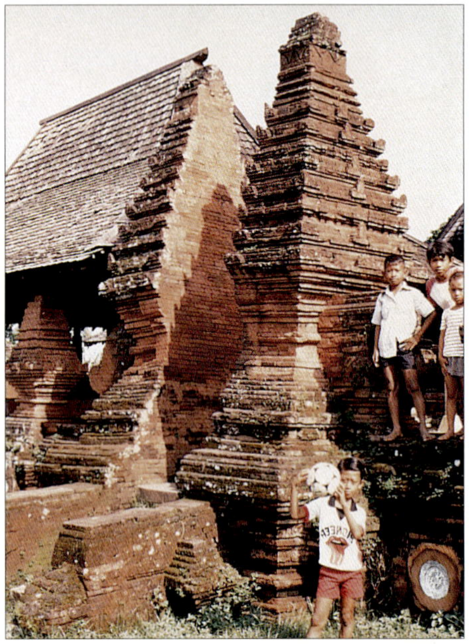
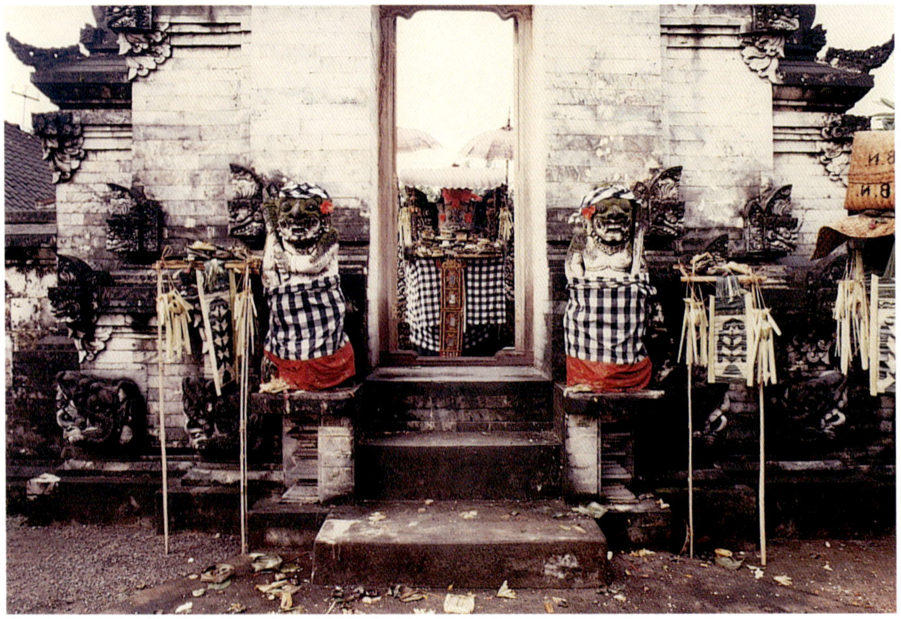
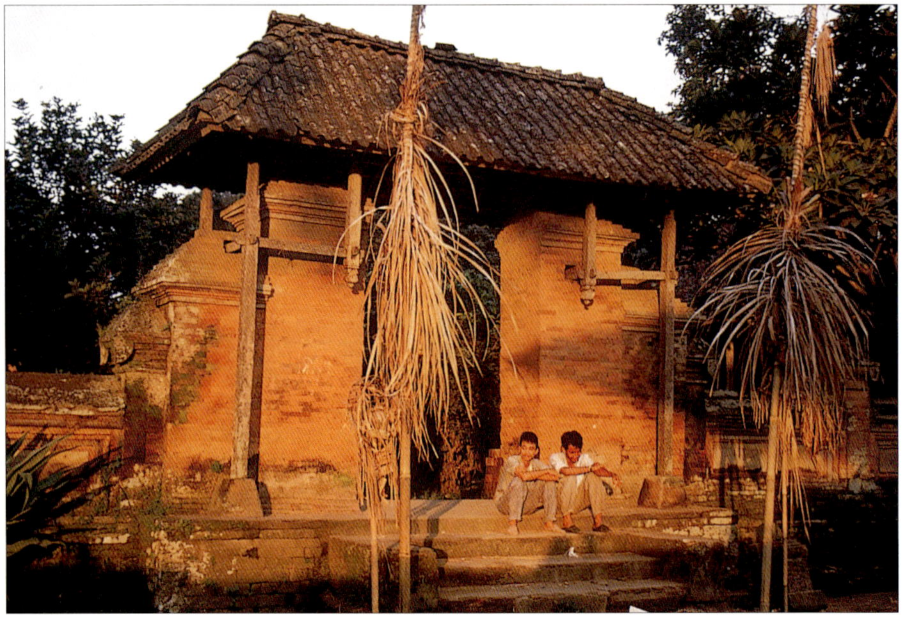

COURTYARD ELEMENTS → **GATES** 4.2

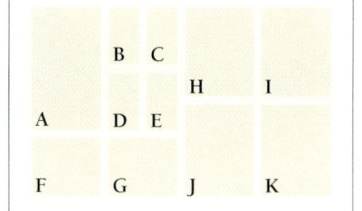

	B	C		
			H	I
A	D	E		
F	G	J	K	

A. *The twin* kori agung *on the terraced sanctuary temple Samuan Tiga, Bedulu.*

B. *In the 19th century most gates had ramps, not steps.*

C. *An exotic gate in Songan village on Lake Batur (1985 photo).*

D. *Subtle beauty: the handsome paras paduraksa gate in the Pura Desa, Guwang, Gianyar Regency.*

E. *A candi bentar or split gate in the Majapahit-era Kasepuhan palace in Cirebon, western Java—an ancestor of Bali's brick architecture.*

F. *Coral temple gate in Banjar Singgi, Sanur (1981 photo).*

G. *A rare gate form in Payangan village, at the entrance to the palace (1985 photo).*

H. *A thatched angkul-angkul gate in a typical village (1979 photo).*

I. *This 1930s photo shows a famous northern Bali temple gate near Kubutambahan.*

J. *Temporary gates are sometimes woven from coconut palm fronds for weddings and other ceremonies when proper gates do not exist.*

K. *House compound gate of carved paras taro in Bukian village.*

71

72

COURTYARD ELEMENTS → **GATES** 4.2

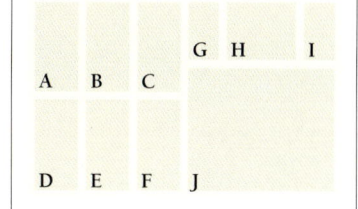

			G	H		I
A	B	C				
D	E	F	J			

A selection of brick, stone, mud brick and carved mud brick house gates from:

A. *The Puri Gede palace in Amlapura, Karangasem (1980 photo).*

B. *The Geria Ketewel, a Brahman compound (1980 photo).*

C. *Iseh village (1985 photo).*

D. *Iseh village (1995 photo).*

E. *Bukian village (1979 photo).*

F. *Ramps and squat split gates were de rigueur in 19th-century palace architecture. This 1985 photo is of the Puri Gede palace in Karangasem.*

G. *An example of the ramp and squat split gate, captured in a 1918 photograph.*

H. *A squat classic candi bentar or split gate at the Pura Desa, Guwang, Gianyar Regency.*

I. *A pig-proof fence is held in place by a bamboo keep on this mountain adobe house temple gate, Bukian village.*

J. *The Uluwatu temple gate is one of the finest on the island. The architect was the famous 16th-century architect-scholar-priest Dhang Hyang Dwijendra, also known as Dhang Hyang Nirartha.*

4.3 Terracing, Gate Steps and *Leneng*

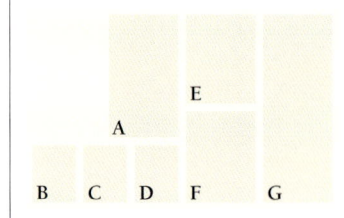

A. Gate steps are the grandstands of courtyard architecture. The Pengerebongan ceremony at Pura Dalem, Kesiman.

B. Images of dancers emerging from temple gates are an old Bali "glamour industry" staple.

C. The garden and flight of stairs that lead to Uluwatu temple in southern Bali.

D. The steps and leneng (low flanking walls) of Balinese gates are communal street furniture.

E. Classic set of temple steps made from volcanic tuff.

F. Grand terraced steps flanked by statues are a feature of many temples in the hills around Ubud.

G. Formal steps and architectural terracing are features of the island's grander temples.

Over the last 500 years the terraced commons of many ancient Balinese villages have been replaced by roads and highways. The gate and its stairs, however, still have a major role in courtyard ritual. The stairs continue to be used for smashing coconuts at the end of a temple festival, for example, or for "grandstand seating" during any rituals taking place in the *jaba* (house forecourt). They are also a general village sitting room, with flanking half-walls, called *leneng*.

Broad flights of stairs shaped from outsized pieces of soapstone with flanking stepped terraces are a pronounced feature of mountain temples, such as Pura Besakih, Pura Batur and the ancient state temple of Bangli, Pura Kehen. In northern Bali temples, the *jeroan* inner sanctum comes replete with high altars on extravagantly carved raised platforms with elaborate stairs.

Steps are the unsung heroes of Balinese architectural design. One always thinks of the towering gate rather than the magnificent flight of steps leading to it. The long stairway at Pura Besakih is deliberately intimidating (see photo A, page 76). The fabulous theatre of the Pengerebongan temple festival in Kesiman is performed on and around the steps of the great *kori* gate. And what would the performance of the *garuda* bird in the *legong* dance be without steps?

The elegant use of stairs and terraces at the Bali Oberoi in the early 1970s influenced a generation of architects. However in the last five years stairs have become like barriers or tank-traps in many Bali Modern projects.

COURTYARD ELEMENTS → **TERRACING, GATE STEPS AND LENENG 4.3**

76

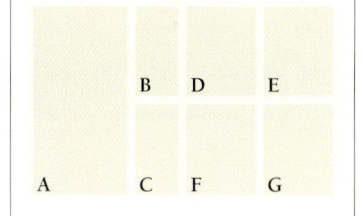

COURTYARD ELEMENTS → **TERRACING, GATE STEPS AND LENENG 4.3**

	B	D	E
A	C	F	G

A. Besakih temple's stairs with their "doormat for the gods" during the mammoth Eka Dasa Rudra ceremonies in 1978.

B. A cement gate in the mountain-deco style in Trunyan, on Lake Batur (1979 photo).

C. Paduraksa ceremonial gate of the famous Pura Kehen in Bangli, decorated for a temple festival, or odalan.

D. Pura Ulun Swi, in Kintamani, also known as Pura Batur, is the second most important temple in Bali, after Pura Besakih. The main paras ukir entrance gate (1980 photo) is understandably grand, flanked by naga dragon statues and other Hindu guardians.

E. Steps may be used as an outdoor sitting room.

F. A ramp on a house gate in Tenganan, eastern Bali.

G. Detail of the main piasan shrine of the ancient Pura Puseh in Tenganan (see photo A, page 28) showing a wide stair suitable for the loading and unloading of largish votive statues and offerings.

77

4.4 Ground Surfaces

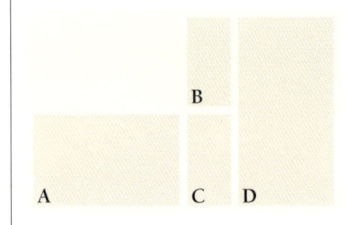

A. *The beautiful serene jeroan courtyard of Pura Besakih (the mother temple) with its compacted volcanic ash floor. Note the twin kul-kul towers, pemegat sot pavilion and matching bale lantang (long pavilions).*

B. *House courts are often pebbled or paved to accommodate ritual activities that take place on the courtyard floor.*

C. *Compacted swept sand courtyard floors were once typical in Sanur village homes. This courtyard in the Villa Bebek is a homage to Jimmy Pandhi's old garden, still partially visible in Emily Gandha's garden at the Baruna Beach Hotel in Sanur.*

D. *Courtyards in Bali often have many ground surfaces on numerous levels. This Villa Bebek entrance court shows a transition from the cement tile of the entrance path—with rhino skin pattern, an old favourite in the 1960s—to the paras batu and grass combination of an adjacent garden court.*

The courtyard floor and the pavilion floor are both reception areas in Balinese courtyard architecture. The courtyard floor in a traditional compound is a functional space: it is an outdoor living room. At any time it can become a dance hall, a place for prayer sessions or an assembly hall.

Traditionally courtyard floors are tightly packed mud, sand, red bricks or stone pavers. At the same time, the surface needs to be soft enough to accommodate temporary structures—to drive in bamboo stakes for a priest's pavilion, for example, or to erect ceremonial parasols. In some temples the floor is well-clipped grass. Stepping-stone rows of worn river pebbles or stone pavers are not uncommon: they are often removed with the arrival of the dry season (March–November).

Courtyard floors are swept twice daily, as they are communal waste bins for fruit peels, offering off-cuts and general courtyard lifestyle detritus. It is the job of the children to sweep the courts with bundles of palm wisps: the rhythmic swishing is a quintessential Balinese sound, as the morning radio raga is to India.

Courtyard floors should be simple, to offset the often ornate pavilion or shrine bases. The sandy courts of coastal temples in Sanur, for example, inspired many famous gardens, notably the Bali Hyatt's foreshore grove-gardens, the La Taverna hotel's garden courts and Jimmy Pandhi's old residence in Sindu, now the Baruna Beach Hotel.

Apart from purely aesthetic concerns, a courtyard floor needs to have enough compacted or paved space for mass prayer sessions or to take the chairs and tables that spring up at wakes, weddings and other house ceremonies.

Sadly the swept dirt temple courtyard floor, an attractive garden surface, is fast disappearing, as village populations grow and more all-weather surfaces in temples are demanded. During the 1990s, architects and landscapers developed many clever ground surfaces for hotels to accommodate trolley and buggy traffic. The Four Seasons Resort at Jimbaran, for example, has a compacted limestone path that is part white sand, part white cement, and part limestone powder.

COURTYARD ELEMENTS → **GROUND SURFACES** 4.4

4.5 Organizing Space in a Courtyard

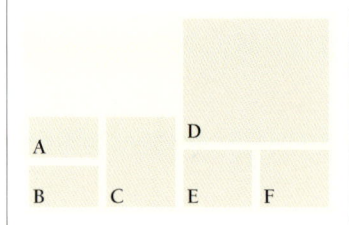

A		D	
B	C	E	F

A. *My bedroom suite during the years 1980-88 (the platform bed is in the pavilion to the left) in Jero Kubu, Sanur, and the raised house shrine I donated to my landlord's family in 1982.*

B. *Taken from inside a dining terrace at the Bali Style Villa Angsa in Mertasari, Sanur, this image illustrates how covered and open spaces—verandahs, pool decks, and open pavilions—interact in Balinese courtyard architecture.*

C. *A high priest climbs off a temporary* pewedan *platform which has been erected in a courtyard for a wedding ceremony.*

D. *The main courtyard of the patih temple at Pura Luhur, Uluwatu, showing the priests and the praying zone, various temporary platforms that spring up in a Balinese temple court at times of* odalan *anniversary festivals.*

E. *The* merajan agung *house temple of the Puri Agung Kesiman palace has large tracts of water garden between its principal shrine buildings. Space for ritual activities is provided between the ponds and courtyard walls.*

F. *Laundry, prawn crackers and coffee beans vie for a place in the sun in this typical mountain courtyard scene. The two elevated structures are rice barns.*

---

*Following pages: Unusual rice barn in the north Bali village of Sudaji. The rice barns (*lumbung*) of north Bali often feature carved doors and elaborate gargoyle-like column bases. A long work platform is suspended on the thick posts which support the structure.*

Balinese courtyard architecture is ideally suited to a tight-packed, low-tech tropical lifestyle. The open spaces of house compounds are used for sun-drying (laundry, harvested rice or prawn crackers), for crowded domestic ritual ceremonies, or as impromptu work sites. Verandahs, porches and open pavilions provide shelter where one can retreat to if it rains or if the sun is too fierce. Pavilions also allow for functions to be isolated—kitchens, for example, with their traditional smoky fuels, are in separate buildings—and patches of garden with useful flowering plants are interspersed between pavilions.

In larger compounds—particularly in the *jero*, *puri* and *griya* houses of the nobility—the public courtyards are used to entertain guests at times of ritual ceremonies, whereas the family courts are where the servants *(paraken)* and close family members make offerings or generally hole up.

Many courtyard spaces are designated "clearways", where temporary porches, called *taring*, are built to take stands of offerings or give shelter to a large gamelan orchestra.

In palaces large spaces are left open for marshalling mammoth cremation processions, for reception halls and theatrical performances for palace weddings and tooth-filings. Space is always left for the occasional *panggung agung*, a large but temporary shrine which sprouts up during house temple anniversaries, or a *pewedan* priest's pavilion, built for major rites of passage (see photo C, below).

At times of major ceremonies, such as cremations and tooth filings, temporary pavilions called *bale payadnyan* or *bale pawedan* are erected for the high priest and his offerings *(yadnya)* west of the *bale bali* ceremonial pavilion.

The traditional house always has a forecourt, called a *jaba*. These ceremonially important *jaba*, called *ajeng pura* in a temple, can be a large court, or as small as a welcome mat. Behind the house is the *teba*, or backyard—the communal toilets of old and, traditionally, the area for pig sties and growing bamboo. The *jaba* and *teba* are also spill-out zones during large gatherings.

COURTYARD ELEMENTS → **ORGANIZING SPACE IN A COURTYARD** 4.5

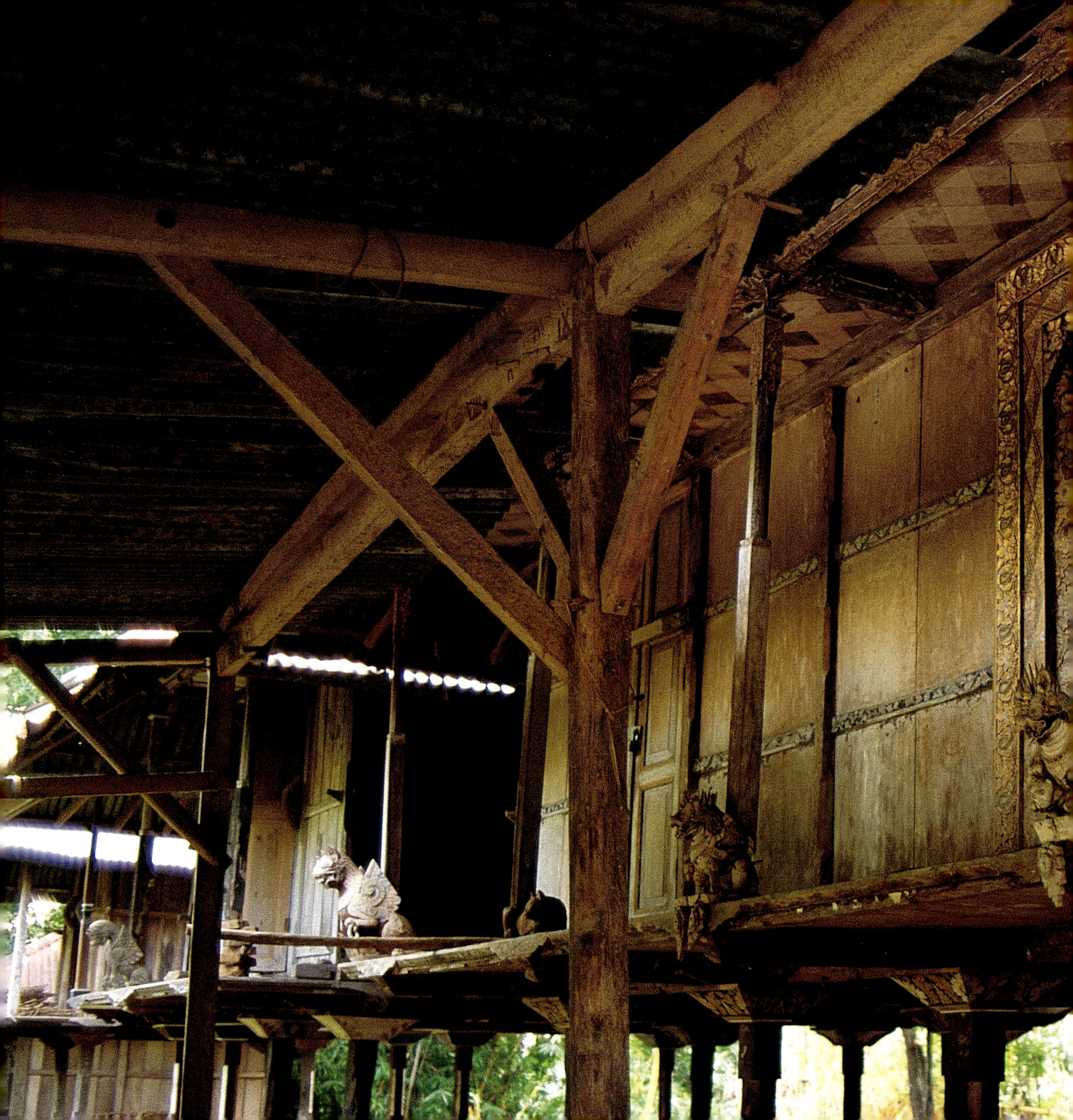

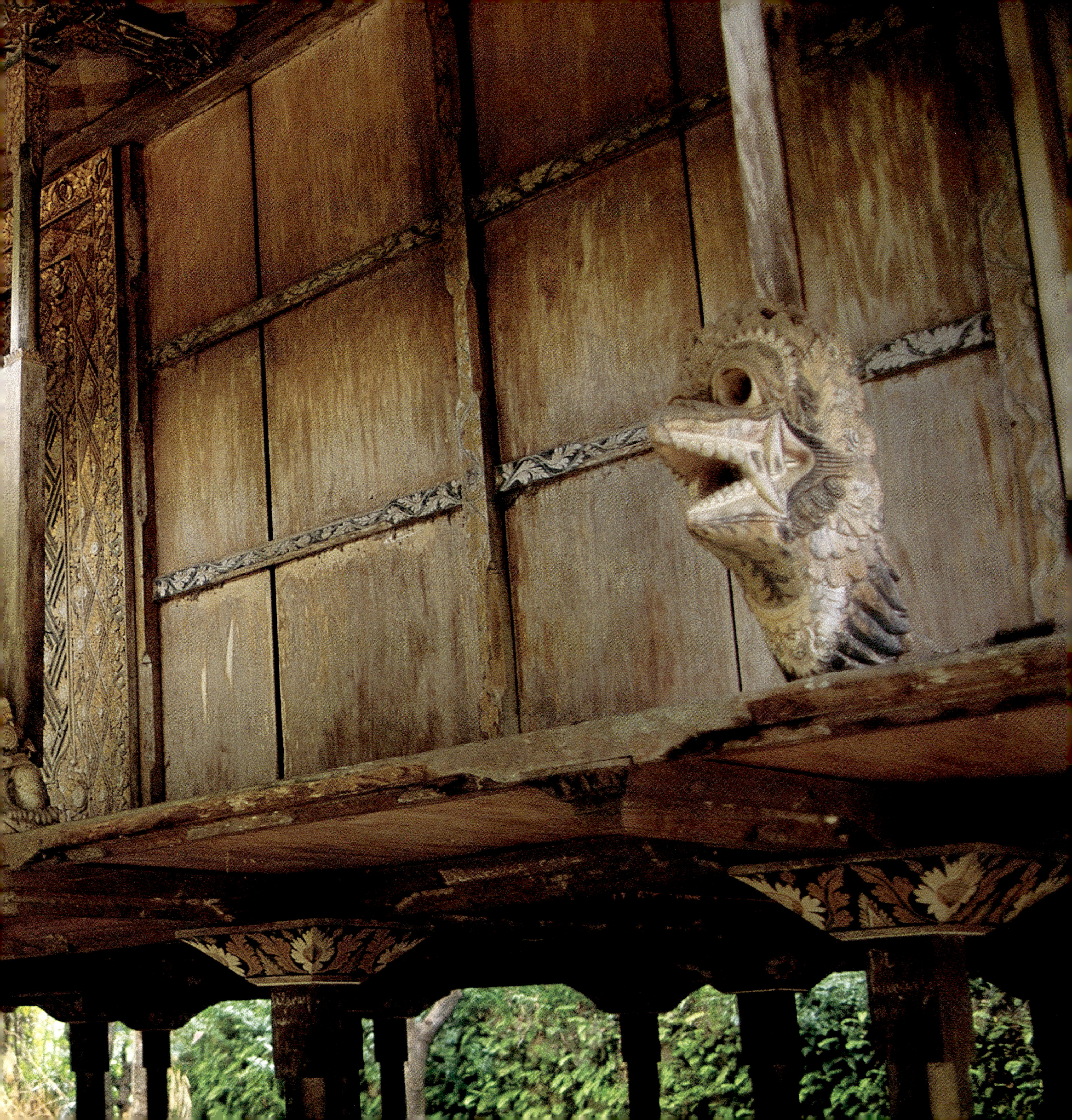

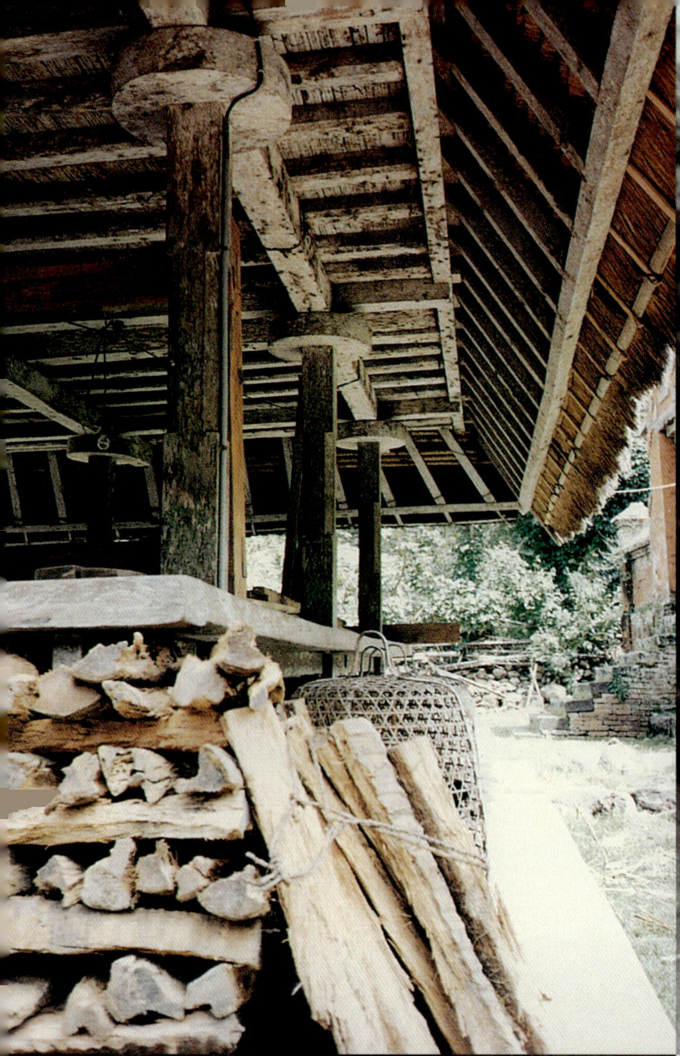

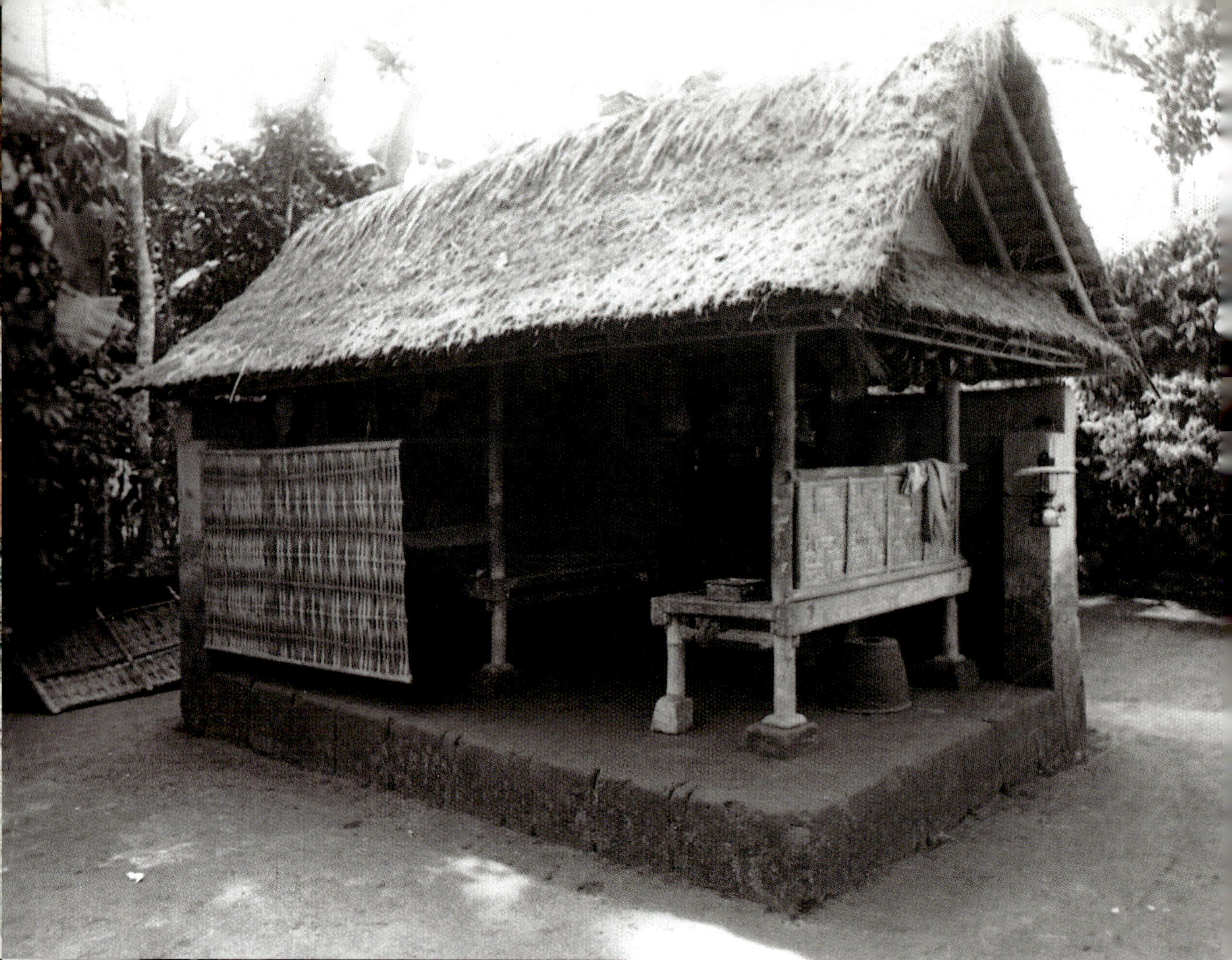

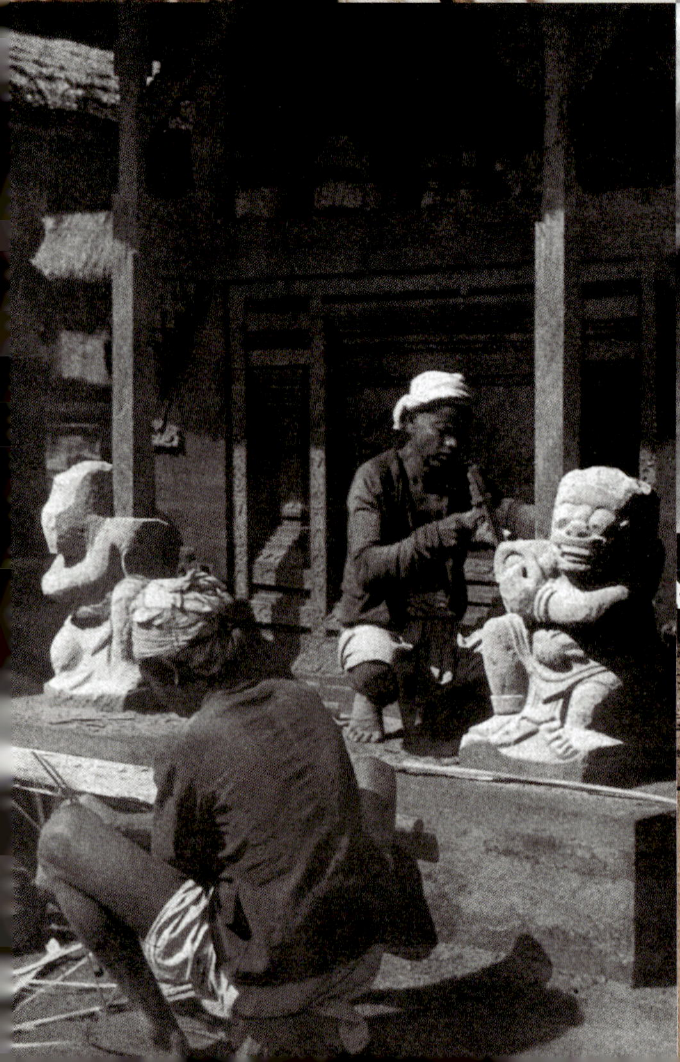

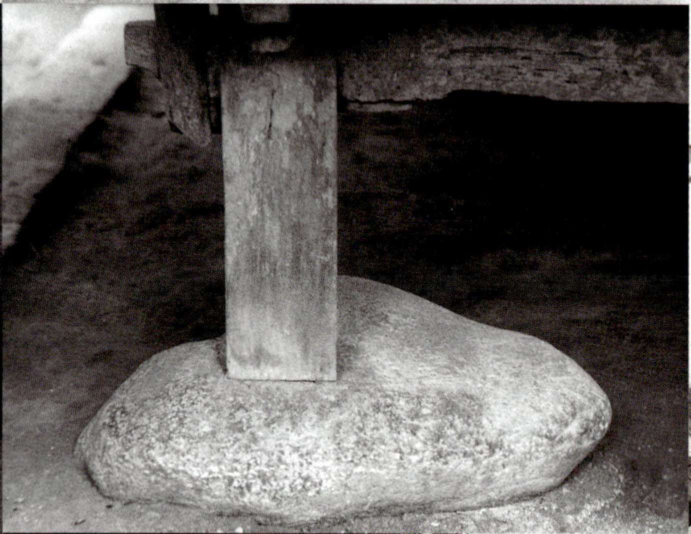

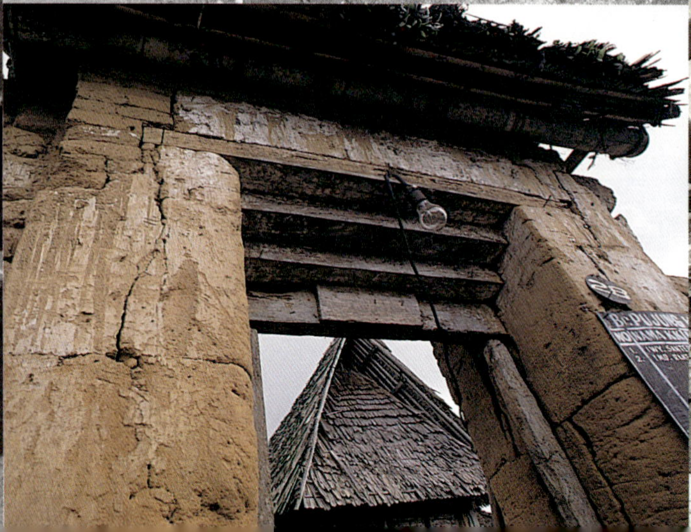

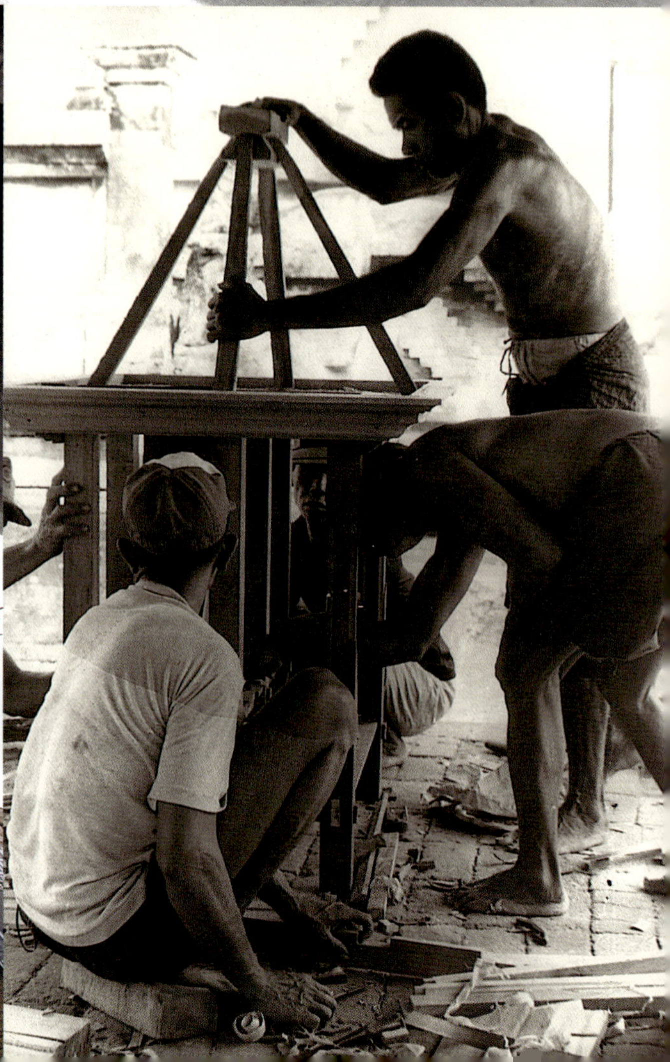

Chapter 5

PAVILION ELEMENTS

5.1	Basic Pavilion Construction	86
5.2	Bases and Foundations	90
5.3	Steps	92
5.4	Post Bases	94
5.5	Columns, Beams and Buttresses	96
5.6	Built-in Platforms	102
5.7	Walls and Screens	106
5.8	Doors	110
5.9	Windows and Air Vents	112
5.10	Roofs and King Posts	114
5.11	Organizing Space in Traditional Pavilions	118
5.12	Storage	120
5.13	Dividing Space in Modern Pavilions • Puri Ganesha • Villa Tirta Ayu • Amandari	122

Pavilion Elements

Pavilion forms are generally categorized by the number of columns (see 3.1 Types of Pavilions). Defining pavilion elements is like describing a model kit: it contains the main parts, such as the stylobate, called *bataran*, bollards (*sendi*) and columns (*tiang*), then optional elements such as built-in platforms (*taban*) which wrap around four columns, and bracing elements or buttresses (*canggahwang*). There are roof plates (*lambang*), rafters (*iga-iga*), king post supports (*tugeh*), apex plates (*dedeleg*), roofing material (*rab*) and the ridge covers called *dore*. This kit can be raided to design and construct any of the multifarious pavilion forms. This chapter will give an overview of all these pavilion parts and show how they can be fused to make interconnected pavilions, and how these can be enclosed or semi-enclosed with walls and screens.

Traditional pavilion structures are difficult to manipulate to make them usable for modern all-under-the-one-roof lifestyles. There are invariably columns in the way or too little space between columns for furniture. How then to retain the traditional forms, but live a modern lifestyle, without having to entertain on mats on the floor as is traditional for the Balinese? How to integrate en suite bathrooms into a traditional architectural scheme? Three projects that have solved such problems have been chosen as case studies for the final section of this chapter (5.13 Dividing Space in Modern Pavilions). These three designs have maintained the simplicity that is inherent in Balinese pavilion design, while using a more generous scale. This allows the occupants to have bedroom and bathroom and sitting areas under one roof.

Many architects and home-makers have dipped into the kit of Balinese pavilion parts for their modern Bali Style homes but with limited success. They often don't understand the simplicity of the structural elements and the principles of successful space planning in courtyard architectural design. Instead many go for Balinese ornamentation applied, like icing or postage stamps, to ungainly forms.

When designing Bali Style, one should first design the pavilions and then choose decorative accents that are suitable. Before deciding on pavilion types, scale and proportion—and the inclusion and adaptation of various indoor-outdoor architectural spaces like verandahs and terraces—a good understanding is needed of pavilion elements and construction techniques.

A	B		
	D		
C	E	F	G

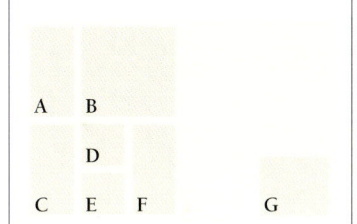

A. *View under the eaves and the side of a big* lumbung *rice loft pavilion.*

B. *The six-post pavilion, called* bale sakenam, *is most commonly used for kitchen buildings.*

C. Tukang ukir *carvers fashion guardians out of the large blocks of* paras *that support the pavilion posts in most Balinese temples.*

D. *A pavilion's* sakti, *or spiritual strength, is found in its* sendi, *the bollard-like bases that support the entire structure.*

E. *A bamboo shingle kitchen roof viewed through a mud brick gate in Pujung village, north of Ubud.*

F. *Shrines are pure pavilion forms too.*

G. *Elevation of a shrine showing details of the construction techniques of the post and beam elements.*

5.1 Basic Pavilion Construction

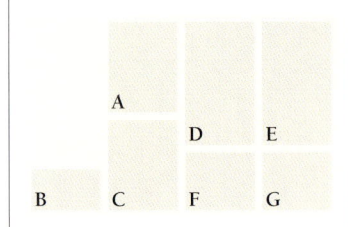

	A		
	D	E	
B	C	F	G

A. *The timber columns of larger shrine buildings are often situated outside enclosed vaults or shrine boxes. In this example, in a temple in Banua, Kintamani district, a low temple-style wall also sits on the edge of the top tier.*

B. *Cross-section of a ceremonial pavilion in a temple (see also photo G).*

C. *Lumbung rice barn under construction.*

D. *Cross-section through an open pavilion, showing all the elements.*

E. *Cross-section through an enclosed pavilion, another standard pavilion type.*

F. *The bale agung opposite Pura Desa, Guwang exhibits the compact Old Bali proportions often found in the Ketewel-Guwang area: the metal stays in front of the temple are there as supports for table-loads of offerings at festival time.*

G. *A classic bale Garuda Makaam in a mountain temple. Note the twin taban platforms and the extra row of columns on an outer stylobate, a prerogative of sacred pavilion structures.*

The traditional *bale* is mocked up on the ground and then pieced together atop column foundations, called *jongkok asu* (see construction sequence diagram page 88). The main elements of the roof structure—the *lambang*, *pementang*, *pemade* and *pemucu*—are then deftly assembled on the timber columns and joined up to a carved block of wood at the apex, which has "ports" to take the roof frame elements. Traditionally, wooden pegs, and not nails, are used. The rafters are then trimmed and the eave plates, called *kolong*, secured. Plumb lines are dropped down to define the edge of the stylobate below, and the stylobate's perimeter walls are then constructed and filled in. The foundations thus reinforce the bamboo rafters *(iga-iga)*, the horizontal keeps *(apit-apit)* are placed and the batons of thatch or rows of tiles are then tied on or secured.

Finally, masoned screen walls, when they are needed, are built on top of the stylobate. The walls are non-load-bearing, that is, they do not touch the pavilion's frame, as the pavilion structure needs to sway during earthquakes.

The Balinese divide the pavilion into three main parts: the head, being the roof structure; the shoulders and the body (posts and beams); and the hips and legs (the *bataran* or stylobate). The style and measurements of each of these three parts is determined after choosing a suitable pavilion form. A standard four-post pavilion form will vary, as will the materials used to make it, for example, according to whether it is a shrine box, a *kul-kul* tower or a garage. An understanding of the basic parts is informed by the rules of the building code or, in the case of a Bali Style home, just by good taste.

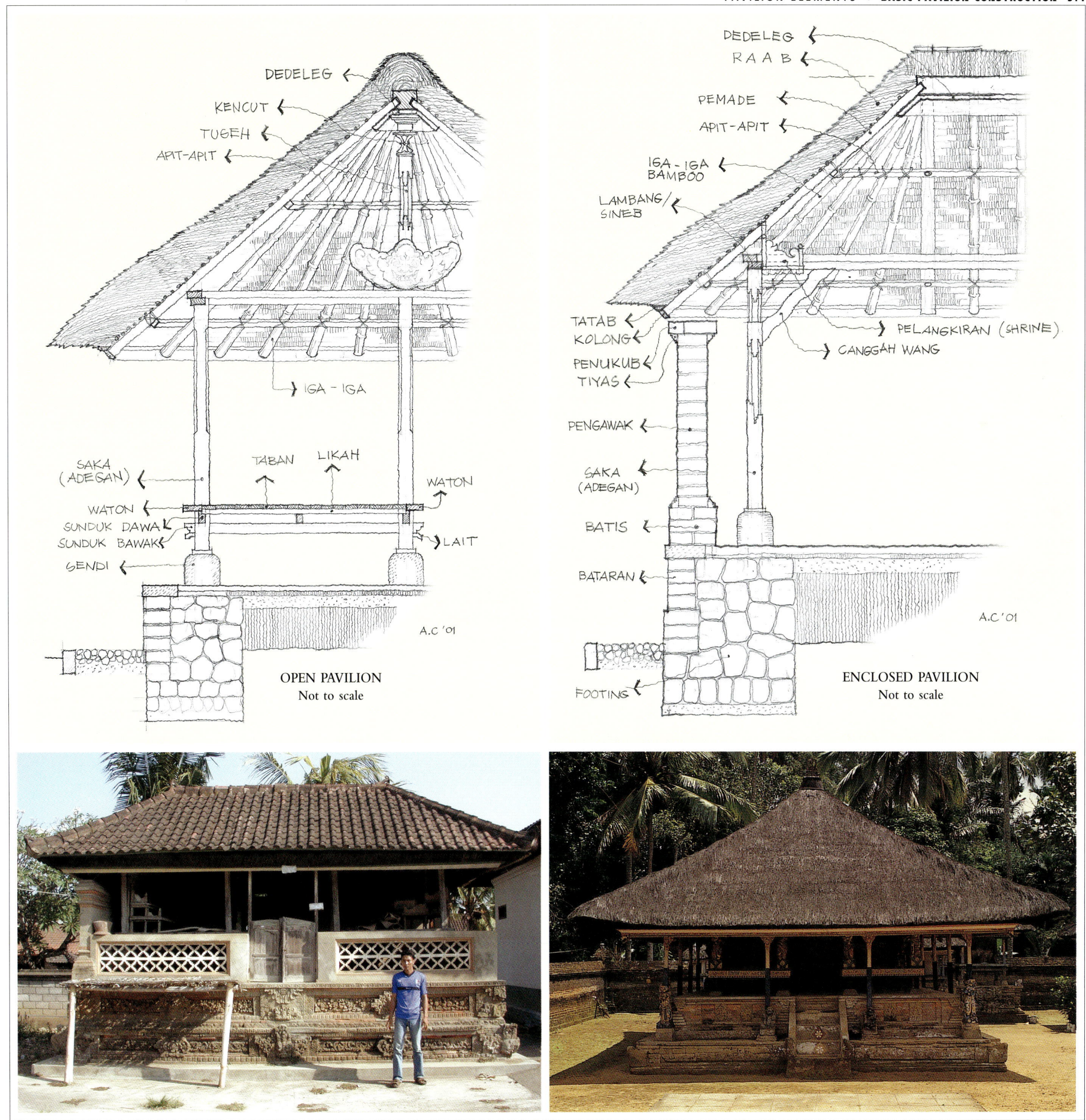

PAVILION ELEMENTS → **BASIC PAVILION CONSTRUCTION 5.1**

OPEN PAVILION
Not to scale

Labels: DEDELEG, KENCUT, TUGEH, APIT-APIT, IGA-IGA, SAKA (ADEGAN), TABAN, LIKAH, WATON, WATON, SUNDUK DAWA, SUNDUK BAWAK, LAIT, SENDI

ENCLOSED PAVILION
Not to scale

Labels: DEDELEG, RAAB, PEMADE, APIT-APIT, IGA-IGA BAMBOO, LAMBANG/SINEB, TATAB, KOLONG, PENUKUB, TIYAS, PENGAWAK, SAKA (ADEGAN), BATIS, BATARAN, PELANGKIRAN (SHRINE), CANGGAH WANG, FOOTING

A.C '01

87

88

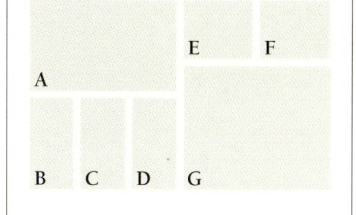

PAVILION ELEMENTS → **BASIC PAVILION CONSTRUCTION 5.1**

		E	F
A			
B	C	D	G

A. *Construction sequence of a typical sakenam pavilion.*

B. *A corner of a classic pavilion frame. The two-decked tie beams (lambang) interlock in the corner, supported by a post and two bracing buttresses, called canggahwang.*

C. *Tight bundles of alang-alang thatching grass are thrown up to the catcher working on the ridge portions of the roof (other portions take long batons of thatch).*

D. *A wall rises off the stylobate, heading for the pavilion's eaves (see diagram A).*

E. *Bamboo scaffolding is required for the labour-intensive work of assembling the pavilion and laying the roof.*

F. *Starting from the eave, batons of alang-alang thatch are secured from the inside, with bamboo string ties wrapped around the bamboo rafters.*

G. *Cutaway view of a typical mountain farmer's cabin showing how this house form utilizes more basic construction methods. The cabin features all the family's activity and storage rooms under one roof.*

89

5.2 Bases and Foundations

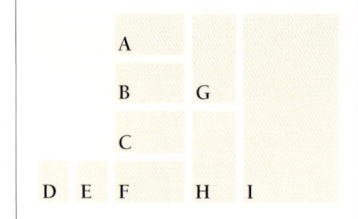

A				
B		G		
C				
D	E	F	H	I

A. *My own Bali dream kitchen, at the Jero Kubu, Batujimbar, Sanur (1981 photo).*

B. *Retaining walls are made of river stones in most areas.*

C. *This 12th-century Hindu temple pavilion base in Tulungagung, central Java is similar in form to those still constructed in Bali today.*

D. *Articulated bataran base of a lumbung pavilion in Tenganan village. Note the sophisticated village drainage system.*

E. *Timber tie-beam base on a mountain pavilion at Belantih village, near Kintamani (1979 photo).*

F. *Pavilions in palace courtyards have more pronounced bataran bases. This courtyard is in the Puri Gede palace, Amlapura, photographed in 1981.*

G. *Holy water vessels line up on a mid-level tier of a high bataran shrine base in the Pura Desa, Guwang.*

H. *Three-tiered bases are common on kul-kul pavilions.*

I. *Architect Cheong Yew Kuan's flying Dutchman rampart, Hardy residence, Sayan (1991 photo).*

The stylobates in classical architecture are raised podia on which pavilion forms sit; in Balinese architecture they are called *bataran*. Practically all pavilion, porch and courtyard spaces are public areas, but the stylobate sets the "polite" space—the pavilion floor and its sections—apart from the courtyard floor where the chickens, pigs and other muddy things dwell. The bases of courtyard pavilions, ringing a central open space as they generally do, are the garden furniture of traditional Balinese architecture.

Stylobates in Bali are built of packed mud, masoned stone or brick and plaster. Temple pavilions and shrines are distinguished by their high, tiered stylobates, which are often elaborately carved. In many north Bali temples, such as the famous Pura Beji Sangsit, the shrine bases are marvels of Bali Baroque ornateness.

Aesthetically, the style, height and treatment of the pavilion base—be it with steps all around, as in many *wantilan* halls, or with extra high decorative *bataran*, as in the *bale agung* assembly halls of the gods—tells us a lot about the pavilion's primary use. *Bataran* in the homes of the gentry, for example, are higher, bolder and more massive in proportion.

Bataran have been shrinking since the tourist-era building boom of the 1970s. Today, most architects have forgotten how to treat a *bataran* with respect—that is, by using biggish building blocks to make it stand proud.

In modern Bali Style homes the stylobate height is often reduced: clambering up and down building bases, after all, is impractical. The resultant lean and mean architectural style looks Balinese but lacks that special courtyard alliance between built space and courtyard/garden space that high stylobates ensure.

PAVILION ELEMENTS → **BASES AND FOUNDATIONS 5.2**

5.3 Steps

A. The phantasmagorical steps to the shrines in the famous Pura Beji, Sangsit, northern Bali.

B. Gunung rata stepped base on a classic nine-posted workhouse pavilion.

C. Strong masoned stone steps lead to a raised pavilion platform in this mountain temple.

D. Unusual sculptural step design leads up an exaggerated stylobate in a Legian dream home of the Rustic Charm school.

E. The inter-pavilion steps at the luxurious Amankila hotel, eastern Bali.

One tends to notice the handsome pavilion rather than the elegantly proportioned tiered base or beautifully crafted steps. Yet steps are an incredibly functional part of pavilion anatomy. Steps are the grandstands of Balinese courtyard theatre, and the spare seats of a thousand banquets, so the step treads are often on the high side, 20-30 centimetres. Pavilion steps sometimes run fully around the base of, say, the gamelan pavilion in the *jeroan* courtyard or the *wantilan* pavilion in the *jaba* forecourt.

Steps are for scraping thongs on in the wet season, for drying prawn crackers in the sun, and for kicking dogs down after a bad hand of dominoes. At temple festivals, steps fill up with celebrants who watch the comings and goings in the courtyards. And where would aristocrats be without steps on which to sit and be higher than their inferiors?

PAVILION ELEMENTS → **STEPS** 5.3

5.4 Post Bases

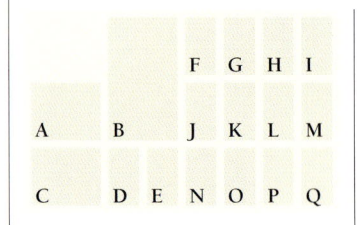

	F	G	H	I	
A	B		J	K	L	M
C		D	E	N	O	P	Q

A. *The* sendi *bases on these pavilion posts in a Cirebon, western Java palace have been exaggerated, giving an even more exotic look to this magnificent west Javanese-Art Deco pavilion hybrid.*

B-Q. *The* sendi *are where architects and carvers can display their decorative prowess. A selection of sendi on pavilions and shrines around the island:*
C and O are whimsical sendi *carved by Made Jojol of Taro for Geoffrey Bawa's museum building at Donald Friend's old house in Batujimbar, Sanur; E is a gargoyle-like* sendi *by artist Wayan Cemul; I and J, by artist Dewa Japa of Ketewel, is in the Sentul Culture Centre, west Java; N is in the Griya Ketewel.*

The *sakti* (spiritual strength) of a pavilion dwells in the post's base, or bollard (*sendi*). Aesthetically the *sendi* provides a plinth, like a statue base, that sets off, or "launches", the top half of a pavilion—the leggy, airy part—from its stolid stylobate.

Traditionally pavilion posts sit unsecured on *sendi*, so they can "jump" a little during earthquakes. A stump of timber protruding from the bottom of the pavilion post sits in a hole in the top of the *sendi* to ensure that the post doesn't slide off its base during turbulence. As *sendi* are often blocks of soft *paras*, the Balinese can't resist carving them or, in the case of temples, carving winged lions on which the posts can sit.

Sendi, the "bobby socks" of pavilion architecture, are often eliminated, or reduced, when a pavilion sits on a high stylobate.

94

PAVILION ELEMENTS → **POST BASES** 5.4

5.5 Columns, Beams and Buttresses

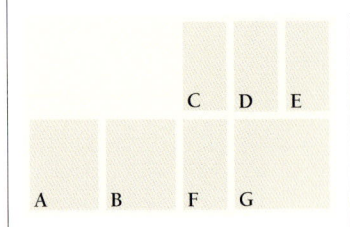

A. *Concrete columns in the ruined pavilion to the moon goddess, Taman Ujung, eastern Bali, built in 1940, and photographed here in 1953 by Luc Bouchage.*

B. *Timber* adegan *posts on a* wantilan *at Puri Ganesha, Pemuteran.*

C. *Twin* singa *(winged lion) statues guard the tie beam of this ornate shrine pavilion in Jero Kubutambahan, northern Bali.*

D & E. *Details of a timber* wantilan *in Sayan (1979 photos).*

F. *Detail from a fancy palace pavilion in Ubud.*

G. Lambang *(roof plate),* adegan *(column) and* pemade *(purlin) meet in the corner of this alang-alang roofed pavilion. Note the neatness of the bamboo string ties and the thinness of the bamboo rafters.*

Pavilion posts or columns are called *adegan* (from *ngadeg*: to stand). Together with the *lambang* (beams) they are the legs, torso and shoulders of Balinese architecture. The buttresses, called *canggahwang*, are the arms: they brace the building, giving it just enough structural support to withstand a heavy rainstorm on a thatched roof, but little more; they are rarely oversized. In temples and palaces, timber columns are of superior timbers, like jackfruit and sandalwood, and are often ornate—gilt or painted, depending on the pavilion's status. A building's elegance is determined by the proportion of column to roof structure to *bataran* base, and the shapeliness of its *adegan* columns. If the "waist" is too long, it is deemed gawky; and if the columns are too short it is called *bontok*, or stubby.

Since colonial times, columns of brick or reinforced concrete (*adegan beton*) have become popular, particularly in large-scale pavilions such as *banjar* halls. Round or octagonal coconut columns called *dolken*, traditionally found in *wantilan* halls, have been appropriated by modern architects for use in large lobby buildings or over-scale pavilion homes.

Limestone or stone-clad columns, descended from the plaster and brick Doric columns of colonial-era pavilions, have become fashionable since the era of expatriate architectural influence. Often they are oversized to create surfaces against which folding doors can rest.

Shrine boxes, called *plangkiran*, are found perched on columns in the corners of the pavilion frame—they are for the spirits who dwell in the pavilion's roof, a pavilion's godly area.

Since the 1980s a strain of concrete framework pavilion, in which the detailing common to timber pavilion structures has been plastered onto the concrete members, has become popular. This is an example of how the Balinese-ness of a building is often perceived, incorrectly, through its ornamental touches. More honest—that is, where form follows function—concrete pavilions have sprung up in the late 1990s as better urban architecture has seeped into the tourism market through the so-called Zen end.

PAVILION ELEMENTS → **COLUMNS, BEAMS AND BUTTRESSES 5.5**

97

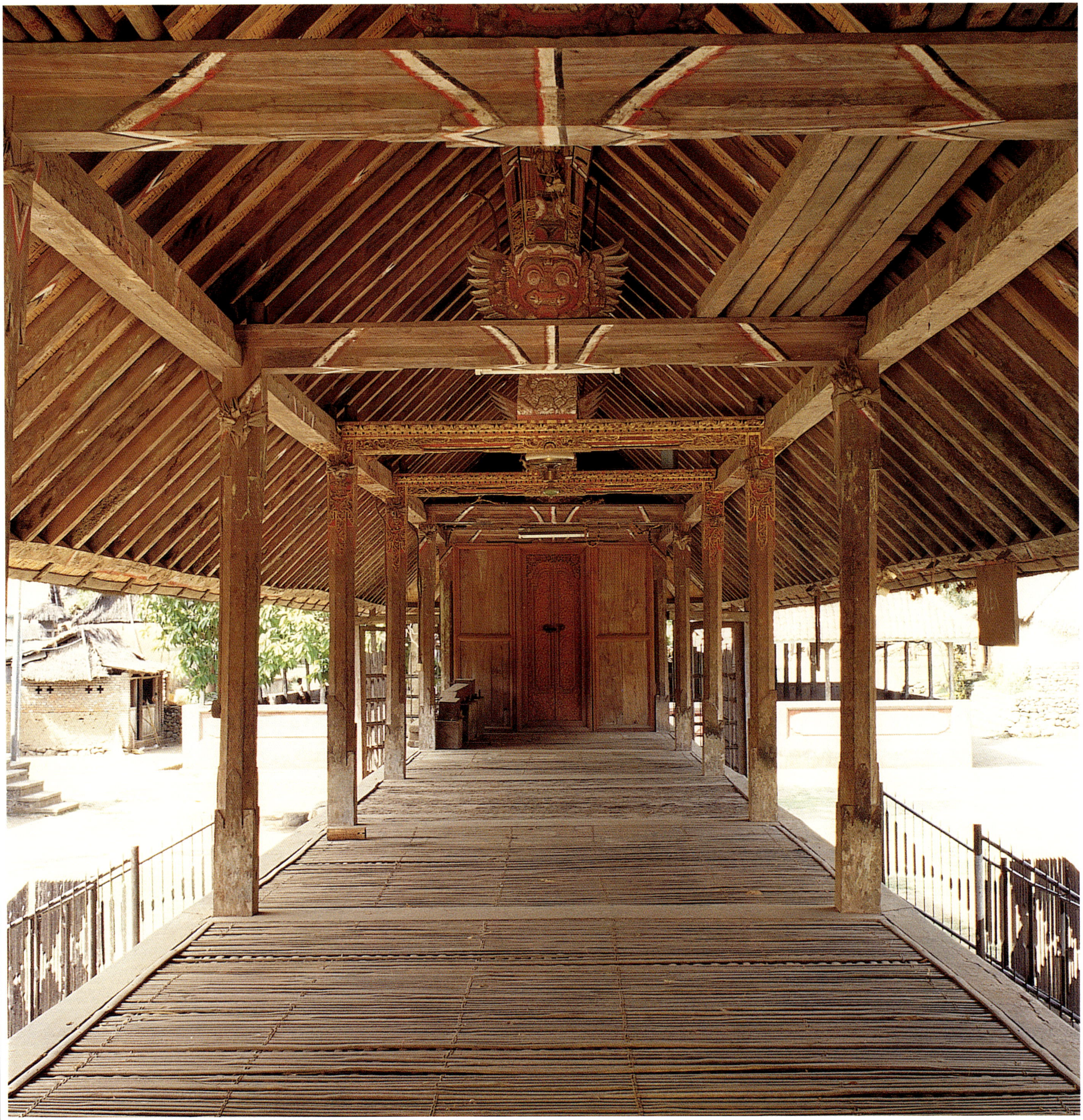

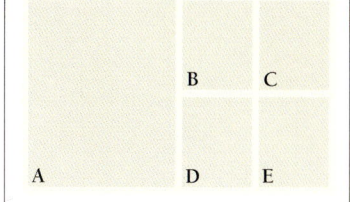

PAVILION ELEMENTS → **COLUMNS, BEAMS AND BUTTRESSES** 5.5

	B	C
A	D	E

A. *One of Bali's most handsome pavilions, the ceremonial long pavilion (bale lantang) in Tenganan village, east Bali. The proportions and scale of the pavilion elements are typical of east Bali architecture. The decoration is strikingly Bali Aga, with ancient pre-Hindu tri-coloured stripes (earth, water, fire) on the tie beams. The Boma decorative king post support (tatakan tugeh) is also impressive.*

B. *Traditional Bali Aga (pre-Hindu mountain culture) Klengan Tebu motif paintwork on a pavilion in the Pura Desa, Guwang. Red, white and black decorative paint finishes appear in ancient villages across Southeast Asia and the Pacific. Very similar decorative paintwork can be found on traditional pavilions in Yunnan, China and also Nagaland, India.*

C. *In the mountains the canggahwang are often just shaped and left uncarved. In villages such as Suter (this photo), Songan and Trunyan, adegan posts are often pinched above the shoulders, as it were, in a more indigenous aboriginal style.*

D. *Exquisitely carved and coloured post, tie beam and roof plate junction in a ceremonial pavilion in central Bali. The elaborately carved and gilded canggahwang buttresses are typical of grand palace or high temple pavilion design.*

E. *Beautifully carved Majapahit-style set of canggahwang brackets and posts in the corner of a pavilion of a nobleman's house in eastern Bali.*

Following pages: Courtyard floors sometimes become operating theatres during tooth-filing ceremonies, which normally take place on taban platforms built on pavilion posts. This 1978 painting is by Sanur artist Ida Bagus Rai, a pupil of Donald Friend.

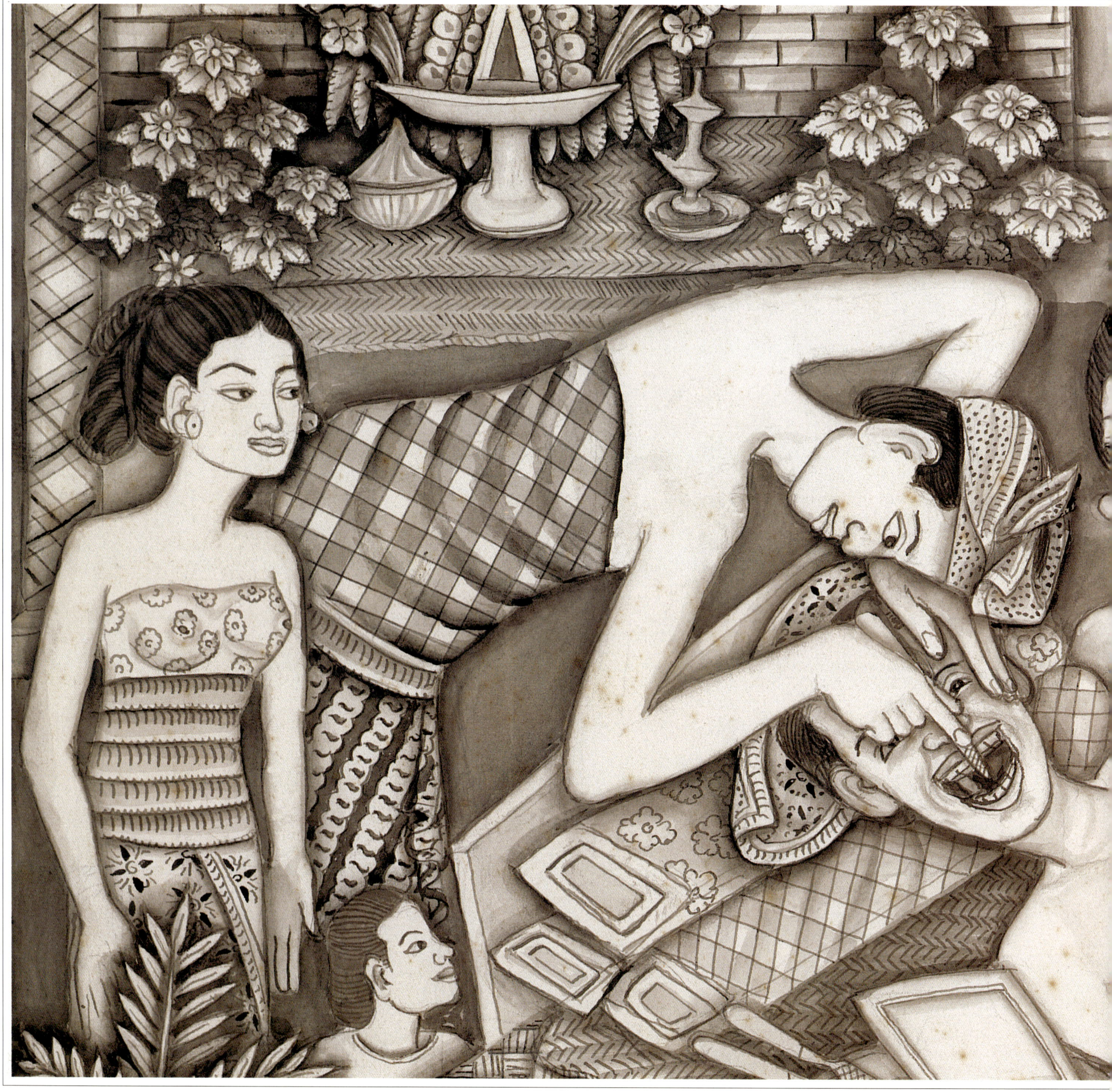

PAVILION ELEMENTS

5.6 Built-in Platforms

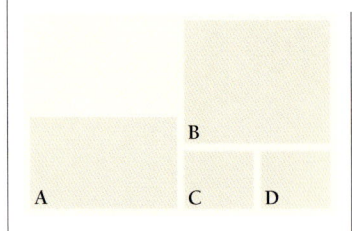

A. A six-post pavilion with a full taban wrap-around platform is depicted in this bas-relief, found on the 16th-century central Javanese temple, Candi Sukuh, outside Solo.

B. An unusual twin-taban bale pemegat sot (oath-taking pavilion) of a pura puseh temple of the origins near Ubud, Gianyar Regency. Note the holy black ijuk thatch.

C. Detail of the joinery in a complicated stepped taban.

D. A rare offering platform taban outside an even rarer timber gedong at the 10th-century Pura Puncak Penulisan near Kintamani (1982 photo), presently under threat from architectural revisionists.

Bed-like platforms wrapped between timber *adegan* posts, *taban* are the interlocking modular lounge suits of Balinese pavilion space. They are found in all *bale bali* (ceremonial pavilions) and, in various configurations, on Balinese timber shrine pavilions and other temple buildings. *Taban* are vital to various rites of passage—such as births, puberty, marriages and deaths—in the family courtyard. Bodies are laid out, marriages consecrated and teeth filed on them.

Balinese long-houses (*bale lantang*), like those found in Pura Batu Karo, Tenganan and Pura Batur, are just one long *taban* with a long roof above, used as platforms for high-level "pow-wows" or ceremonial banquets.

Gods returning from the annual *melis* processions to the sea sit in state for some days on elevated *taban* in *bale agung* temples at the village's centre. These temples are descended from mountain long-houses. Some ancient temple gates are flanked by *taban*, as are the "oath" pavilions (*bale pemegat sot*) found in very old village temples (see photo A, page 104).

For any major domestic ceremony, a *pedanda* high priest will dedicate the offerings on a *taban* in the *bale bali*. The priest sits on the *taban*, facing the offerings, to conduct his rituals. To have both priest and offerings up high, closer to the gods, *taban* are slung almost a metre off the pavilion floor. Protection from marauding dogs and pigs is another reason.

Often a roof extension or awning, called *emper*, is an architectural ploy to provide another *taban* work platform (see photo D, page 105). *Taban* of this type are sometimes appended to mountain temple buildings (see photo D, opposite) and are used as platforms for placing offerings to the gods who are seated within the shrine pavilion, or *gedong*, proper.

Peter Muller was the first to utilize the *taban* as a hotel bed at the Kayu Aya (now the Bali Oberoi) in 1972. The platform's traditional bamboo or wooden slatting allows air to circulate beneath the mattress. Some deluxe *taban* use timber strips as slats between the *taban*'s frame.

PAVILION ELEMENTS → **BUILT-IN PLATFORMS 5.6**

103

104

PAVILION ELEMENTS → **BUILT-IN PLATFORMS** 5.6

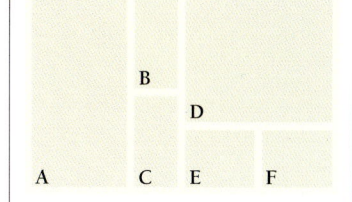

A. Taban *are often slung between columns in temple pavilions like this* bale piasan *in Pura Pulaki temple, north Bali. Usually only priests or* sadeg (*trance mediums*) *sit on temple* taban.

B. *Nasty double-decker "Lucy in the sky with diamonds" structure in the holy Pura Pulaki, on the island's northwest coast, features an extra long* taban *in a giant twelve-posted ceremonial pavilion.*

C. *During the pemelaspasan inauguration rites afforded a traditional Balinese pavilion, the beams and posts are "wed" in a small, stylized rite of passage.*

D. Taban *and* emper *awning tacked on to poet John Darling's Ubud rice field house kitchen (1982 photo).* Taban *are also found inside most traditional kitchens.*

E. Taban *are often found as* tingklik (*bamboo xylophone*) *platforms.*

F. *An elegant carved platform is slung between ornate columns in this classic* bale piasan *shrine pavilion near Kintamani.*

105

5.7 Walls and Screens

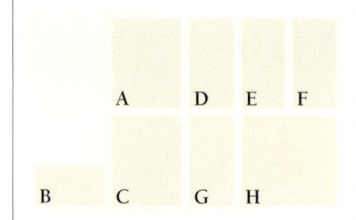

	A	D	E	F
B	C	G	H	

A. *Low balustrade of paras ukir on a shrine pavilion near Kintamani.*

B. *In a northern coast warung food stall, an ingenious wall, fashioned from coconut palm fronds, is pinched in sections to create ventilation windows.*

C. *This privacy screen, hung on the eaves of a simple pavilion, is fashioned from plaited coconut leaves.*

D. *Detail of a Tenganan bale lantang enclosing screen.*

E. *An improvised bamboo screen provides some privacy yet still allows a view of the statues in the entrance to the Villa Angsa in Sanur.*

F. *A thin, timber lattice screen keeps the chickens out of this ceremonial long-house in Tenganan village, eastern Bali.*

G. *The decomposing corner of this east Bali meten pavilion shows how the enclosing non-load-bearing wall is constructed from mud brick balls. Firewood, leaning against the pavilion base, is being dried.*

H. *A woven bamboo strip fence in Pemuteran, north Bali. Bamboo derivative building materials do not do well when exposed to the elements over a long period of time.*

Walls in a *bale* are traditionally not load-bearing. They are more screen than wall. Often they are just woven split bamboo sheets called *bedeg* framed with bamboo and fixed between the *bataran* edge and the eaves' barge plate. Privacy screens (see photo C) come in many styles: sometimes they are woven panels of bamboo slats, which hang like blinds from the eaves.

Lighter screens are occasionally put in place to keep dogs and chickens from *taban* laden with offerings (see photo C, page 108). Masoned walls sometimes enclose half or all of a pavilion's space. Half-walls appear, balustrade-like, in some pavilions, where they act as tables or counters; full walls close off pavilion ends exposed to the elements. Sets of columns are fully enclosed to create rooms.

Walls in Balinese ceremonial pavilions are essentially screens: their function is to define sacred spaces. During tooth-filing ceremonies and other confinements, special semi-sacred enclosures are created for the celebrants on the wide verandahs that are left over when a portion of a pavilion is walled off.

Masonry screen walls in pavilions are often thick. Thick walls insulate, and also allow room for bulky decorative door jambs and windows. They are often ornate.

Since the 1970s pavilion walls have largely replaced the traditional well-carved, well-joined post-and-beam configurations as the principal load-bearing elements in contemporary pavilion architecture.

The tops of solid screen walls—those made of brick or *paras* or mud—provide an excellent ledge for storing *dulang* offering trays, oil lamps, cigarette lighters and magazines (see 5.12 Storage).

PAVILION ELEMENTS → **WALLS AND SCREENS 5.7**

107

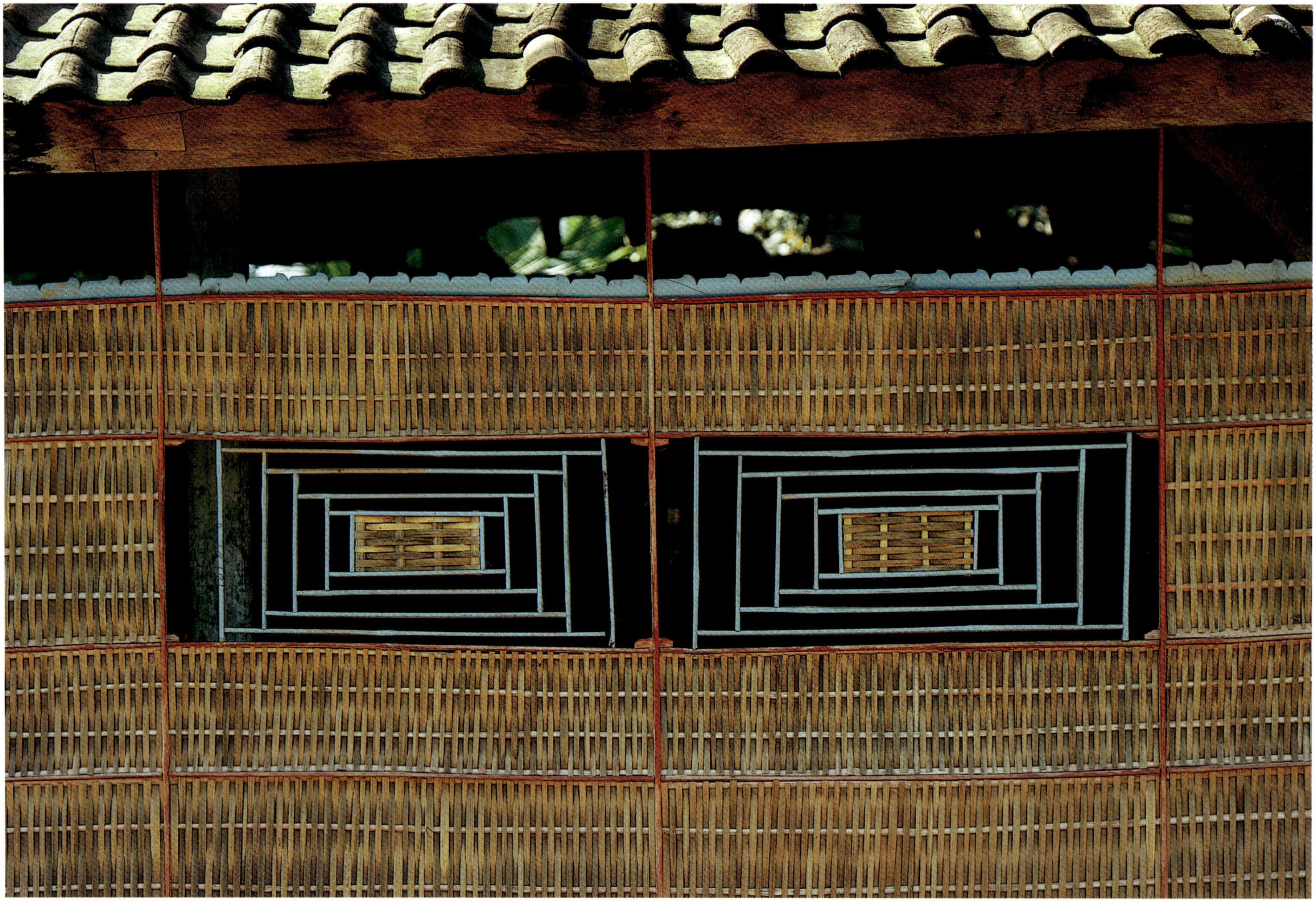

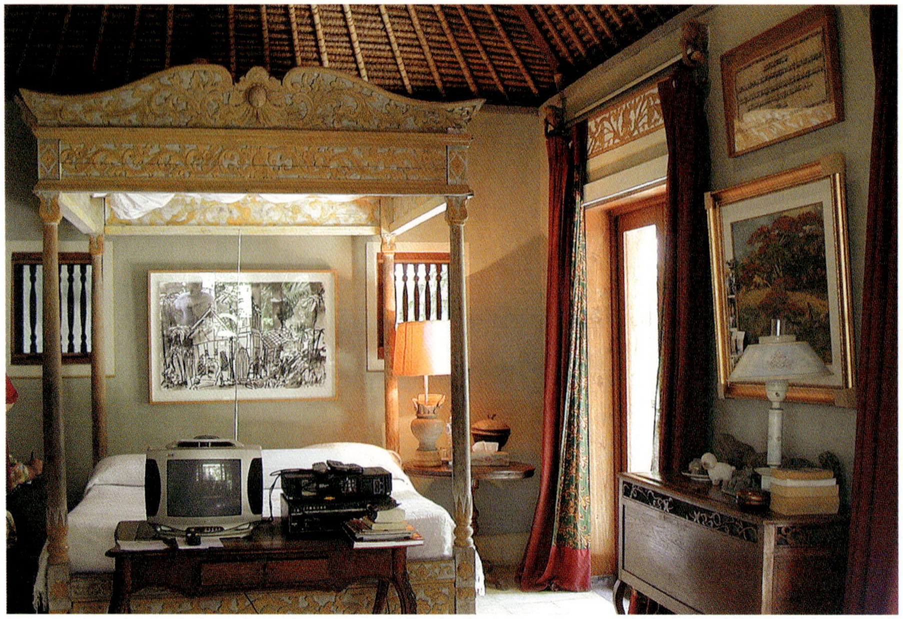

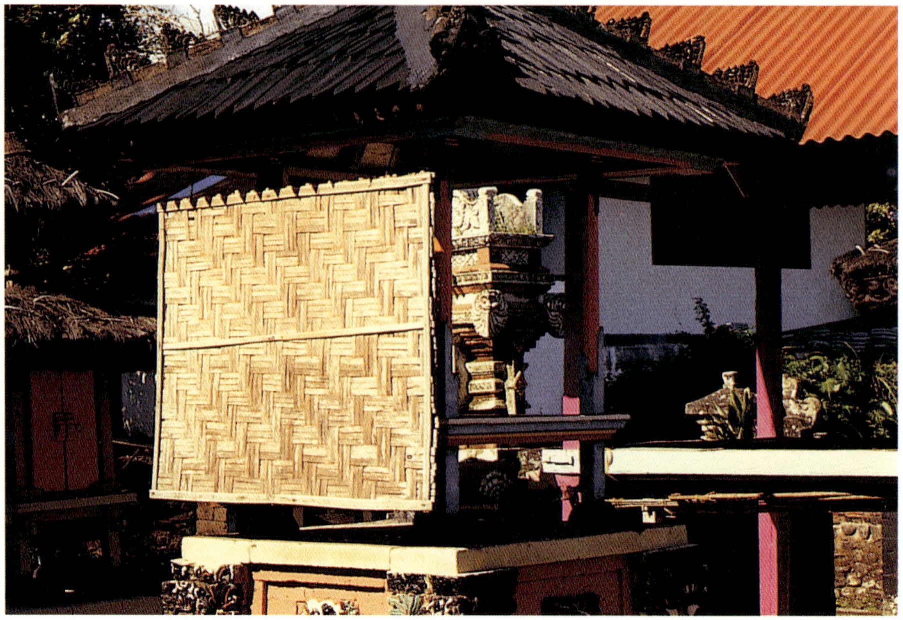

PAVILION ELEMENTS → **WALLS AND SCREENS 5.7**

|A| |
|B|C|D|

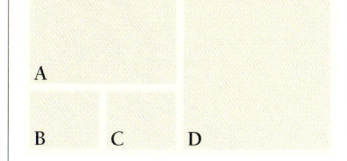

A. Woven bamboo privacy screens are parts of a Balinese pavilion's accessory kit. Hanging from the eaves or the bargeboard, as in this photo, the partitions are often pierced with perforated patches, to allow through cooling breezes.

B. The cottage at the Villa Bebek in Sanur exhibits the traditional pavilion form but with load-bearing walls and no columns, as championed by Peter Muller in the early 1970s.

C. Bamboo screens also keep the sun off the offerings on a Balinese shrine.

D. Living room in one of Putu Suarsa's bamboo houses at Big Bamboo, in Sidakarya. Note the bedeg walls, and the coconut tree growing through the living room (this often creates problems with water-proofing as trees sway in the breeze).

109

5.8 Doors

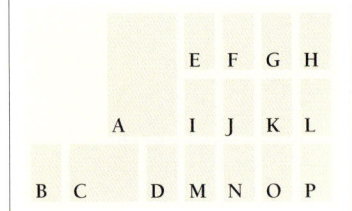

	E	F	G	H
A	I	J	K	L
B	C	D M	N	O	P

A. *An exquisite eastern Balinese door from the Waworuntu collection, used here in a Bali Style building in Batujimbar, an estate famous for its collection of over 500 antique doors.*

B. *A classic door pull.*

C. *Details of door entablature.*

D. *Handle on a Majapahit-style door.*

E. *This door on the Fountain of Youth shrine at Taman Narmada gardens, western Lombok, has a dramatic fiery surround (1985 photo).*

F. *Shrine door on a northern coast temple in the Dutch colonial style. Shutters on the windows of estate outhouses in Holland often have this same ornamentation.*

G. *Balinese house compound doors are left ajar until the occupants retire for the evening.*

H. *The magnificent Majapahit-style doors of the Pura Lingsar temple, western Lombok.*

I. *Note the contrasting colour schemes on Majapahit-style twin-leafed doors.*

J. *Door in the Villa Bebek showing traditional urus (post and lintel) hinging mechanism.*

K. *Classic northern coast, Old Bali shrine doors.*

L. *Elaborate entablatures are a feature of doors in the old imperial capital of Klungkung.*

M. *Chinese-style doors were popular from the 19th century onwards.*

N. *Ancient form of temple gate—a pavilion with a portal between a pair of taban—at a mountain temple in the Kintamani area (1985 photo).*

O. *All the doors at Four Seasons Resort, Jimbaran were painted by Australian artist Stephen Little.*

P. *Nineteenth-century door from Nusa Penida Island, now utilized in the Taman Bebek, Sayan.*

In an archipelago of extraordinary door types and styles, the typical Balinese door is unique. It is closely related to the twin-leafed doors of southern India—particularly the pavilion doors in Tamil Nadu architecture—not only in construction but also in colour, door handle style and locking mechanism. The Balinese version has had, over the centuries, many decorative phases, from the simple tri-colour favourites of the old mountain villages to the elaborately carved and wildly painted chinoiserie doors of the Gianyar, Klungkung and Karangasem palaces, popular throughout the 20th century.

The indigenous mountain Bali door, as opposed to the typical Bali door, is single-leafed and can be found in the family huts of ancient mountain villages such as Belantih and Trunyan, and on the small islands off Bali's southern coast. Some of these single-leafed doors are similar to the Majapahit-era doors (see photos H and I, and photo B on page 50). The carvings and designs are very similar to those still found in some of the ancient 16th-century mosques of eastern Java, particularly at Sendangduwur near Bojonegoro. Temple gates, shrines and house gates always have double-leafed doors. The courtyard's principal *meten* pavilion and the *paon* kitchen pavilion often have single-leafed doors. Sliding bamboo kitchen doors are common in traditional homes in rural areas.

The frame, its *petitis* lintel piece and the surrounding architrave are where the decorative skills of the designer, and the craftsmen who create the pavilions, are on show. The architrave on a *meten* or *bale bandung* door is sometimes carved *paras* stone with a Boma or Sai protective talisman figure worked into the ornamentation (see photo L).

Balinese twin-leafed doors traditionally have brass ring handles which are mounted on stylized *padma* (water lily flower) base plates. Locks can be secured between the two rings.

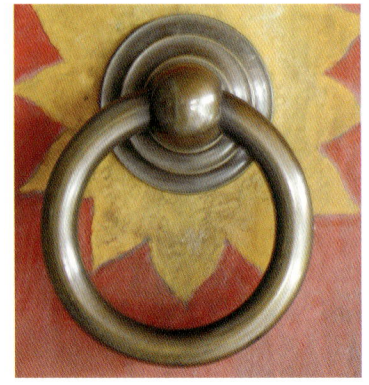

PAVILION ELEMENTS → **DOORS** 5.8

5.9 Windows and Air Vents

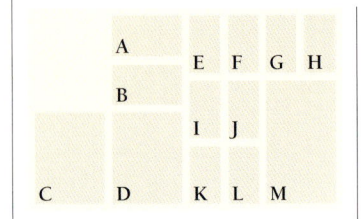

A		E	F	G	H
	B			
		I	J	
C	D	K	L	M

A. *A traditional Balinese window of the* jaro-jaro *type.*

B. *Ventilation holes in a mud brick kitchen wall.*

C. *Typical timber swing window, on a colonial-era design outhouse hut in a north coast village.*

D. *Windows in rice field huts, called* pondok, *were often just flaps of woven bamboo.*

E-L. *A selection of window types on the island.*

M. *A small traditional Bali window was worked into this sophisticated Bali Style villa—with paint finishes by Stephen Little—at the Taman Bebek, Sayan.*

Before the modern era, the traditional timber shutter window (see photos E, G, I, K and M) were partly ornamental and partly practical: they were used for ventilation and to let some light into sleeping chambers during the day. Most daytime activities took place in open pavilions; the exception was the kitchen, which tended to be very gloomy. Glazed windows, which came with the Dutch colonial era, were never successfully married with traditional structures until Peter Muller's sliding glass doors at the Kayu Aya (now the Bali Oberoi), which disappeared into recessed double masonry walls. In 1987 Muller employed Japanese-style mullioned sliding glass doors for the villas at the Amandari, a design now used to enclose pavilions around the tropical world.

Decorative grilles and air vents, in a variety of designs, are an essential part of any tropical architecture, but in Bali they have been elevated to an art form (see also 7.3 Stone Air Vents). Timber grilles, with lathed spokes painted in candy-stripe pastel colours, are another form of Balinese window/air vent.

PAVILION ELEMENTS → **WINDOWS AND AIR VENTS** 5.9

113

5.10 Roofs and King Posts

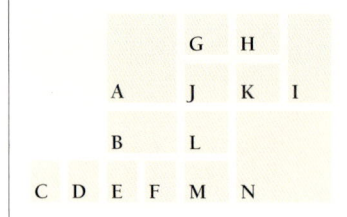

	G	H		
A	J	K	I	
B		L		
C	D E F	M	N	

A. *A Boma king post support, king post and carved and painted top "knuckle" which supports the ridge plate of the main bale lantang of Tenganan village (see photo A, page 98).*

B. *Hanging swing shrines, called* plangkiran gantung, *similar to those in Indian temples, were traditionally found in the northeast corners of ceilings, above babies' cribs.*

C-E. *Classic* tatakan tugeh *statues,* betaka *and* dedeleg, *which sit on the* pementang *central tie beam of the pavilion.*

F. *A classic garuda statue used as a decorative king post support (called a* tatakan tugeh*) is connected to a square decorative roof plate, called* betaka. *Longplates are called* dedeleg.

G. *Painted ceiling and carved and gilt elements in a shrine at Puri Nyalian.*

H. *Well-laid, tight-packed alang-alang makes for a beautiful decorative ceiling.*

I. *Architect Reda Amalou used timber purlins and rattan ties in this impressive roof.*

J. *The gods' palanquins, called* jempana, *and temple umbrellas are stored above the tie beams in ceremonial buildings.*

K. *Chinese red (*kinju*) and gold-leafed (*prada*) carvings are in stylish contrast to the eau de nil-coloured rafters on this temple pavilion* betaka.

L. *Interior of a bale lantang (ceremonial pavilion) roof showing a* bedeg *lining between the rafters and the ijuk thatch.*

M. *The batons of alang-alang thatch are laid more tightly between the last apit-apit purlin and the bargeboard, so that the thatch has a slight upturn near the eaves for a better dispersal of rainwater, and presumably for a more Chinese profile.*

N. *Sophisticated yet traditional bamboo* kolong *bargeboards provide interesting roofing detail.*

Balinese roofs are exquisitely crafted, both inside and out. (see also 6.3 Thatch). They rival even the Japanese traditional thatched pavilion for elegance and simplicity. Ceremonial buildings with hipped roofs often have elaborate king posts which sit on the back of carved *singa* (winged lion) or *garuda* king post supports. The entire thing is then perched on richly carved tie beams called *pementang* (see photo F).

Before being selected for rafters (*iga-iga*) in roof structures, bamboo poles are sorted for perfection of form. The rafters meet at an apex, actually penetrating neatly into the four sides of carved roof ridge plates called *betaka*, if square, or *dedeleg*, if elongated.

Roofs are judged on thickness of thatch, fineness of bamboo string ("like an angel's eyelashes"), and regularity of tying as much as on the beauty of their carved structural elements. *Tali ijuk* (string made from the fibre of the sugar palm) is used to pinch-tie the *iga-iga* stays, while fine bamboo string is used to tie the batons of thatch, called *ikatan*, onto the *iga-iga* rafters.

Some roofs have unusual shapes. The *lumbung* and the *jineng* roof has a curvaceous form like the upside-down hull of a boat. This shape is formed by bending thin, malleable bamboo rafters which are tied between ribs of coconut wood. The pagoda-like *meru* shrines have complex roof structures which are built to wobble in the event of earthquakes.

In western Bali, thin rafters of coconut wood (*seseh*) sometimes replace bamboo as *iga-iga*. In such buildings, the *alang-alang* grass thatch is tied on with rattan string. The finished product is very handsome (see photo I).

PAVILION ELEMENTS → **ROOFS AND KING POSTS** 5.10

115

116

PAVILION ELEMENTS → **ROOFS AND KING POSTS** 5.10

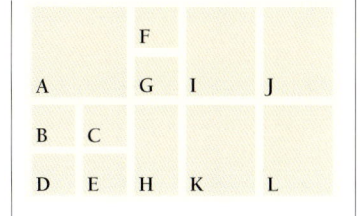

	F		
A	G	I	J
B	C		
D	E	H	K	L

A. The corner "hump", called pemugbug bucu, of a bamboo-shingled roof.

B. Bamboo shingles and corrugated iron roofs stack up in handsome display in Bayunggede village, near Kintamani.

C. A klangsah (coconut palm frond) roof on a northwest coast lumbung rice loft.

D. Ridges of roofs on gates are often decorated with Chinese or southern Indian-style decorative motifs.

E. Rolls of black ijuk sugar palm fibre between the tiered roofs of a meru pagoda. Black ijuk thatch is reserved for temple roofs as the ijuk palm is the tallest on the island.

F-I. Corrugated iron is used as a substitute for thatch in many mountain villages. In Balinese architecture it is the proportion, not the material, which often determines a pavilion roof's beauty.

J. The inner workings of a typical lumbung rice loft roof are revealed here.

K. Rows of mountain meten pavilions, with bamboo-shingled roofs, in Bayunggede village, near Kintamani (1995 photo).

L. A large alang-alang wantilan roof and a smaller klangsah thatch roof.

117

5.11 Organizing Space in Traditional Pavilions

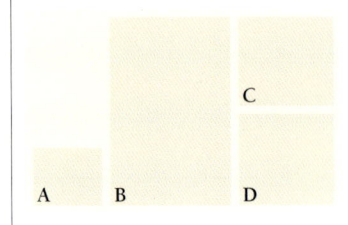

	C	
A	B	D

A. *The bar in the main dining pavilion of the Amankila hotel, eastern Bali.*

B. *Architect Kerry Hill has practised the fine art of timber pavilion design for over 30 years: the main lobby building of his award-winning Amanusa hotel is pure and simple, with space-defining stone walls placed architectonically (the Balinese way).*

C. *Ceremonial* bale lantang *long pavilions in Bali Aga villages often have one section enclosed, creating storage rooms for gamelan instruments or other ceremonial objects.*

D. *Traditionally, indoor spaces are for storage or sleeping and therefore tend to be dark. Activities that require light, such as reading, writing or painting, take place in public view on a shaded porch. This 2001 photograph was taken in the Pura Desa, Guwang.*

Various elements, including walls, windows, doors and *taban* platforms, are fitted to pavilion bases and columns after the completion of the basic pavilion construction. *Taban* are added to provide work or sleeping platforms: for example, kitchens need work platforms, and ceremonial pavilions need platforms on which to set out offerings.

The function of the courtyard pavilion can expand, concertina-like, from that of a bedroom into a community hall by tweaking the screening, or organizing, elements. Raised stylobates can become comfortable row seating, for example, if treads are deep enough; beds can become wedding altars if the *taban* space is decorated with special bunting and *ulon* cloth.

A well-designed traditional pavilion has built-in storage space on top of the thick screen walls or in attic platforms in the voluminous roofs, particularly in the *lumbung* rice lofts and *bale bali* ceremonial pavilions.

Screening elements define zones of private and public space, or just keep out the sun and rain. Curtains are often added around *taban* platforms in open pavilions to keep the chickens off the offerings or provide privacy for slumber chums.

Wantilan and *bale agung* rarely have vaulted or screened areas, the exception being mountain *bale lantang* where the village gamelan may be housed in a compartment built into the long pavilion. *Wantilan* floors are often sunken, or articulated, to create stages and cockfight pits. *Bale banjar*, once completely open, now have offices and storage rooms built into their hindquarters.

PAVILION ELEMENTS → **ORGANIZING SPACE IN TRADITIONAL PAVILIONS 5.11**

5.12 Storage

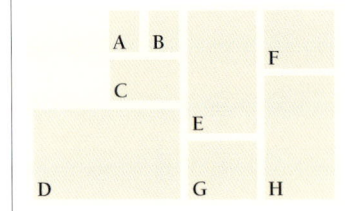

A B		F
C		
	E	
D	G	H

A. *Offering elements are often stored in the thatched roof above head level to protect their purity.*

B. *Ingenious use of woven bamboo wall sheets to hang cans of lighter fluid and other things in a traditional kitchen.*

C. *Large temples often have storage rooms—for offerings and ceremonial paraphernalia—which act also as kitchens and dormitories at temple festival time.*

D. *The space between the pavilion wall or base and the bargeboard is an excellent place for storing bikes, old doors or baskets of chickens.*

E. *A jineng (four-poster rice loft) with mossed-over ijuk roof in the mountain temple sanctuary of Batu Karo.*

F. *Above the tie beams is a cavity ideal for storing palanquins and temple umbrellas.*

G. *A typical bale bali (ceremonial pavilion) between festivals. Note how kites are stored in the ceiling courts and dulang trays above the thick screen walls.*

H. *Many temples now have tower-like "safes" in which the arca god effigies (often priceless) are stored.*

Balinese *bale* design allows for many nooks for unusual storage possibilities. Ceremonial umbrellas and palanquins can be stored above the tie beams, for example, in the open roof cavity. The area between the non-load-bearing screen walls is another good spot: it attracts wooden trays, called *dulang*, (used for transporting offerings to the village temples) and other household goods. These often thick walls have niches set into them, too, for storing such things as playing cards and lamp-cleaning equipment. Mats are stored under the *taban* bed platforms; old doors, farm equipment, *krupuk*-drying mats and bikes are kept under the broad eaves between the splash zone and the stylobate, together with fighting cock baskets.

Other household storage is done in large armoires or cupboards, which are always locked—temptation is not polite in a Balinese home—or in large baskets, called *keben*. *Keben* are stored in the kitchen on platforms of various heights.

Sheaves of rice are stored in *lumbung* rice lofts, if the loft hasn't been sold to some tourists for a honeymoon suite.

PAVILION ELEMENTS → **STORAGE 5.12**

121

5.13 Dividing Space in Modern Pavilions

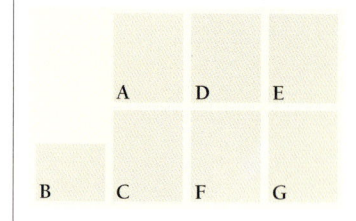

	A	D	E
B	C	F	G

A. *This villa overlooking Jimbaran Bay was designed by Grounds Kent Architects' Guy Morgan and shows a radical use of pavilion overhang.*

B. *Architect Glen Parker cleverly divides space within a space at his Pantai Lebih beach house.*

C. *Screen walls, with Balinese doors inserted, divide two pavilion forms at the Taman Bebek hotel, Sayan.*

D. *At the Villa Bebek in Sanur a similar space to photo C has been divided by placing timber planks and carved Javanese house panels between columns.*

E. *Designer Ed Tuttle's innovative interpretation of Balinese architecture in this lobby building for the Amankila hotel.*

F. *Philip Lakeman and Graham Oldroyd's Ubud home displays modernist examples of dividing pavilion space.*

G. *The sensational Serai hotel, with interiors by Terry Fripp for Kerry Hill Architects.*

In 1972 Peter Muller designed a series of residential pavilions for the Kayu Aya (now the Bali Oberoi). The villa kept the proportions of Balinese pavilion architecture but effectively eliminated the columns and replaced them with load-bearing walls. The foundations and walls were reinforced to withstand earthquakes. An air-conditionable space, without rows of columns in the way, was thus achieved. This style had existed on the island previously as the traditional *kantor* (office) style.

By the 1980s all sorts of between-column and column-eliminating solutions had sprung up: full louvres between columns, as in the Australian "Queenslander", appeared on beach front bungalows; pavilion walls supported sawn-off columns (see photo E); and the idea of an architecture within an architecture developed (see photo B) whereby the internal space allocation and construction has little or no relation to the pavilion framework.

The best of its generation of trad-mod hybrids is surely Sri Lankan architect Geoffrey Bawa's ingenious 1973 adaptation of the classic assembly pavilion to create Australian artist Donald Friend's air-conditioned museum in Sanur. Bawa vastly enlarged the pavilion, raising the stylobate to create an insulated ground floor on which sat a spacious open-air pavilion. Since then, architectural adaptation knows no inhibitions.

Today there are any number of innovative space-dividers in Bali Style homes: metal-framed room dividers, glass panels which disappear into the floor and roll-down blinds with hyper-real looking photo art on them. "Anything goes" is the spirit of New Age Bali.

Three case studies of dividing and organizing space in Bali Style pavilions conclude the chapter.

PAVILION ELEMENTS → **DIVIDING SPACE IN MODERN PAVILIONS 5.13**

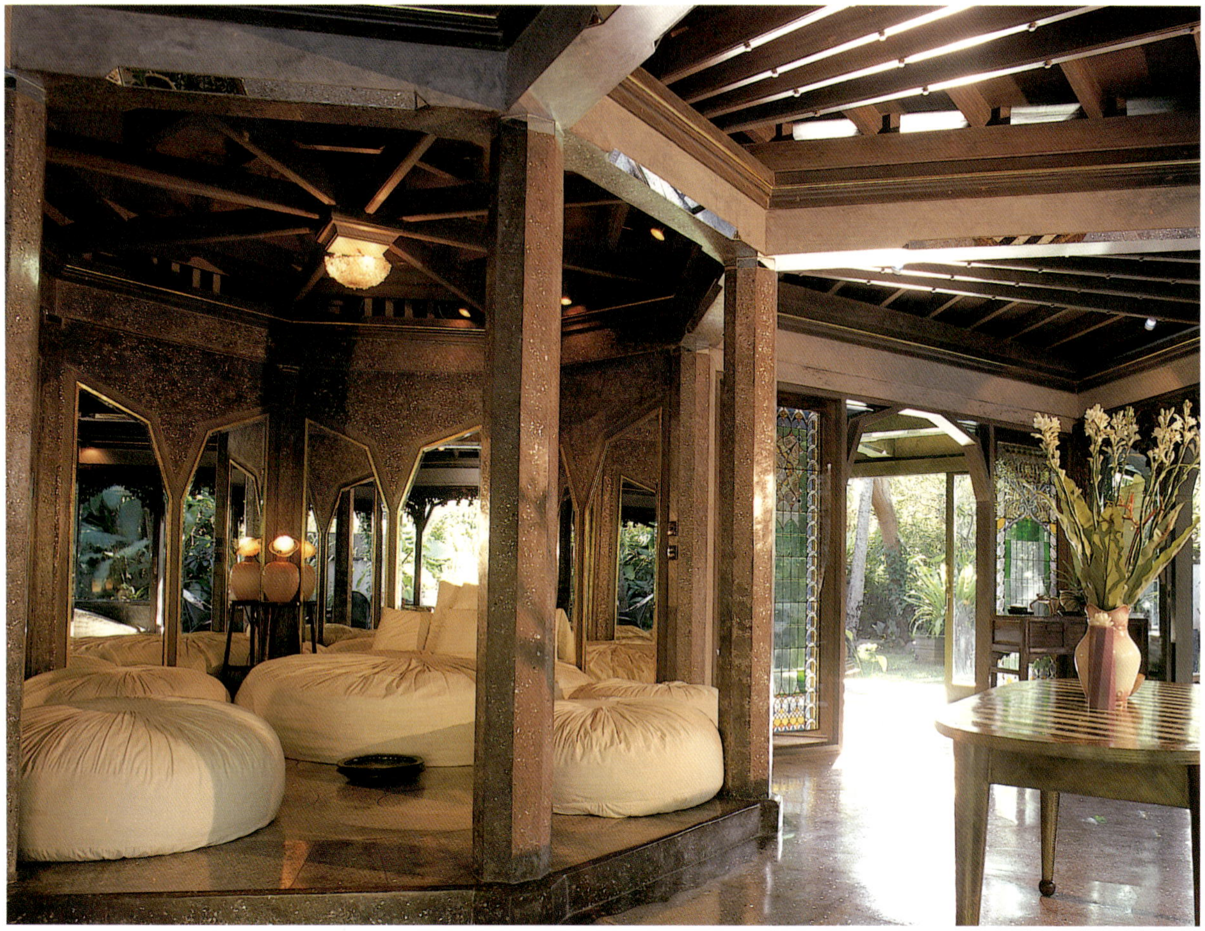

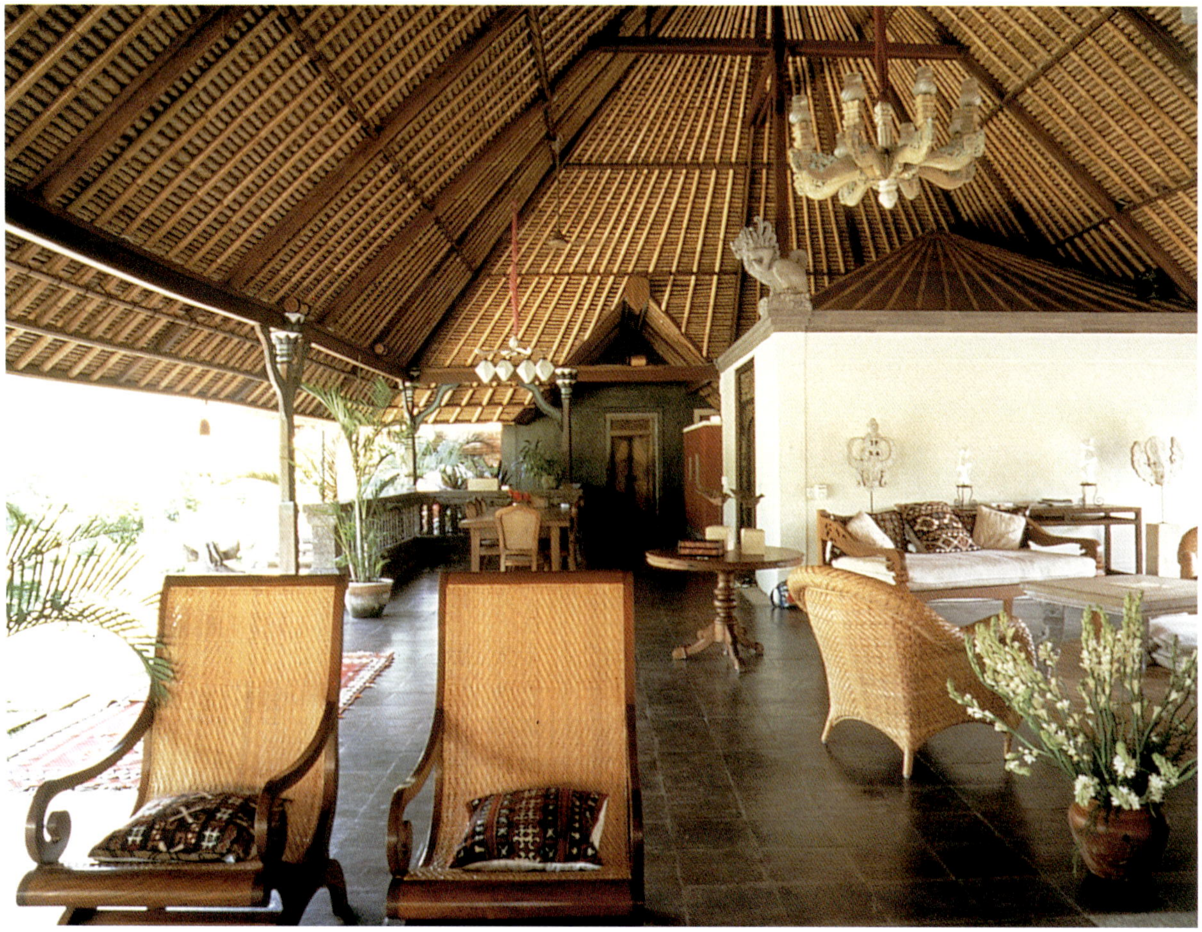

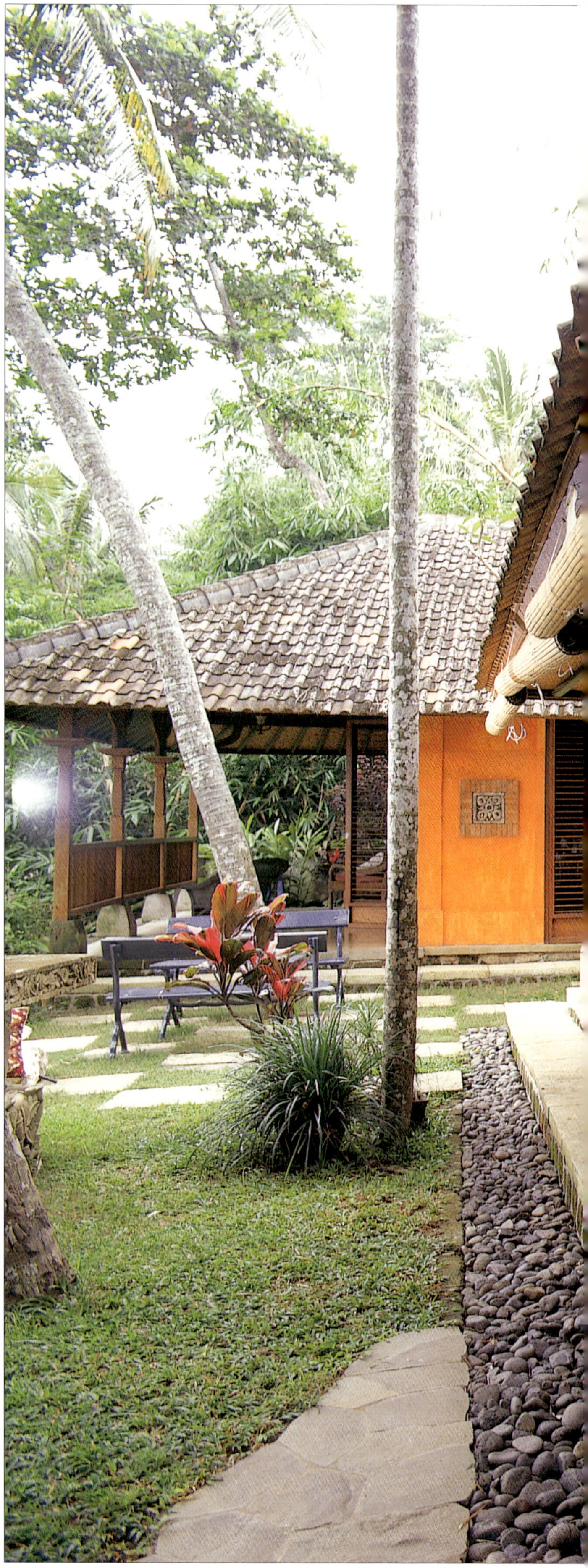

PAVILION ELEMENTS → **DIVIDING SPACE IN MODERN PAVILIONS 5.13**

A	
B	C

A. *The Legian house of Italian fashion designer Milo is based on an octagonal form that is not wholly traditional: the use of Balinese materials (coconut wood and thatch) and the neat divisions enforce a Balinese feel.*

B. *Two "box bedrooms" have been dropped into a cavernous open pavilion at the Canggu Puri Mertha in Canggu.*

C. *The living room of the Presidential Suite at the Taman Bebek villas, Sayan, is essentially one half of the ground floor space of a traditional* wantilan *building. The other half is divided into an entrance hall, bathroom and spiral staircase (to an upper floor bedroom). In the background, a traditional* sakutus *(eight-poster) form has been divided into terrace, bedroom and garden bathroom.*

Puri Ganesha

Designer Diana von Cranach has used the *wantilan* form with delightful effect in the far northwest coast hotel, the Puri Ganesha.

Firstly, the four two-bedroom villas *look* wonderful, spread sparsely along the coast in grassy meadows thinly planted. The only other elements of the landscape vying for attention are the hills behind and fishing boats skimming past on the Bali Sea.

Secondly, the duplex villas are a heroic exercise in wasted space, with expansive reaches of loggia, verandah, corridor and dining alcoves. In their construction, the structures are quasi-traditional. Concrete was used in the main inner *wantilan* frame to allow for a bathroom upstairs (on a concrete slab floor) and a column-free bedroom downstairs (a tad non-U Hindu, but one must be prepared to sacrifice one's principles for beauty).

Whitewashed brick coursework walls, elegant timber, *bedeg* (woven bamboo) screens and carved wooden elements—Lombok doors and Javanese fretwork screens—have been used to partition off activity spaces and to provide privacy, security and romance.

All this, plus super-high ceilings, has been achieved without losing the traditional *wantilan* proportions and the traditional *wantilan* appearance from the outside.

Each villa has an "outsider" six-poster pavilion by the pool and, some 50 metres away, a northern coast *jineng* rice loft with *klangsah* (woven coconut) roof, as a beachside belvedere.

GROUND FLOOR
Not to scale

UPPER FLOOR
Not to scale

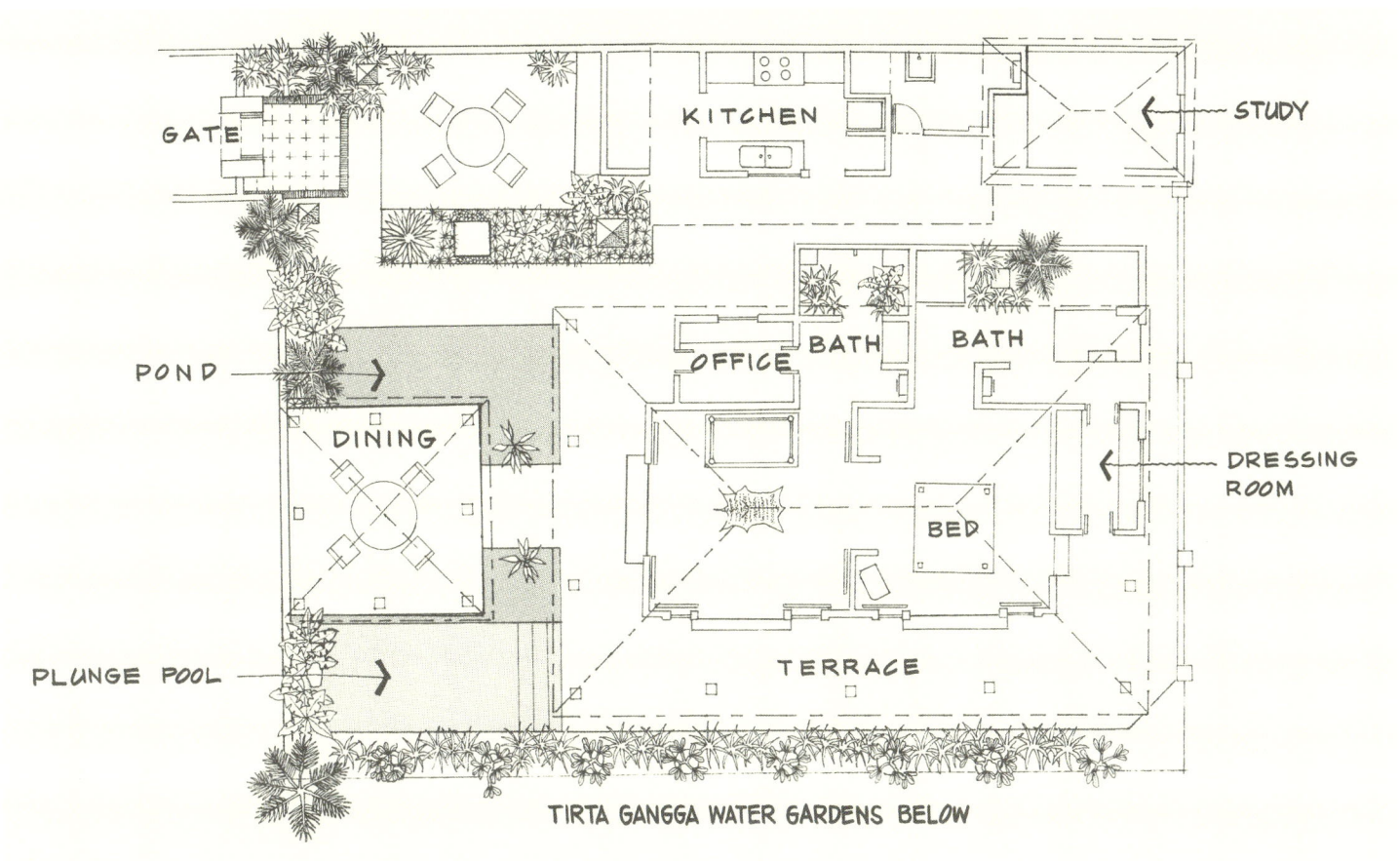

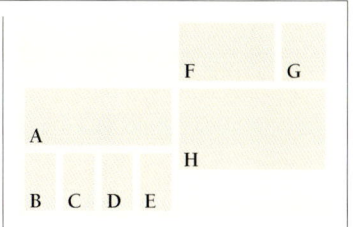

PAVILION ELEMENTS → **DIVIDING SPACE IN MODERN PAVILIONS 5.13**

A. Ground floor and upper floor plans of the main wantilan villa at the Puri Ganesha.
B. Front elevation of the main wantilan villa.
C. The loggia, which holds the timber spiral staircase.
D. Detail of roof construction.
E. The corner support is part masonry column, part post.
F. The dining pavilion of Carole Muller's residence, Villa Tirta Ayu.
G. The bedrooms.
H. Plan of the compounds.

Villa Tirta Ayu

In 1995, famed ergonomic suffragette Carole Muller remodelled an existing palace recreation pavilion, called a *loji*, to create a Bali Style residence for herself.

Ms Muller acquired a neglected palace courtyard overlooking the fabulous Tirtagangga royal water gardens in eastern Bali. The original tiered structure was maintained and cleverly divided by the deft use of shoji-like sliding screens and mirrored doors.

The lower tier became the verandah and the upper tier became glamorous bed platforms, complete with canopied *taban* beds in neo-traditional style (by Symon of S.I.L.I). All the rooms in this pleasure pavilion survey a sublime view of the water garden fountains and lily ponds, with the Lombok Straits beyond.

127

Amandari

Architect Peter Muller used the proportions of a small *wantilan banjar* building near the Taman Ayun royal temple in Mengwi for the bones of his award-winning single-storey villa design for the Amandari hotel.

The floor plan was fairly basic: the cleverness, however, was in the system of sliding screens (by Carole Muller and artist Symon), the Japanese-style sliding windows and the private nature of the walled compound concept. Muller's proportions make for a very refined, very glamorous, but wholesomely Balinese feel.

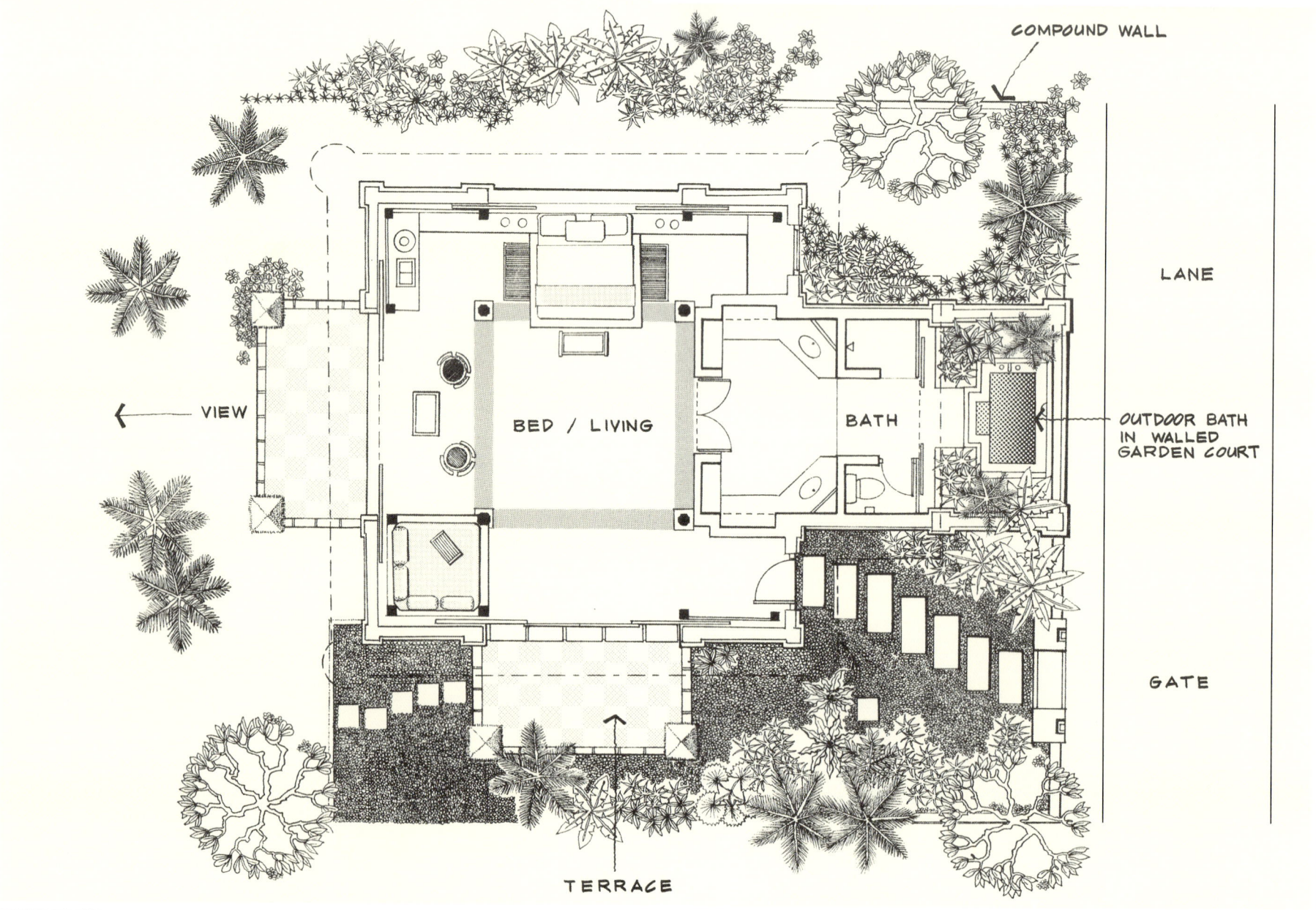

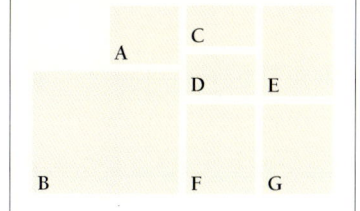

PAVILION ELEMENTS → **DIVIDING SPACE IN MODERN PAVILIONS 5.13**

A	C	
	D	E
B	F	G

A. *The outdoor bath in the bathroom's garden court of an Amandari hotel villa.*

B. *Plan of a villa compound at the hotel.*

C. *High walls enclose each pavilion courtyard.*

D. *The garden courtyard of the duplex pavilion has its own private pool.*

E. *Cleverly designed sliding windows and screens help modulate light and air.*

F. *A village lane in the Amandari hotel.*

G. *The pavilion suites are built using traditional materials and techniques.*

Following pages: A medley of Balinese artisans and tradesmen.

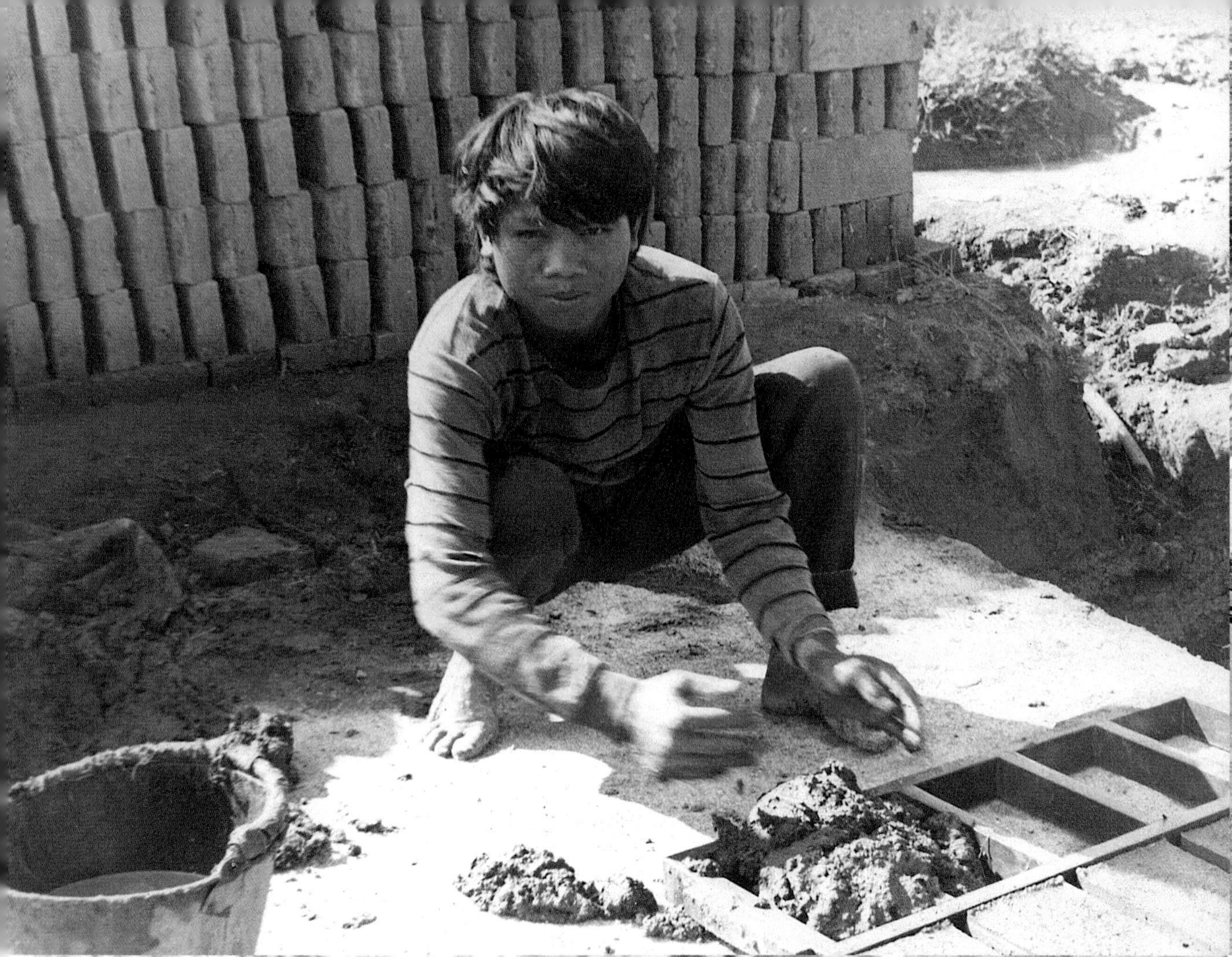
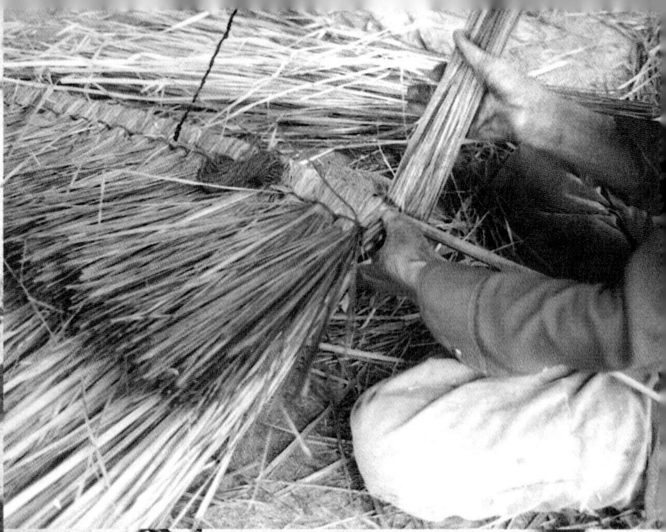
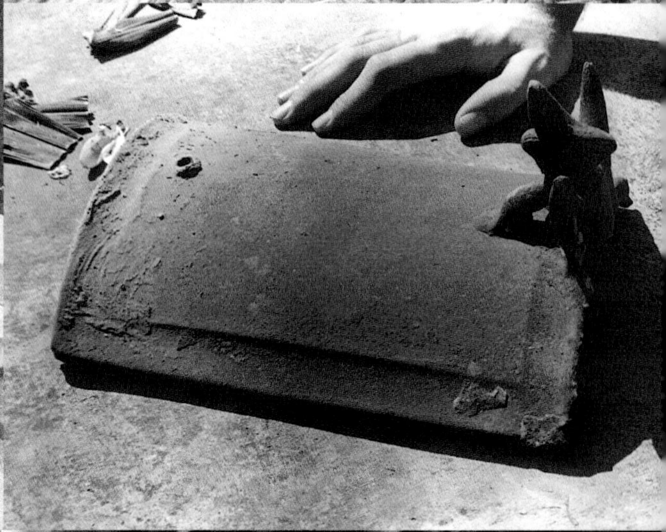
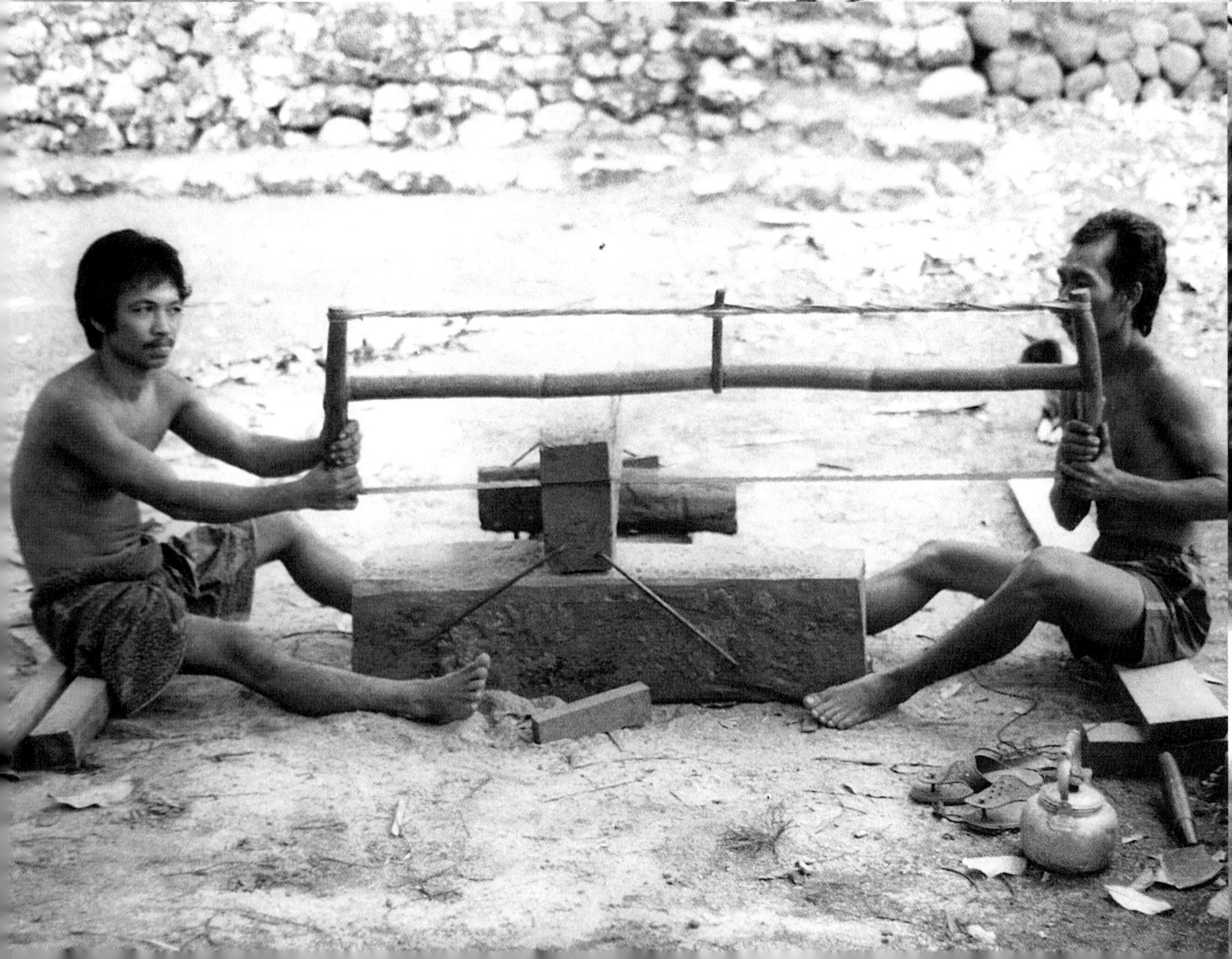
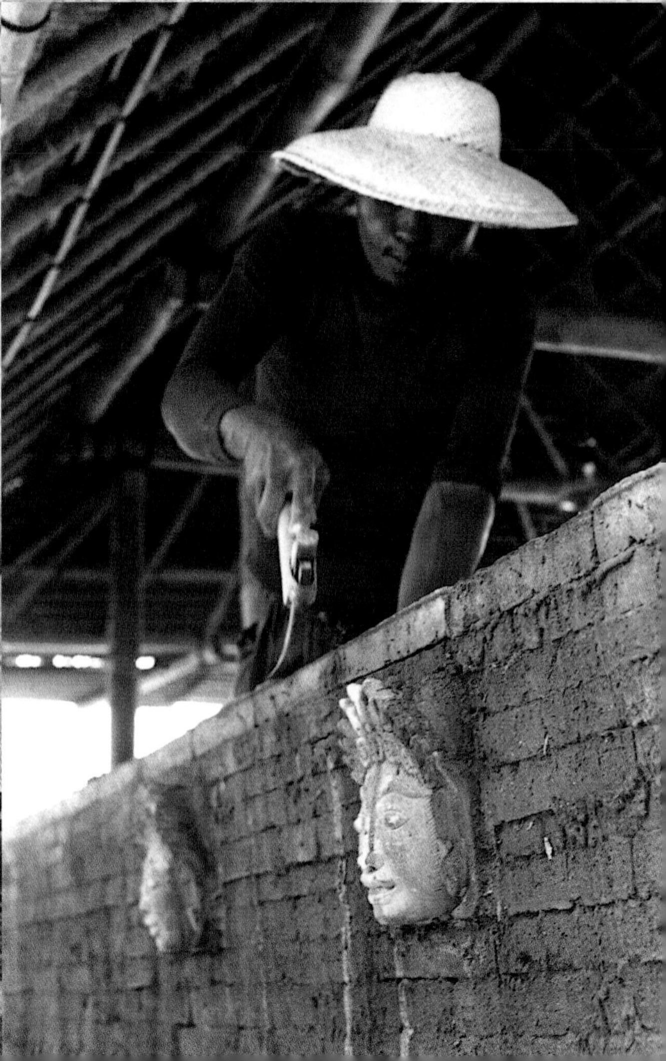

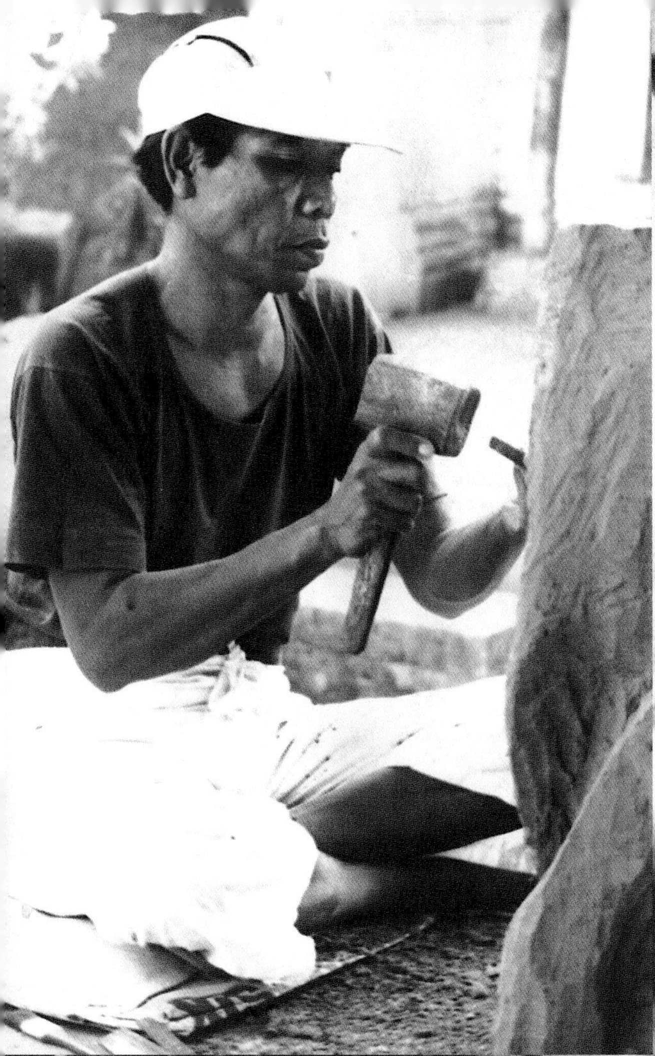
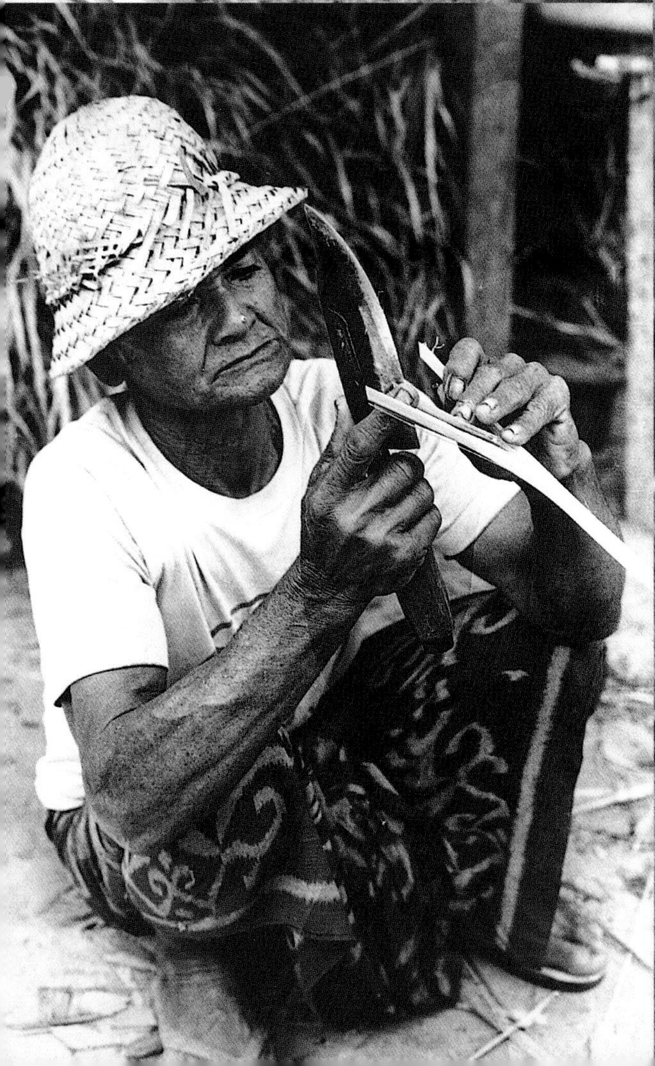
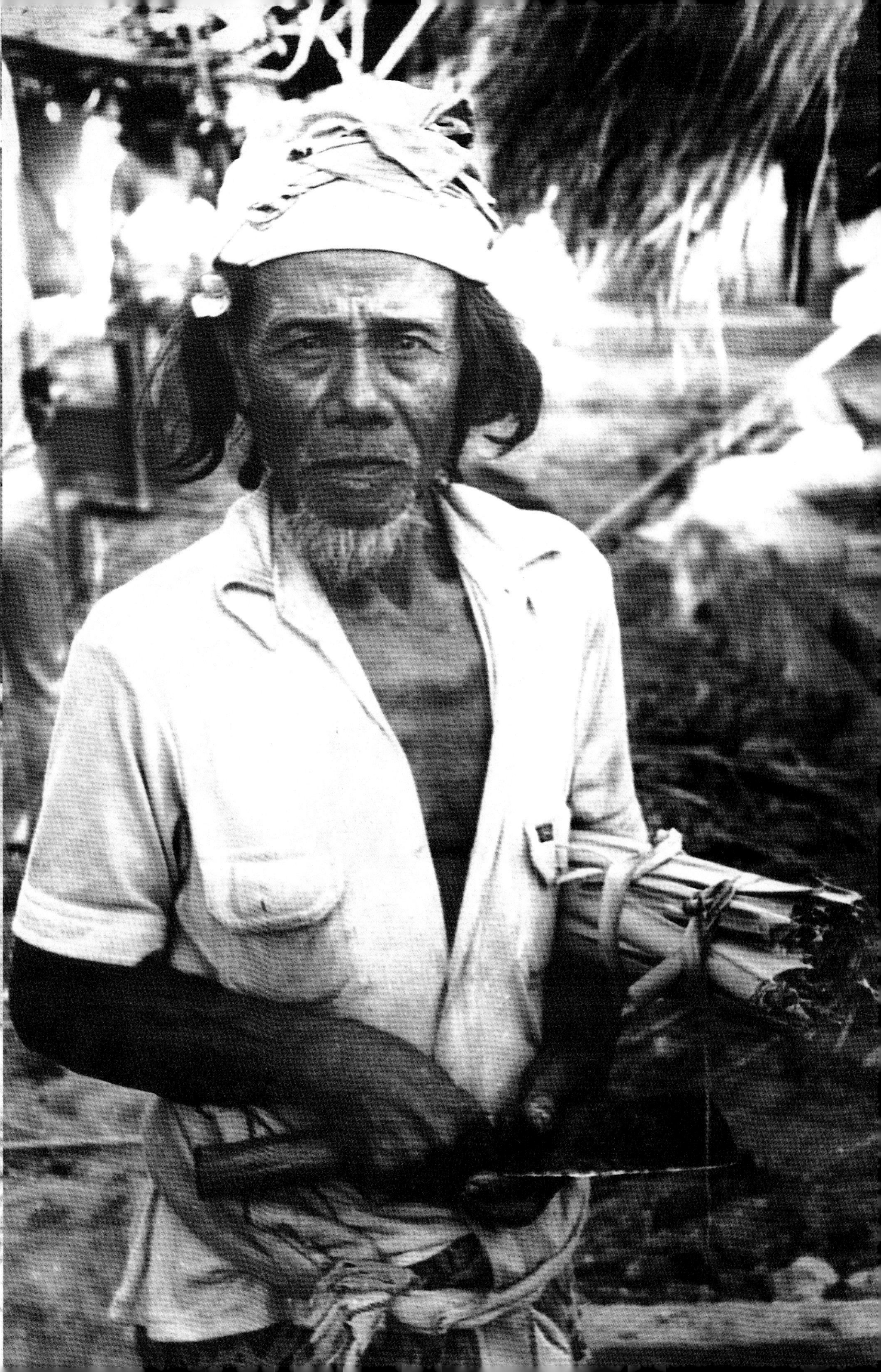

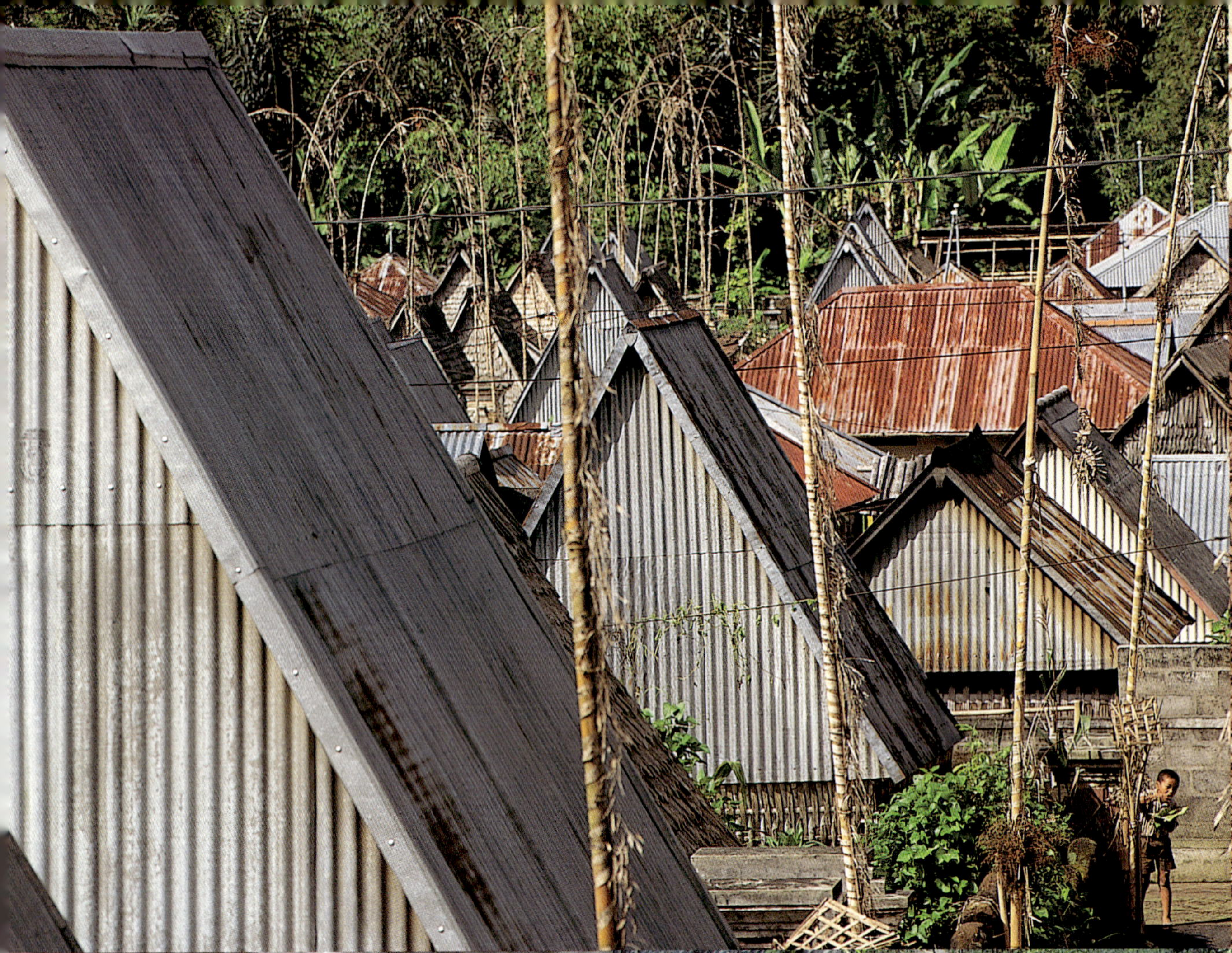
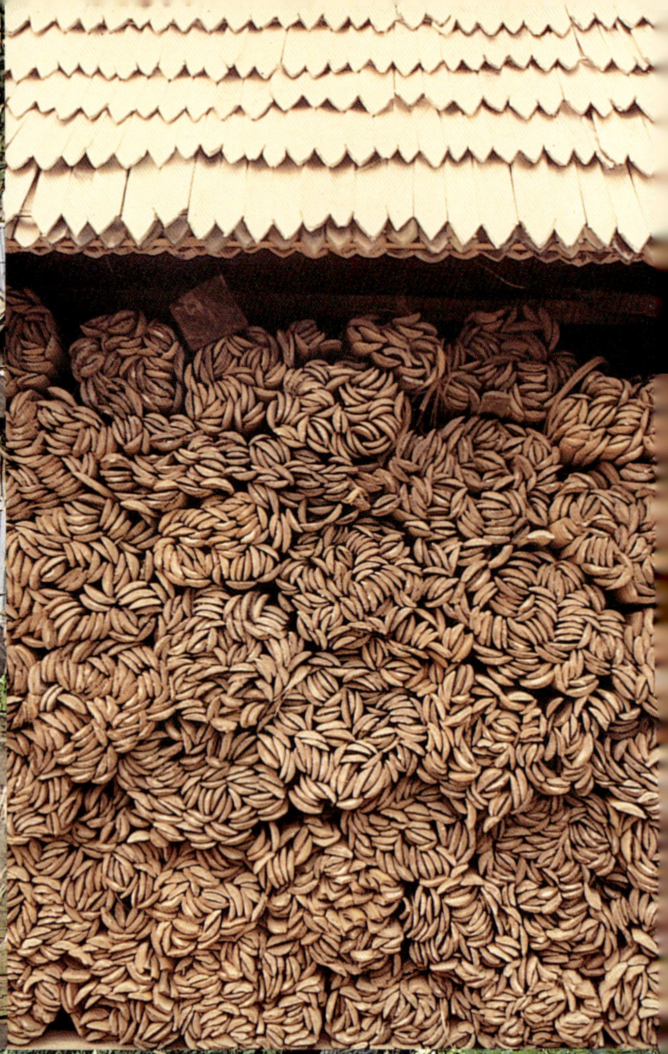
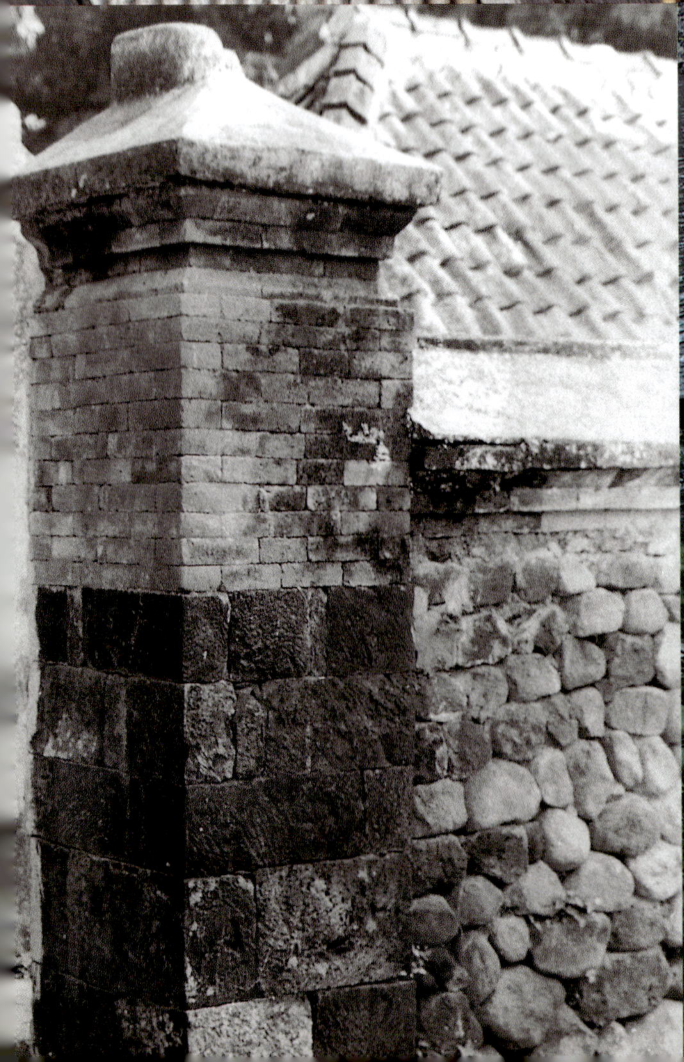
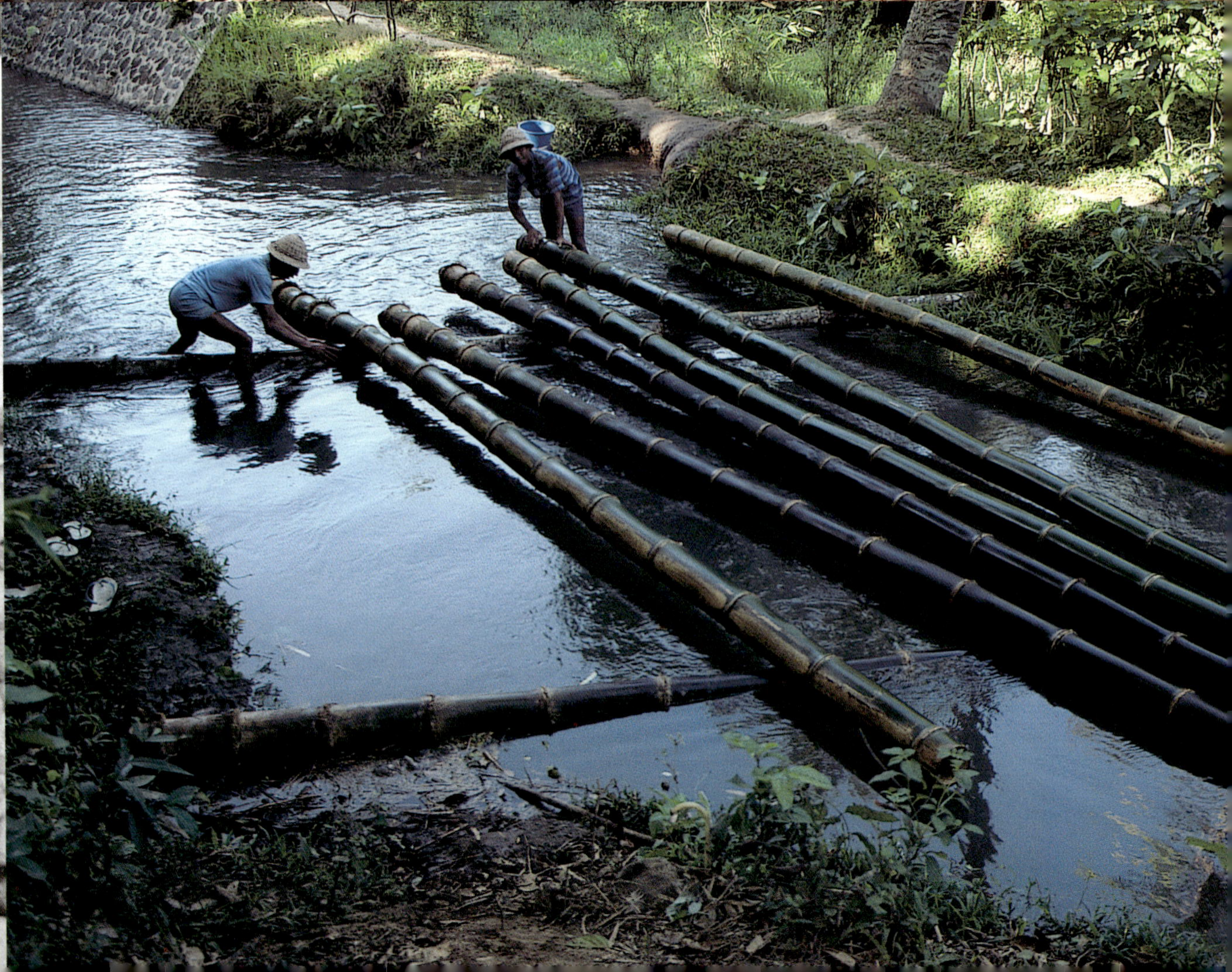

Chapter 6

BUILDING MATERIALS

6.1	Timber	134
6.2	Bamboo	136
6.3	Thatch	140
6.4	Temporary Architecture	144
6.5	Stone	148
6.6	*Paras*	152
6.7	Coral and Limestone	156
6.8	Earth and Brick	158
6.9	Terracotta and Terrazzo	160
6.10	Cement and Plaster	162
6.11	Ceramic	164

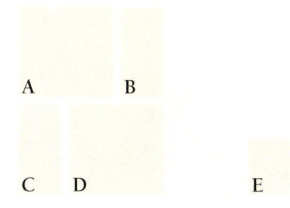

Building Materials

Bali has a wealth of building materials positively bursting from its rich volcanic soil. Nearly everything can be worked by hand with the appropriate carpentry, masonry, thatching and bamboo-working tools.

For hundreds of years architectural splendours were constructed without importing cement, paint or steel. In fact, if one excepts the iron age (when adzes from China were traded across the archipelago for sandalwood and nutmeg) and the age of Indian, Arab and Chinese traders (when Gujarati textiles and kitchenware Ming plates were traded), Bali has been pretty much self-sufficient.

These days everything is available—titanium louvres, two-way glass, laser-simulated hand carving—but the best Bali houses are still built the old way, by hand, using local materials and methods. By "local" I mean particular to the immediate locality: coastal houses and hotels, for example, are more apt, more geographically-referenced, if they use coastal materials such as limestone, beach-sand (for courtyards) and coconut wood (for truss work). In the mountains, bamboo shingles, volcanic tuff and dark timbers work with the landscape and with the climate. This chapter showcases an array of building materials available in Bali, and, in most cases, the structures shown are built in materials from their locale. The use of local materials lends authenticity to design.

Decorative stone finishes are too often forced onto Bali Style houses and hotels, rather than growing naturally out of a design process informed by local traditions and a choice of materials based on suitability.

Traditionally, Balinese building practices were "honest"—that is, true to the craft and the material. Since the tourist boom, however, all sorts of cost-cutting and time-saving practices have become standard, particularly the use of stone as an appliqué, fixed in thin veneers. A study of traditional materials and building techniques leads to a better understanding of Balinese architecture and a feel for Balinese proportions. Beauty is in the proportion of forms and in the correct selection of materials for the form chosen and the location. While a wide range of materials may be available, often the most common is the most suitable.

A. Corrugated iron roofs in Bayunggede village, Kintamani.

B. Bundles of bamboo roof shingles stacked in a bamboo storage shed in a mountain village.

C. The corner pilaster of a courtyard wall in Padangkerta, eastern Bali. Three materials are used: river stones, honed andesite and red brick. The capital is of cement render.

D. Giant green bamboo being washed in a village pond.

E. In eastern and northern Bali, the use of sun-dried mud balls in construction is commonplace.

6.1 Timber

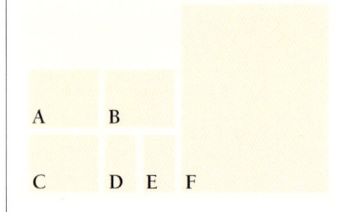

A B
C D E F

A. The Villa Kirana in Sayan has covered walkways with timber ribs modelled on traditional Laotian houses.

B. Colonial-style timber bungalow in Petang village in the mountains.

C. An exquisite late-19th-century window/air vent from a jero palace meten pavilion near Singaraja, northern Bali. The lathed spindles, five Majapahit-style carvings and lively puppet-style paintings at the centre are all very fine.

D. The main gate of the handsome Pura Batur in Kintamani (before its 1997 renovation).

E. This single-leafed meten door in Guwang village, Ketewel, is carved in the classic Majapahit style, with traditional eggshell paint finish.

F. Before its 1995 renovation, the main bale lantang long-house inside Pura Batur temple had thick timber elements and very masculine proportions. Note the "sawn-off" sendi.

Bali has a variety of both hard and soft woods. Coconut wood *(kayu seseh)*, jackfruit wood *(kayu nangka)* and teak *(tegeh)* are the most widely used for columns and beams and truss work. Jackfruit timber planks are also fashioned into door and window leaves. Temples use rare scented woods like sandalwood, durian or nutmeg for their spirit houses.

The wood of the tall, straight coconut palm is the workhorse timber of Balinese pavilion architecture. Large *wantilan* structures, for example, use *kayu seseh* with the bark removed in long sections, called *balok*. Rafters, roof plates and beams use coconut timber taken from the outer layers of the tree trunk, as the inside is pulpy.

Teak and ironwood shingles, called *sirap*, were introduced from Java in the 1970s. While the Balinese pavilion is one of the most beautiful structures in the world, it should be said that, as far as mill work goes, the Balinese are far better carvers than they are carpenters. Pavilions are timber structures pieced together rather miraculously. The importation of modern carpentry tools might change this: let's hope their arrival doesn't sweep out traditional timber pavilion construction skills.

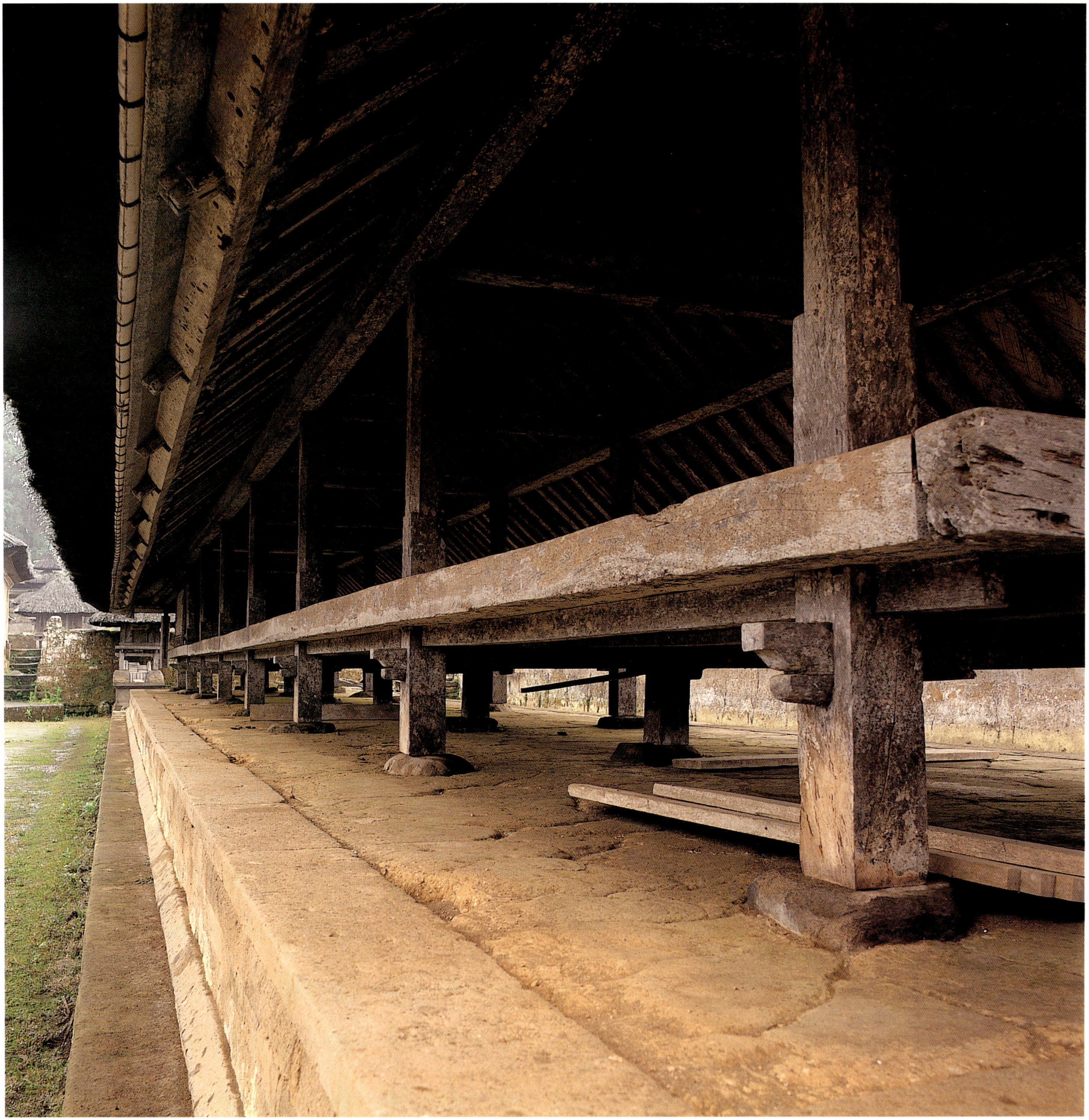

6.2 Bamboo

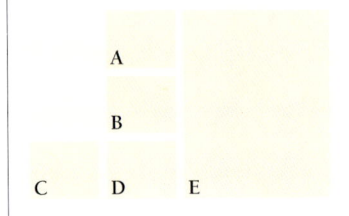

A. Bundles of bamboo roof shingles on the roadside.

B. A simple bamboo fence and a bamboo plant in a garden at Puri Ganesha, Pemuteran, northern Bali.

C. Detail of bamboo shingles on the corner of a mountain rice loft.

D. Adobe and bamboo are staples of mountain architecture.

E. A corner of designer Putu Suarsa's house in Sidakarya.

One of nature's most versatile wonders, bamboo (called *tiying* in Balinese) is widely utilized in Balinese construction. It is most noticeably used as rafters *(iga-iga)* in thatched roofs. Whether split and shaped into roof shingles, sliced and woven into panels called *bedeg*, or shredded to make the bamboo string used in thatching, it is a cheap and effective material. Strong in compression, bamboo makes excellent supports, particularly for temporary offering platforms (see 6.4 Temporary Architecture) and makeshift huts. In some rural areas whole kitchens are constructed almost entirely of bamboo, and adobe-bamboo combinations reach levels of high art.

Unfortunately, tropical bamboo suffers from a blight, called *bubuk*, which causes small particles of dust to rain down from the rafters after a few years. Canopies need to be put over beds in thatched buildings to protect from the *bubuk* dust. When the thatch is changed, the bamboo rafters are often replaced too.

Bamboo is most commonly used as *bedeg* panels in bamboo or timber frames. Its botanical structure—long hollow tubes joined by hard nodules—makes it strong and flexible. It is a grass which reproduces rapidly through rhizomes and it is environmentally desirable because it prevents soil erosion along Bali's steep river gorges.

Putu Suarsa of Big Bamboo in Sidakarya and Linda Garland of the Environmental Bamboo Foundation in Nyuhkuning are two designers who are dedicated to the promotion of bamboo as a building material.

BUILDING MATERIALS → **BAMBOO** 6.2

138

BUILDING MATERIALS → **BAMBOO 6.2**

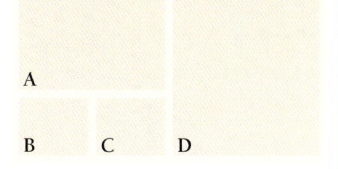

A. *A simple mountain meten with woven bamboo (bedeg) screen walls. The roof shingles, baskets, conical rice steamers and the platform on which they are drying are all made of bamboo.*

B. *Detail of the main bale lantang at Pura Batur, Kintamani, showing the exquisite combination of timber, bamboo and black ijuk string elements (1980 photo).*

C. *A clever utilization of exaggerated overhang in a Java-style bamboo pavilion at Linda Garland's estate.*

D. *A guesthouse at the Linda Garland estate, centre of an environmental research foundation devoted to the promotion of bamboo. The house is constructed almost entirely of bamboo.*

6.3 Thatch

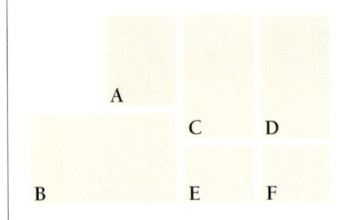

A		
	C	D
B	E	F

A. *Edge of an ijuk (sugar palm fibre) thatch. Growth on the eaves like this indicates that the consecration ceremonies were performed well.*

B. *A thatched roof pitch should not be too steep (nor too flat): this tobacco-drying hut is purely temporary.*

C. *Ijuk (sugar palm hairy bark fibre) thatch on a mountain temple gate, Bukian, near Kintamani (1982 photo).*

D. *Alang-alang thatch, with bamboo keeps on a wantilan building in the Puri Ganesha, Pemuteran.*

E. *Thatch roof on a temporary pavilion in the Puri Mengwi palace, during cremation ceremonies.*

F. *Old Bali villages had ketan rice stalks, called* sumi, *as a rough thatch on adobe courtyard walls.*

Bali has many types of thatch, called *rab*. There is *rab klangsah*, made from woven coconut leaves; *rab ijuk*, made from the fibre on the trunk of the sugar palm and used exclusively for the roofs of important shrines; *rab sumi*, made from rice stalks; and, most famously, *rab alang-alang*, made from elephant grass which is gathered and tied to long bamboo spines to form brush-like batons of thatch.

Each thatch type has an individual method of fabrication and application, but all are laid from the bottom (eave plate) up, over timber or bamboo rafters. The piquant Balinese roof profile, that signature "bustle", results from packing the thatch tighter in the lower portions of the roof, or the addition of an extra skirt of roof called a *gerantang*.

Even cement- or tile-roofed buildings emulate the slight up-turn, to achieve the more Chinese look typical in ceremonial structures like the *bale bali*, the *kul-kul* tower and shrine buildings. The roof of a Balinese building is a dwelling place for deities.

BUILDING MATERIALS → **THATCH 6.3**

142

BUILDING MATERIALS → **THATCH 6.3**

A. Thatch made from plaited coconut leaf, called klangsah, on a simple four-posted pavilion.

B. A combination of roof styles and roofing materials in this 1982 photo of the beautiful Pura Puseh temple, at Bayunggede, near Kintamani.

C. Bamboo bark is used on a temporary ceremonial pavilion in Selat village.

D. Alang-alang thatch is ideally laid on a 40°–42° angle. Bamboo strip "keeps" are often laid on top to stop freak winds flipping up the alang-alang.

6.4 Temporary Architecture

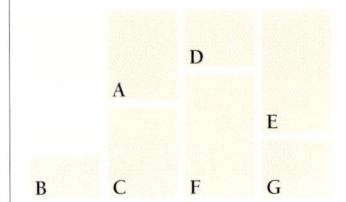

A. The long processional entrance arch at Kuta's society wedding of the year (for the son of the owner of café Made Warung) was created with busung *coconut palm leaf and woven* sampiyan *starbursts*.

B. Special pavilion constructed for a visiting high priest in the suci, or inner, courtyard of the Mengwi Palace during the Pelebon Naga Banda cremation ceremonies.

C. A roadside stall, or warung, on the north coast road shows an ingenious use of klangsah (woven coconut fronds) as both wall and window.

D. Detail of a typical temporary shrine building constructed of bamboo.

E. Tall sanggah agung *temporary shrines have been built with betelnut palm columns and tie bamboo pieces.*

F. Pewedan *pavilions, for officiating* pedanda *priests, are thrown up at graveyards and in house compounds for important ceremonies.*

G. Klangsah *woven coconut thatch only lasts for a year or so, but is cheap and effective for temporary structures such as stables for cows.*

One could write a whole book on temporary architecture, wrapping and decoration in Bali. Much of the island's architecture is built of disposable materials—like bamboo, *klangsah* thatch and betelnut palm—for special ceremonies. Giant bamboo and woven palm enclosures, called *bancingah* or *payadnyan*, are built for the holy *mukur* "purification of the soul" ceremonies and are dismantled after a few weeks. The rites demand that the structures be "virgin", and on virgin land, that is, land previously unoccupied in the village.

The tall funeral biers, called *bade*, are also works of temporary architecture. Besides these sacred ceremonial structures, there are temporary pavilions, called *pondok*, in the rice fields, where a family "hangs out" during the day, between shifts of working the padi. There are temporary shelters-cum-food-stalls, called *warung*, in the marketplace and along roadsides. In many rural areas the kitchen of a compound is often a semi-permanent structure, too, built of bamboo and thatch on an adobe base.

The proportions of temporary pavilions are the same as their more permanent cousins, but the construction methods employed are quite different: good bamboo construction requires a lot more pegging and strapping than joining, for example (see photo D).

Bamboo string is the "universal tetherer" of Balinese temporary architecture, and coconut leaves the "great provider". The Balinese are particularly adept at raiding nature for simple needs, like string fasteners, thatch or even umbrellas fashioned from giant caladium leaves.

BUILDING MATERIALS → **TEMPORARY ARCHITECTURE** 6.4

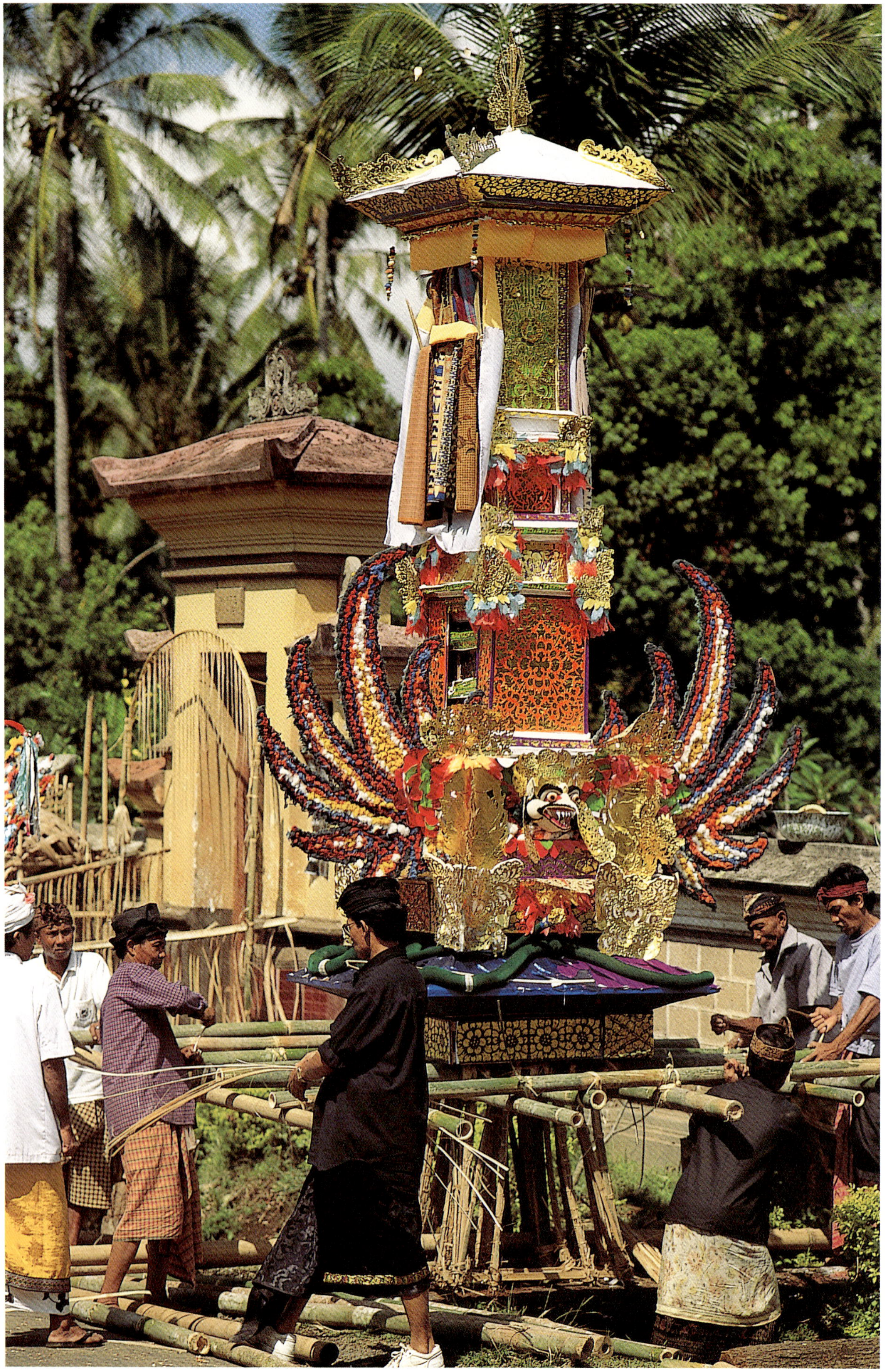

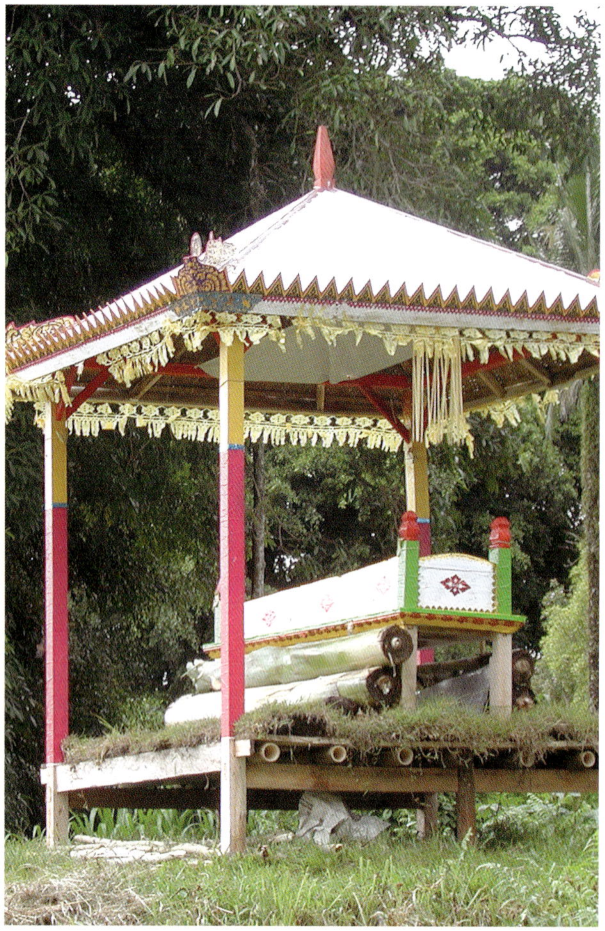

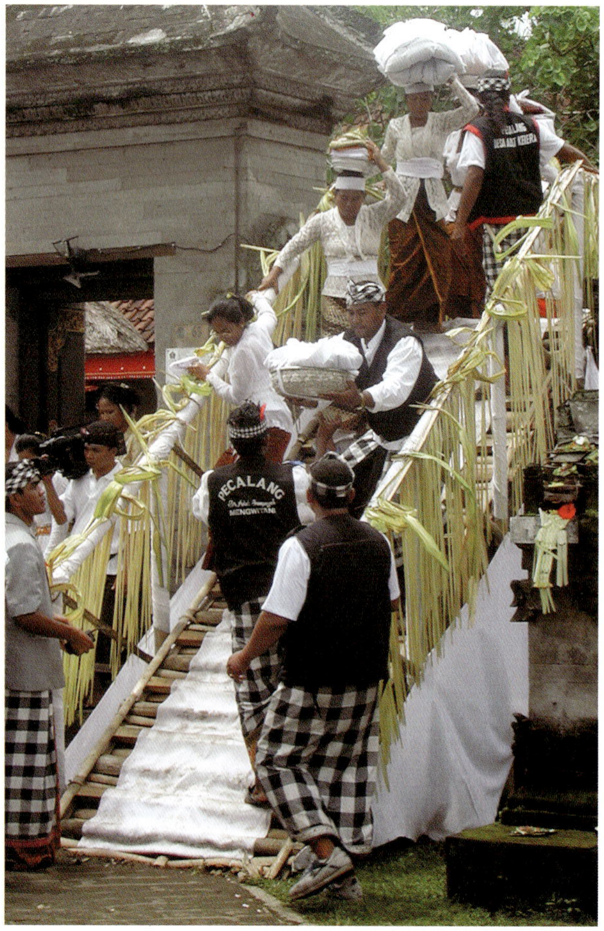
PECALANG

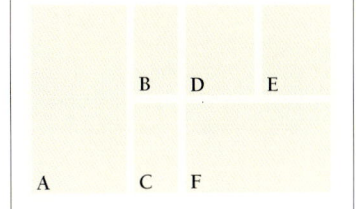

BUILDING MATERIALS → **TEMPORARY ARCHITECTURE 6.4**

A. Cremation or funeral biers, called bade, are made of bamboo and balsa wood. They are burnt at the graveyard after the ceremony.

B. A cremation pavilion in the graveyard of Selat village, Karangasem.

C. A temporary staircase built over the wall of the Mengwi Palace's ancak saji court for the giant Pelebon Naga Banda cremation on 7 December 2001.

D. Built for just one ceremony, this very temporary shrine is constructed of one piece of split bamboo and one woven coconut leaf.

E. Klangsah woven coconut fronds are used for screening and roofing elements.

F. Shade structure off twin shrines at Pura Jagatnata temple, Ketewel.

6.5 Stone

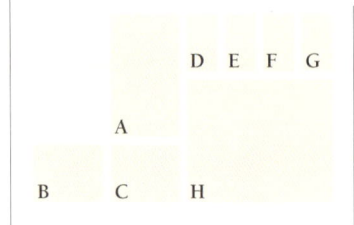

	D	E	F	G
A				
B	C	H		

A. *Tenganan village's plaza and pavilion bases are constructed almost entirely from worn lava rocks and river stones. The baskets on the pavilion's stylobate are for fighting cocks.*

B. *Baris dancer helmets on a lava wall at Pura Jati.*

C. *Detail of the batu candi (andesite) fascia on a decorative wall in the lobby of the Hotel Chedi, Payangan (Kerry Hill Architects).*

D. *Split stone meten pavilion, Padangkerta, eastern Bali.*

E. *Photographer Rio Helmi's northern Bali slate house gate in Ubud.*

F. *House gate, Padangkerta, eastern Bali.*

G. *Temple stairs and shrine in Padangkerta village, eastern Bali.*

H. *Pura Pulaki on Bali's northern coast was recently refurbished. The base of its giant kul-kul tower was given a veneer of limestone.*

Following pages: Limestone fascia on concrete pillars at the Amankila hotel, eastern Bali.

Architecturally-speaking the best Balinese buildings have more masculine materials at the base of a structure and finer materials working up.

Traditionally, building foundations in Bali were mixtures of river sand and split river rocks, rough limestone or volcanic lava rock. Moving up, stylobates were fashioned from *paras batu* (pitted volcanic tuff, *batu* meaning stone in Balinese), and the body of walls and gates were made of a finer, lighter *paras* or were cement rendered (see 6.6 *Paras*).

Rocks used in building are usually metamorphic; they are found, pre-tumbled, on river banks or in dried river beds during the dry season. The architecture of the northern coast, the mountains and eastern Bali uses lava rocks found in the vicinity of recent eruptions: these areas are particularly rich in stone architecture. The architecture of Bali's Stone Age survives in Bali Aga (aboriginal or mountain culture) villages such as Tenganan, Padangkerta, Songan and Trunyan. In these villages, one finds ramps, pavilion bases, gates and courtyard walls of split metamorphic rock.

Lately limestone, called *palimanan*, from the hills of western Java, has been used extensively throughout Bali and exported, as "Bali stone", to the rest of the tropical world. It is a friendly stone, easily honed, which also comes in streaked and softer, cheaper varieties. Slate, called *batu teplek*, from either northern Bali or western Java, has recently been re-discovered as '60s-style feature walls in Bali Style homes.

BUILDING MATERIALS → **STONE 6.5**

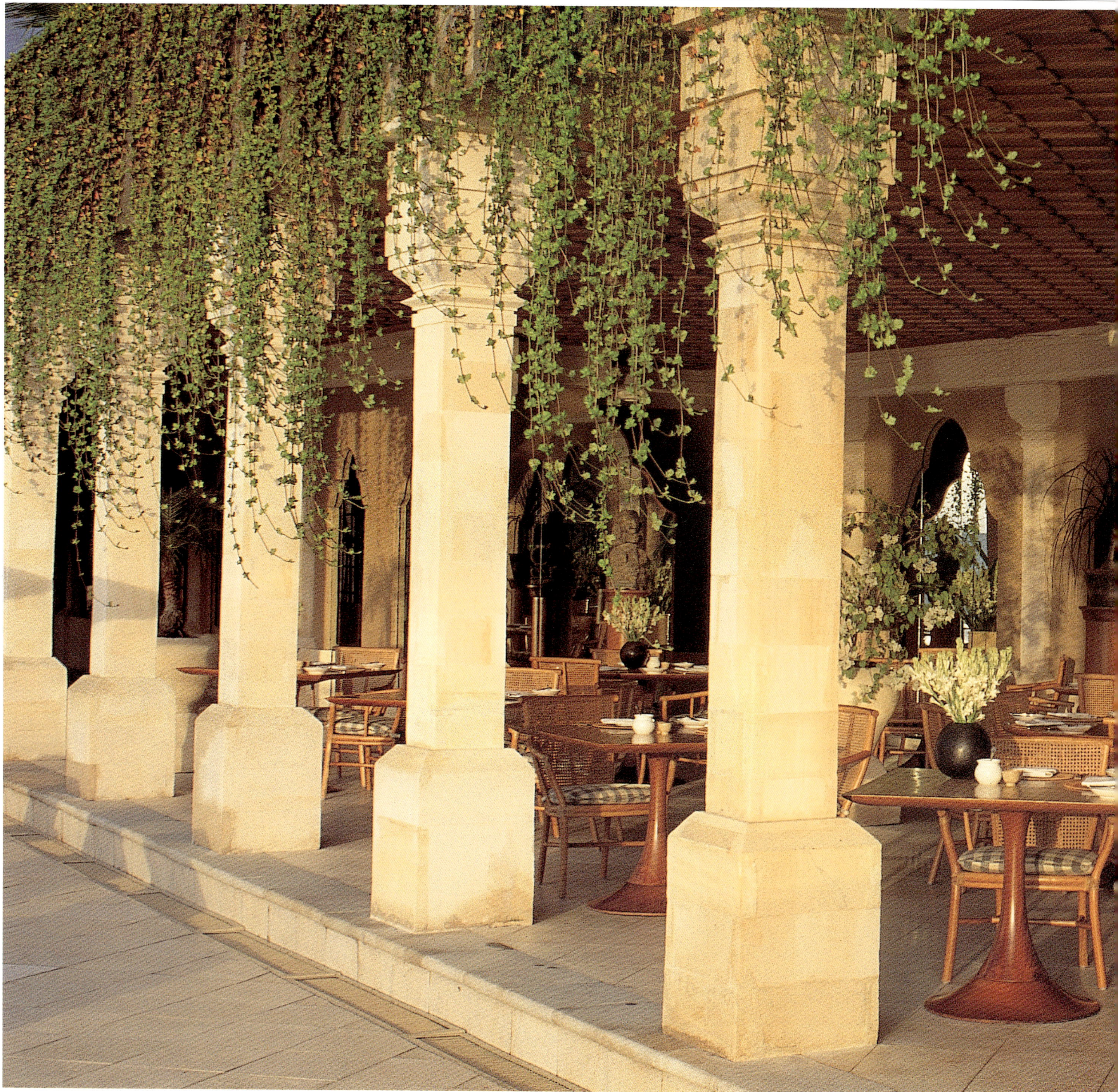

BUILDING MATERIALS

6.6 *Paras*

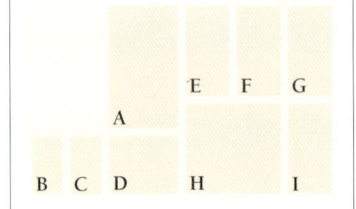

	E	F	G
A			
B	C	D	H	I

A. *A mason shapes a block of paras ukir at a riverside quarry.*

B. *Papalihan and simbar coursework using paras ukir brick, called paras tempelan.*

C. *Pink paras carving on a Pura Beji, Sangsit, northern Bali, shrine base.*

D. *Simple brick and paras rosette as a gate decoration at the Villa Bebek, Sanur.*

E. *Photographer Rio Helmi and designer Ela Helmi designed this paras feature wall for their Ubud home.*

F. *Paras taro quarried in blocks and carved in situ on a Bukian village (central Bali) house gate.*

G. *Carved paras ukir panel as a decorative element in a Bali Style house.*

H. *Female dancers' and angels' faces are often found carved in paras on north coast temple walls. This example, over 100 years old, is on the wall of the famous Pura Beji, Sangsit.*

I. *A paras ukir frame around an offering niche on a paras batu gate.*

Sometimes referred to as volcanic tuff, *paras* is a sedimentary rock similar to sandstone. It is quarried from river banks in coastal and central Bali, in particular on the banks of the Petanu and Wos rivers.

There are many varieties of *paras*. North coast *paras* is often pink. *Paras sanggingan*, from Sanggingan village near Ubud, is streaked with a yellow sulphur stain. There is a pitted *paras*, called *paras batu*, which is widely used in Denpasar and Kerobokan (a rich quarry area near Denpasar and Kuta) and which was championed in hotel architecture by Peter Muller at the oft-cited Kayu Aya.

Paras batu is a landscaper's friend, too, as it is easily worked and most appropriate for courtyard steps, pond edges and even as courtyard paving. *Paras ukir* (*ukir* means carving) is popular throughout Bali for courtyard walls, temple gates, shrines and for the millions of statues on the island. In northern Bali carved *paras* shrine bases and temple gates were often painted in pastel hues.

There is a mortadella-like *paras batik* and a beautiful soft mountain *paras* called *paras taro* which occurs in quarries near architecturally splendid mountain villages such as Taro and Bukian. *Paras ukir* is beautiful on courtyard and pavilion walls and *bataran* foundation coping, but tends to be slippery in the wet season, like Bali bricks, when used on the ground.

In recent years various chipped finishes have been introduced by designers such as Bill Bensley and Anak Agung Yokasara to create fresh and unusual textures.

BUILDING MATERIALS → **PARAS** 6.6

154

BUILDING MATERIALS → **PARAS 6.6**

A. *Paras coursework on a pavilion in the 11th-century Pura Puncak Penulisan, Kintamani.*

B. *Paras batu is a durable stone suitable for courtyard walls. It comes rough hewn from the quarry in 550 x 150 x 110 mm blocks called balok.*

C. *A decorative wall at a petrol station near Sanur boasts three varieties of paras.*

D & E. *The magnificent kori agung temple gate (designed by the great I Gusti Nyoman Lempad, 1862-1978) at the Pura Desa, Ubud.*

F. *Paras taro used as a veneer on a concrete pavilion at the Amankila hotel, eastern Bali.*

6.7 Coral and Limestone

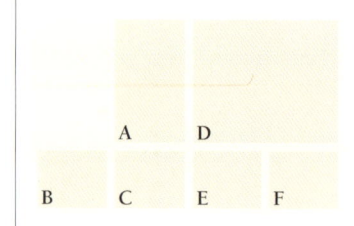

A. Coral architecture was once popular in the coastal village of Sanur. This gate, by Pak Cekog of Taman, Sanur, was built in Batujimbar Estates, copying a gate in Donald Friend's house, designed by Geoffrey Bawa.

B. Natural and hewn coral mosaic veneer by Pak Cekog for Geoffrey Bawa on the old water tower at Batujimbar Estates, Sanur.

C. Coral used on a coastal temple, the Pura Ratu Agung, Suwung Gede (1998 photo).

D. The long wall that leads to the Donald Friend house was built of coral. Designer Ed Tuttle later partly faced it with carved paras.

E. Dramatic use of different types of limestone at the lower swimming pool, Four Seasons Resort, Jimbaran.

F. Limestone rubble pergola at the Four Seasons Resort, Jimbaran.

In ancient times, most of Bali's coastal temples were built of coral. Pura Uluwatu and Pura Sakenan are two striking examples of coral architecture. The Bukit peninsula in southern Bali is one giant raised coral reef: limestone quarried there, called *batu bukit*, was once found only in villages like Pecatu and Sawangan (the latter obliterated, tragically, by the Nikko Hotel's approach road). *Batu bukit* is Bali's most economical and widely used stone. A softer strain, called *paras bukit*, can also be found on the peninsula: it is often used in cheaper housing and for pavilion and boundary walls, despite its tendency to erode when exposed to prolonged rains.

Polished *palimanan* limestone, which actually comes from western Java, from the village of Palimanan, was first used at the Amandari. It is a handsome material, with good colour and texture, but stains fairly easily, unlike its European relatives. It turns grey when used outside but keeps its bone hue, surprisingly, when used on submerged swimming pool steps.

Balinese house walls were traditionally plastered with a thick pasted lime-and-water mix, a process called *mulas*. This whitewashing, often applied to *popolan*, was done with a paint brush made from smashed rice stalks.

Lime wash for walls, and lime-based plasters, have been used for a long time in coastal areas, where lime is readily available. It is now illegal to harvest coral and bake it into lime, but lime quarries have sprung up all over the Bukit peninsula.

BUILDING MATERIALS → **CORAL AND LIMESTONE** 6.7

6.8 Earth and Brick

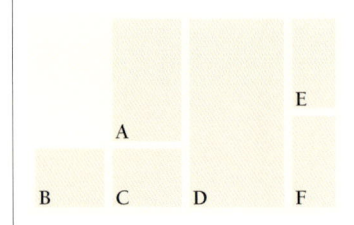

		E
A		
B	C D	F

A. Tiered brick paduraksa gates in the Majapahit style appear in palaces and temples all over southern Bali.

B. Unusual brick-on-brick (partly carved) ornamentation on a temple gedong at Sebatu village. Fine examples of adobe architecture can still be found in mountain villages such as Bayunggede, Sebatu, Bukian and Taro.

C. Carved bas-relief free-standing decorative wall at the Taman Ayun Cultural Complex.

D. Over-zealous antique dealers, in cahoots with under-zealous temple guardians, sometimes gouge out the antique Chinese plates which decorated many late-19th-century red brick shrines and gates, leaving a weird, but magical, pock-marked look.

E. Corner of classic Majapahit gedong vault at Pura Maospahit, Denpasar. Good examples of bata bali temple gates and gedong shrines can be found in and around Kesiman (east Denpasar), Mengwi, Tabanan, Krambitan, Renon, Sanur, Seminyak and Sidakarya.

F. Typical red brick coursework on a temple shrine.

Bali is rich in adobe architecture, particularly in mountain villages. Chapters 4 and 5 have many examples of courtyard walls and gates in adobe (*popolan*) and mud brick, called either *bata matah* or *bata citakan*.

The distinctive *bata bali* is a baked clay roman brick which is used extensively throughout the island. The ancient Hindu Majapahit capital of eastern Java, Trowulan, was constructed entirely of roman bricks and this style was probably brought to Bali during the era of Majapahit expansion. Certainly whole cities of masterful roman brick architecture—Ayutthaya in Thailand, and parts of Katmandu (Nepal), Champa (Vietnam), Pagan (Myanmar) and Angkor Thom (Cambodia)—were built during that era.

Bata bali are easy to build with, either dry laid (*bata pasang*) or shaved and rubbed into place with water (*bata pripihan*). They are also good for pavilion flooring and for coping on courtyard walls. A wall of *bata bali* can be carved to create decorative panels: combined with *paras*, it becomes a distinctively Balinese decorative scheme (see 7.2 Brick and *Paras*).

Used externally as courtyard walls *bata bali* gather moss attractively; during the wet season the rich pelt-like patina is often supplemented by ferns growing on a wall's *paras batu* base. Sadly, *bata bali* are now smaller and more prone to crumbling after five or 10 years of exposure to the weather. But outsized *bata bali* can still be found, or ordered, and are infinitely superior when doing large gates or thick walls.

BUILDING MATERIALS → **EARTH AND BRICK** 6.8

159

6.9 Terracotta and Terrazzo

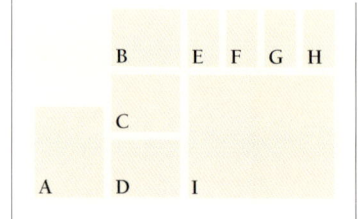

	B		E	F	G	H
			C			
A		D	I			

A. *The Cili motif—that of the Balinese, not Hindu, goddess of fertility—adorns many ceremonial pavilions in Bali. This Cili was worked onto a clay dore roof ridge tile.*

B. *Typical* genteng daun *(or* genteng kodok*) terracotta roof tile used widely on the island.*

C. *Interesting terrazzo-tiled annexe on a large* bale bali *ceremonial pavilion in the Jero Kubutambahan mini-palace, northern Bali.*

D. *Terrazzo steps on a handsome scored plaster palace gate near Sempidi.*

E. *Old-style* pemugbug *apex cap on a temple* meru, *Puri Nyalian, Klungkung.*

F-H. *Terracotta ridge pieces, "pinned" onto thatched roofs with bamboo stakes, help conserve the volatile ridges called pemugbug.*

I. *Terracotta roof tiles, called* genteng, *are first moulded from clay and then left in the sun to bake before firing.*

The use of terracotta for pots and roof tiles in Bali is probably as old as the island's habitation. Terracotta floor tiles appear on ancient buildings of the Portuguese era in Java (16th century), but in Bali were probably introduced, with terrazzo, by the Dutch during the early 20th century. Prior to the 1970s, nearly all of Bali's urban dwellings had either terracotta or terrazzo floors.

Both are now back in vogue: smart designers have discovered the practicality and cost-effectiveness of all-terrazzo bathrooms; and terracotta tiles are back in fashion for the more ethnic Bali Style home. Terrazzo is also widely used for *sendi* bollards, counters and decorative wall finishes (the most famous being the terrazzo in opal hues, mixed with mother of pearl, championed by fashion designer, Milo, and fashionable among Italian high rollers in the garment district). Terracotta, on the other hand, is the most conservative of finishes, suitable for verandah and loggia spaces. It mixes well, colour- and texture-wise, with *paras ukir*, *paras batu* and *batu palimanan*.

BUILDING MATERIALS → **TERRACOTTA AND TERRAZZO** 6.9

161

6.10 Cement and Plaster

Cement and plaster have been around for a few thousand years, but they were not widely used in Balinese architecture—there was no real need—before the colonial era. It must be said that the introduction of reinforced concrete in the early 20th century marked the start of a slow deterioration in the island's building practices and its architecture, particularly in stonework and brick coursework traditions.

The first half of the 20th century, however, saw some imaginative innovations in the use of cement and plaster, particularly in decorative finishes. The last raja of Karangasem, in eastern Bali, led the promotion of cement mouldings as decorative trim on concrete pavilion columns, gates and walls, still visible at the Puri Kanginan and Puri Gede Karangasem palaces in Amlapura. On the north coast, plaster walls have a rich decorative tradition: bas-relief fashioned from cement is more popular there than carved stone.

Many original mixes have been developed since the tourism boom: Geoffrey Bawa used a clay and cement mix for bollards *(sendi)*; Linda Garland pioneered the apricot blush Careyes (Mexico) plaster floor finish; Jack Kent introduced a special combination of white sand, white cement and limestone powder for hotel paths; and rubbed and waxed coloured cement floors and walls have popped up in Expatriate Dream Homes.

For some reason wall plastering has traditionally been the job of women while decorative plastering, similar to stone carving, is a male domain. Otherwise women are relegated to labouring chores on a building site, until the day comes for the all-important house-warming ceremony *(pemelaspasan)* when the women take over.

A. Decorative panels of moulded concrete on the main gate into the Puri Kanginan, Amlapura.

B. In the early 1970s pre-fabricated concrete shrines started to appear in the marketplace. Thirty years later more than half of the island's gates and shrines are pre-fab (and the offerings ordered over the phone).

C. In northern Bali, the art of cement plastering is quite developed. This motif is copied from a classical wood-carving design.

D. Concrete balustrades on the Bale Maskerdam (Amsterdam) at the Puri Kanginan, Amlapura.

E & F. In the colonial era a new architectural language was developed using cement columns, decorative panels, and wall and floor tiles.

G. Cement detail on a Denpasar temple.

H. Beauty is in the proportions, not the materials. On this east Bali shrine, brick and cement are used with minimalist elegance, appropriate to its bold chunky simplicity.

I. Winged lion cement moulding on a pavilion base in the Puri Gede Karangasem palace.

BUILDING MATERIALS → **CEMENT AND PLASTER** 6.10

163

6.11 Ceramic

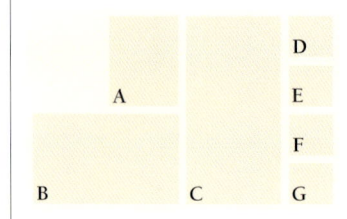

A. Ceramic topknot on Princess Mirah's villa in the Puri Kanginan, Amlapura.

B. Designer Hinke Zieck used ceramics extensively in her interior design for the spa at the Four Seasons Resort, Jimbaran.

C. Chinese kitchenware ceramic plates were used as ornamentation throughout Southeast Asia during the early 19th century.

D. Window of glazed ceramic air vents on Puri Mengwi pavilion wall.

E & F. Part of the range of decorative tiles based on Balinese and Javanese motifs from front-runner Pesamuan Ceramics of Sanur. In 1990, Melbourne ceramic designers Philip Lakeman and Graham Oldroyd set up this high-end decorative ceramics company, making lines of hand-painted decorative tiles that could be used for friezes, table tops and floors. They used local decorative motifs for inspiration as well as the usual goldfish and tropical fruit. The pineapple—a staple in colonial-era architectural decoration since its discovery, speared on 17th-century Arawak tribal gateposts in Barbados—has been joined by mangosteens, snake fruit and melon.

G. The Pesamuan contemporary range, started in 1998, included a wall tile modelled on woven bamboo strip panelling called *bedeg*.

Following page: Offerings placed on a temple pavilion stylobate awaiting consecration.

Bali has few ceramic traditions to speak of, although Chinese ceramic plates have been incorporated as decorative accents on *paras* and *bata bali* gates, walls and shrines since the early 19th century. Machine-made high glaze ceramic tiles were introduced during colonial times for bathrooms and soon appeared as trim on Chinese and Muslim graveyards.

It was not until the 1970s, however, that these mass-produced tiles made their way into traditional courtyards and *kantor-* (office) style homes, where, unfortunately, they have achieved wide appeal. Many of the island's most ravishing shrines have recently suffered from makeovers at the hands of ceramic bathroom tile enthusiasts. Somehow the homogeneity of ceramic tiles often just doesn't go with other hand-finished surfaces and materials.

Since the 1990s west Javan marble and trendy terrazzo finishes have replaced ceramic tiles as the surface of choice at the high end of the building industry.

BUILDING MATERIALS → **CERAMIC** 6.11

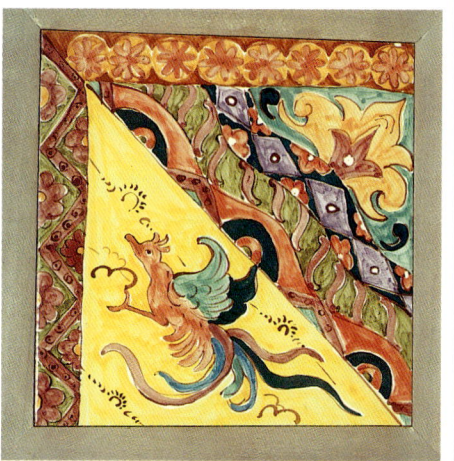

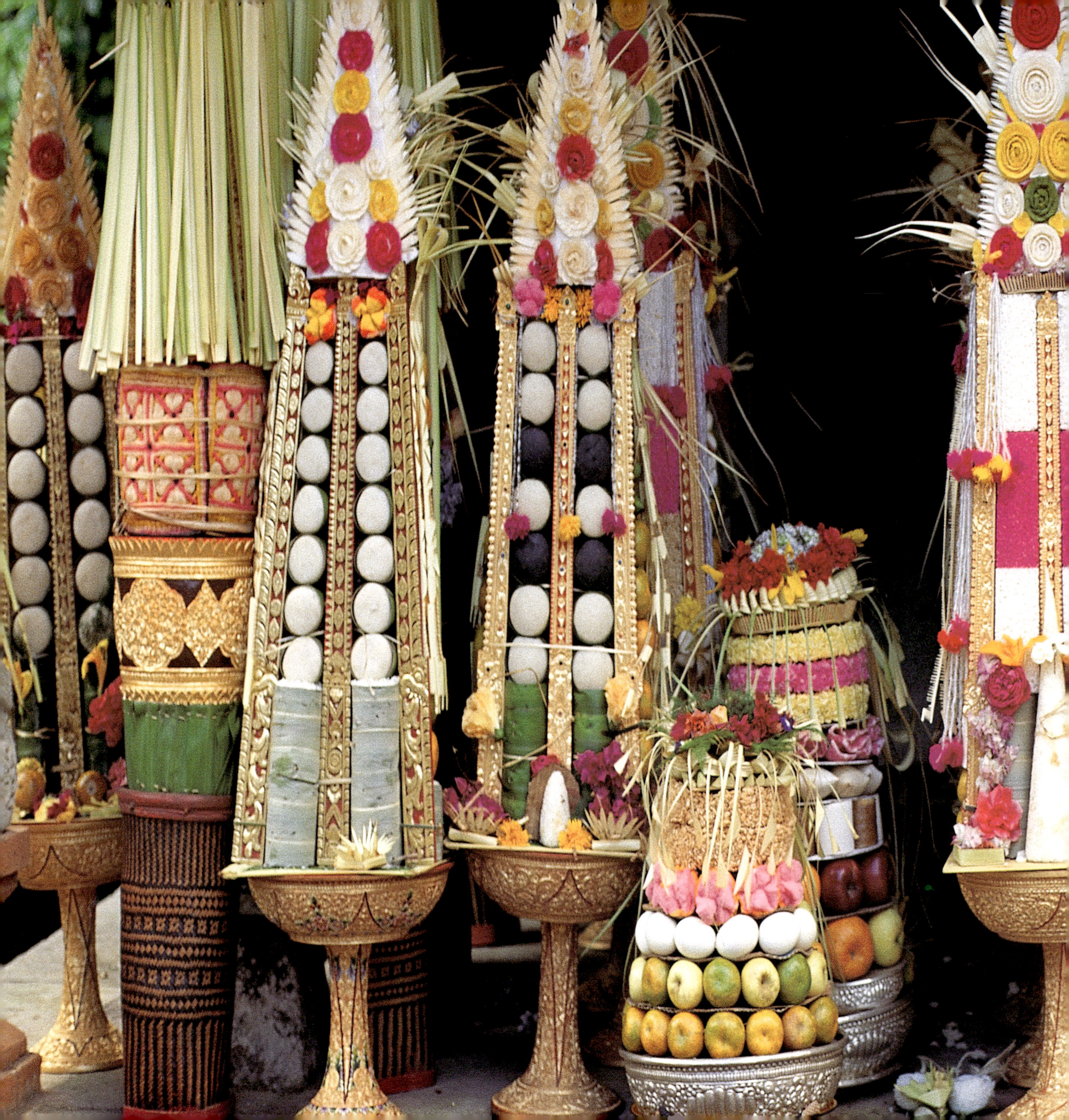

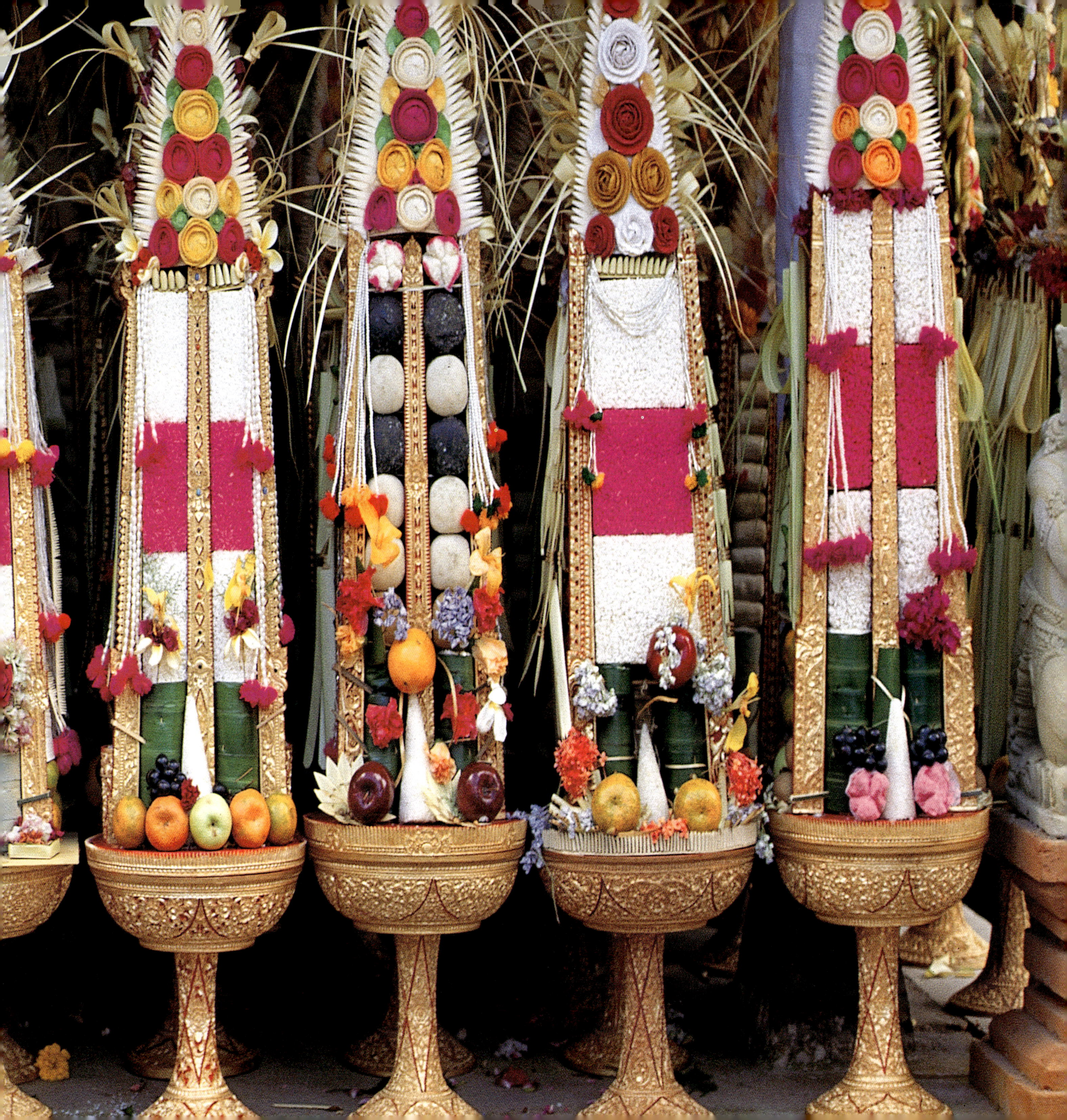

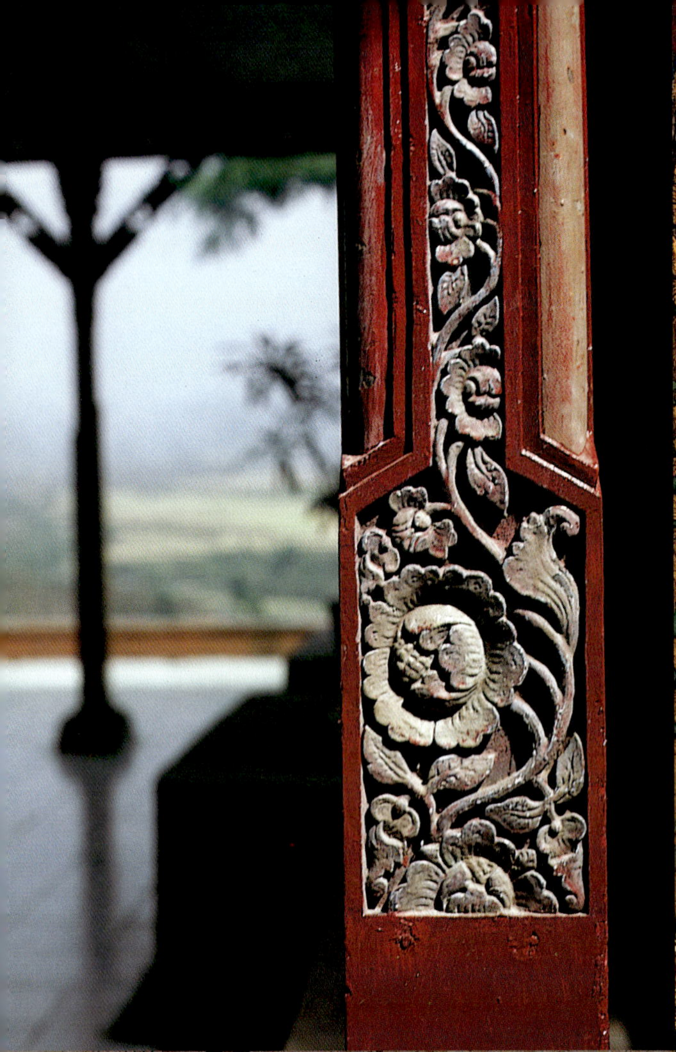

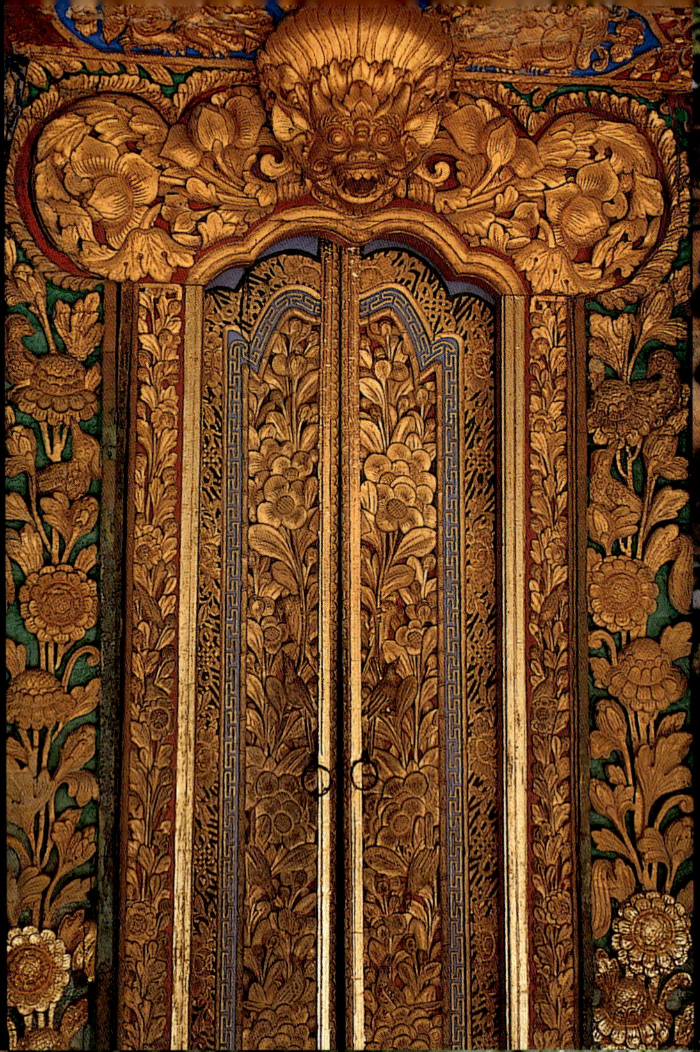

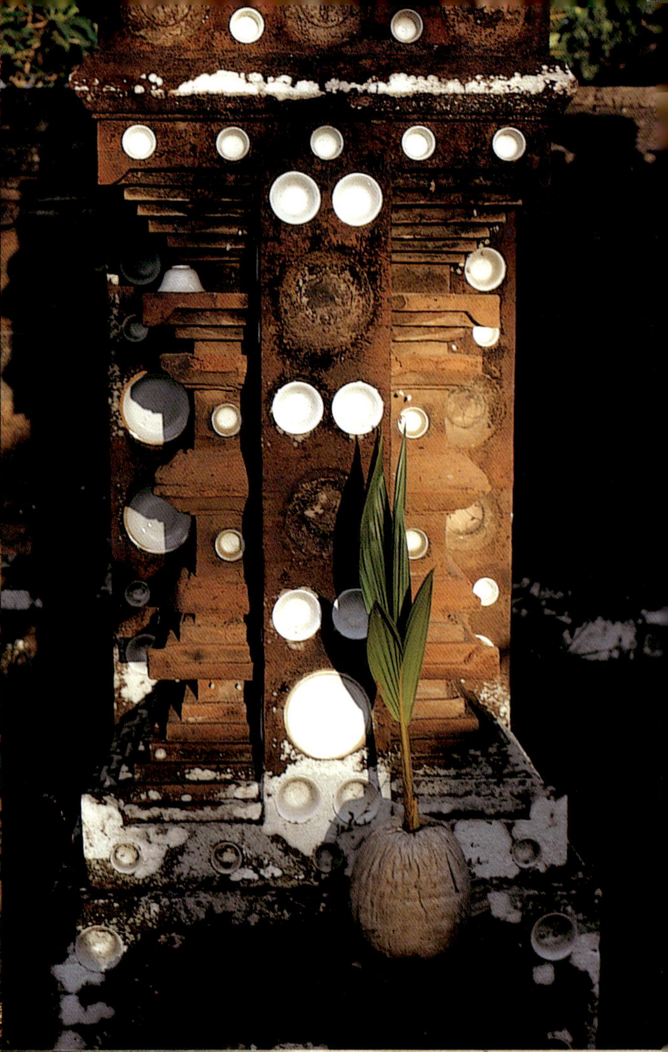

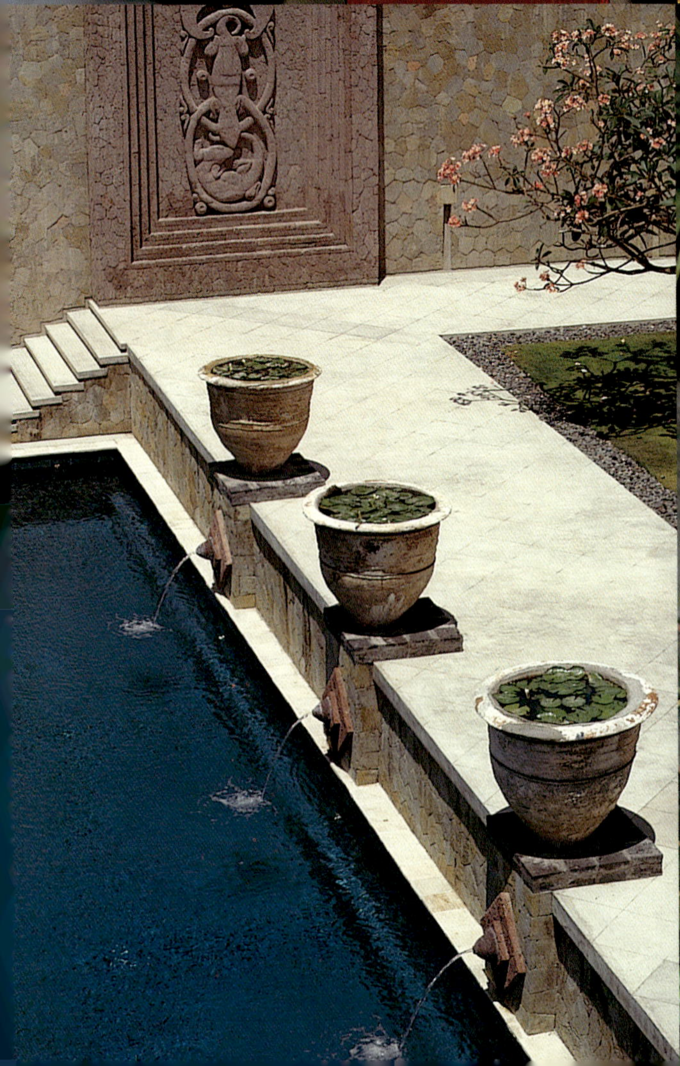

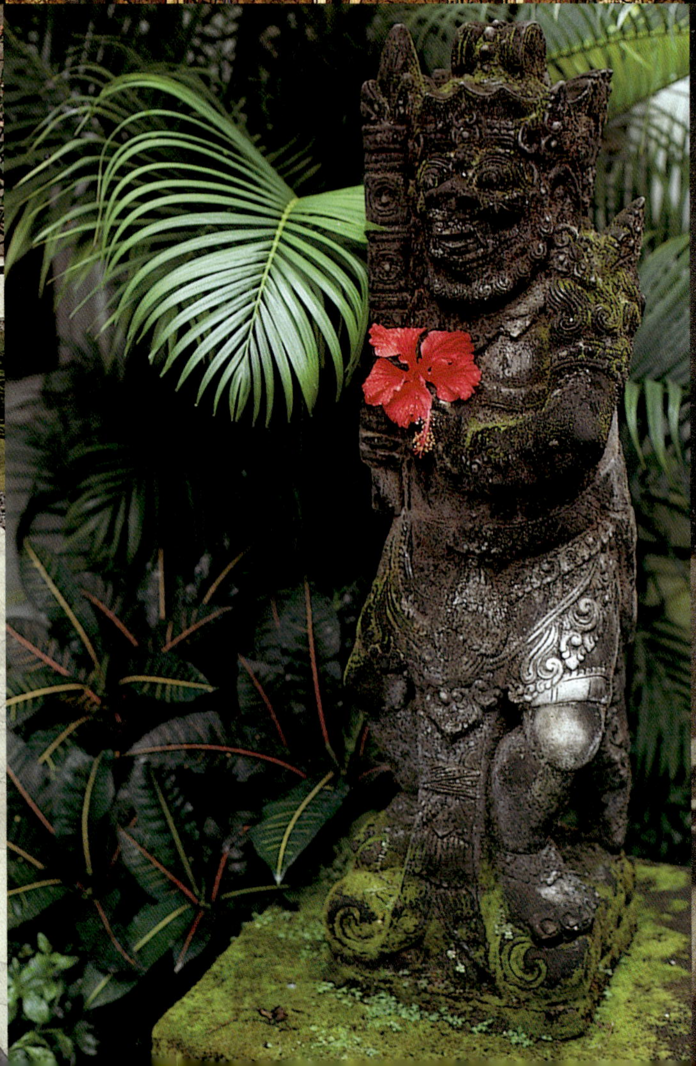

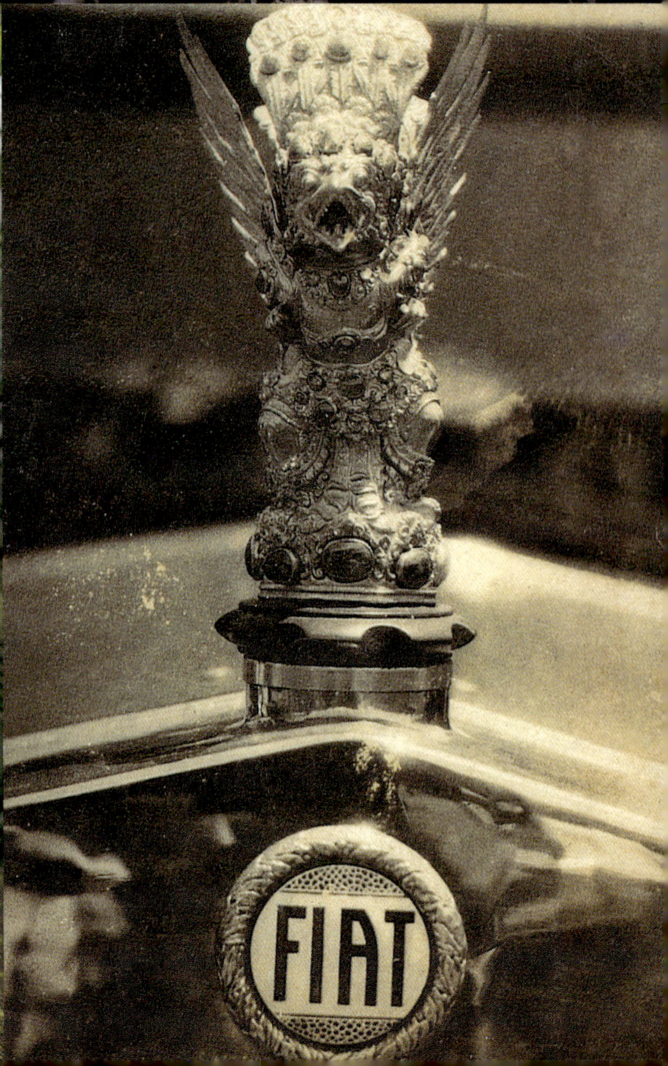
FIAT

CHAPTER 7

Ornamentation

7.1	*Paras* Carving	170
7.2	Brick and *Paras*	174
7.3	Stone Air Vents	176
7.4	Balustrades and Railings	178
7.5	Woven Elements and Cloth	180
7.6	Carved Wood	182
7.7	Colour	188
7.8	Statuary	190
7.9	Boma and Sai	194

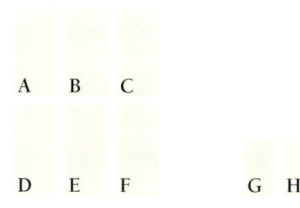

The word Bali is synonymous with decorativeness, and nowhere are the Balinese more decorative than in the ornamentation of their architecture. Traditionally ornamentation in architecture was reserved for the abodes of the gods and the palaces of the nobility but eventually spread to domestic and other buildings.

This chapter covers a full range of Balinese decorative styles: from the ancient aboriginal, through the heavily Chinese- and Hindu-influenced "Going for Baroque" of the 17th and 18th centuries (Bali's Golden Age), up to the present mostly gruesome, but occasionally inspired, modern trends.

On temples almost every element of the architecture is either carved, painted or gilded. During temple festivals the courtyard grows banners, bunting, woven coconut-leaf shade structures and temple sashes in the form of cummerbunds of brocade or chequered cloth wrapped around the pavilion posts. Ornamentation of this temporary type has been included in this chapter.

Traditionally the ornamentation on domestic buildings denoted the occupant's caste. The Ksatriyas (princely caste), in their palaces, for example, had red and gold-encrusted ceremonial pavilions set within handsomely carved, thick red brick courtyard walls. Peasants' houses, on the other hand, exhibited reticence in carved detail, while generally choosing block colour over full-throttle polychrome. There are notable exceptions in mountain villages, such as Sebatu, near Ubud, where the entire village is a riot of colour. Northern Bali villages in particular are fond of very Chinese colour combinations such as yellow and purple, and black and red.

It was once culturally correct not to outdo the gods' houses (the temples) in terms of decoration: in modern times, however, everyone seems busy outdoing their neighbours. Every suburban house, it seems, is trying to look like Gianyar Palace's gatehouse on steroids. Buildings are often just concrete shells, supporting gaudy decoration. Thin veneers of natural stone, encouraged during the Balinisasi (Balinization) programme (1975-95) are now black and mossy with age.

It must be noted, however, that Balinese culture is extremely resilient. It has resisted Islamification, survived colonization and endures, for the most part, under the insidious thrust of tourism. The ornamental quality of today's architecture bears the laurels, and the scars, earned from all these challenges.

A. *Carved and painted column, east Bali palace style, at Walter Spies' old studio abode in Iseh, Sidemen, eastern Bali.*

B. *Ornate door in east Bali chinoiserie style.*

C. *Plates are often used as decorative accents on Majapahit-style bata bali brick shrines.*

D. *Architect Kerry Hill used giant indigo-dipping pots as spout ornamentation along one edge of Bali's largest swimming pool at the Amanusa hotel.*

E. *Mossy statuary is Bali's signature decoration.*

F. *The gold garuda effigy on the front of the raja of Gianyar's car in the 1940s.*

G. *Balinese architectural ornamentation runs from the basic, like these simple mountain air vents, to the baroque (photo H).*

H. *The gate stairs on the main stage at Denpasar's Art Centre.*

7.1 *Paras* Carving

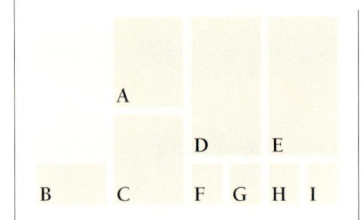

A. *Paras* carving on a payadnyan shrine at Pura Pulaki, northern Bali.

B. Florid *sendi* on a Sempidi village shrine.

C. *Aling-aling*, the demon-deflecting wall inside a temple gate near Mengwi.

D. Offering niche outside a house in Tenganan village has a carved *paras* surround which utilizes a popular *patra mesir*, or Egyptian pattern, wood carving motif. The swastika, seen in the background pattern, is the symbol of Hindu Bali and is also a propitious symbol for the Chinese and Vietnamese.

E. The carved *singa sendi* on the main shrine pavilion at the Pura Beji, Sangsit, are the finest in the land.

F. Simple *padma* lotus petal designs on a north coast shrine base.

G. Whimsical and rare: a winged lion, wielding a Balinese chopper carved onto a temple *sendi* in Bongkasa, Mengwi.

H. Classic design on a temple in the mountains.

I. *Garuda* birds and winged lion motifs are popular throughout Bali. This example, in pink *paras*, is on a northern coast temple.

Balinese architecture's crowning achievement in ornamentation is its rich *paras* carving tradition: nowhere else in the world are artisans still carving stone by the cubic tonne with such verve, originality and intricacy. Of course it is the softness of the *paras* stone which makes it possible. It is this same softness, however, which determines that works of art rarely survive beyond 100 years, unlike the andesite marvels of Candi Borobudur and Candi Prambanan, Balinese carving's direct ancestors.

In Bali, newness is next to holiness and the reconsecration, and often recarving, of a temple's shrine, gates and sometimes walls, every 30 years or so, is a time of great pride for a village. If the village can't afford to have gates and shrine bases remade and recarved, or if time does not allow for the final finishing before the reconsecration rites *(karya agung)*, *paras ukir* is laid in a sort of constructivist style—an abstract representation of the yet-to-be-carved motifs.

The most fabulously carved temples in Bali are to be found along the northern coast, where Balinese Rococo flourished, untempered by the stolid stateliness of the Majapahit styles of the south. Each region has its own unique carving style: some villages, such as Batubulan, Ketewel and Silakarang, are almost entirely given over to ornamental carving studios. Other villages, particularly the Bali Aga villages, have limited carved decorative detailing but this is generally highly original.

New influences in the 1990s—a period of resurgence for the Balinese building industry—resulted in many new trends in the ornamental use of *paras* and other stone cladding.

ORNAMENTATION → **PARAS CARVING 7.1**

171

172

ORNAMENTATION → **PARAS CARVING 7.1**

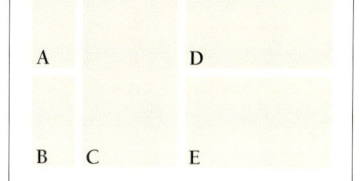

A		D
B	C	E

A. Village musicians, dancers and priestly activities are common carving subject matter on temple gates.

B. Mountain ornamentation is generally more inspired and unique: there are no real rules.

C. Regal pavilion ornamentation, Singaraja-style, on the corner of this palace loji building in Tabanan. The face is a Sai mythological creature. (see 7.9 Boma and Sai).

D. Winged lions (singa) atop garuda masks on the corners of an ornate kul-kul tower near Sibanggede.

E. Wayan Cemul, an Ubud-based sculptor, made this decorative paras wall, depicting a scene from the Balinese fairytales, called Tantri.

173

7.2 Brick and *Paras*

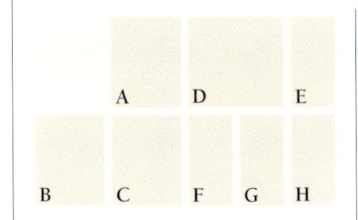

A	D	E	
B	C	F	G	H

A. *The main shrine of the Pura Dalem Pengerebongan in Denpasar is a classic example of brick architecture with* paras *ornamentation.*

B. *Many Balinese temples, particularly larger temples, have one door for the gods and priests, and another for the devotees. Both of these are expressed in brick and paras in this typical Denpasar area temple front.*

C. *A mix of the ornate and the simple on this shrine base at Puri Nyalian palace, Klungkung.*

D. *Striking rosette of carved brick on a shrine building, Puri Nyalian palace.*

E. *Temple gate near Puri Nyalian, Klungkung. The ornamental use of brick and paras in Klungkung seems more refined than in Denpasar and Gianyar. A sprinkling of artistically carved paras on a predominantly red brick gate is often more handsome than the reverse, which seems overly encrusted.*

F. *Simple brick and paras base on a shrine in Tenganan village.*

G. *Classic pair of early-20th-century Denpasar area Majapahit-style temple gates probably designed by the great Pedanda Sidemen of Sanur (1890–1980).*

H. *Detail of the main paduraksa gate at Pura Puseh, Guwang.*

The sublime combination of brick and *paras* ornamentation is Bali's own invention—it is Balinese sparkle meets Majapahit handsomeness. During the 19th century the *paras ukir* decorative elements were often applied sparingly, displaying an Assyrian-like romantic austerity. By the 20th century gates were fully florid with drapery of deeply carved botanically inspired, or anthropomorphic, Balinese motifs.

Paras is often sold in units that fit with *bata bali* brick sizes, making it easier to create protruding sections that may then be carved. This makes it perhaps too easy for young architects, struggling with ornamental issues, to over-use this decorative device.

Since the Balinisasi programme of architectural atrocity (1975-95), when all public buildings had to have 5% brick and *paras* ornamentation, truly inspired decoration has become harder to find: so much of the island's unique architecture—unusual temple gates in particular—has been re-done in the regulation "47B Gianyar: *Paras* and Brick Motif" style.

ORNAMENTATION → **BRICK AND PARAS 7.2**

175

7.3 Stone Air Vents

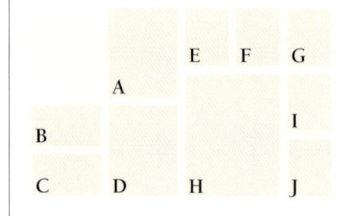

	E	F	G
A			
B			I
C	D	H	J

A. *Pre-Hindu style air vent, probably from the Batur region, in a small garden courtyard wall at the Villa Bebek.*

B. *Classic position of air vents in a gedong temple pavilion.*

C-H. *A variety of* batu galang—*all of traditional design.*

I. *An ancient* batu galang *decorative motif, from a 17th-century shrine building in Trunyan village.*

J. *This* batu galang *was designed by Ubud sculptor Wayan Cemul and painted by Stephen Little.*

Air vents are the eyes of Balinese architecture: they are most traditionally found flanking a *meten* pavilion's mouth-like door. Air vents can be ceramic (imported from Vietnam during the golden age of trade, 1800–1930) but are most commonly *paras ukir* or, recently, limestone. Often the *batu galang* is not "*galang*" (light-filled) at all but blunt and unperforated, fulfilling a purely decorative function that merely imitates its perforated confrères (see photo F). Once simply a ventilation element, the humble air vent has lately been elevated to star status as a decorative decal on Bali Style homes; it can be found across the tropical world applied, rather mindlessly, to building facades.

In Singaraja air vents became elaborate artworks decorating *meten* pavilion walls. Borrowing from both Indian and Chinese models, these north Bali air vents/windows are being reproduced to this day.

In 1983 Australian artist Stephen Little revived the art of painted *batu galang* (see photo J) which had been lost in the mists of time.

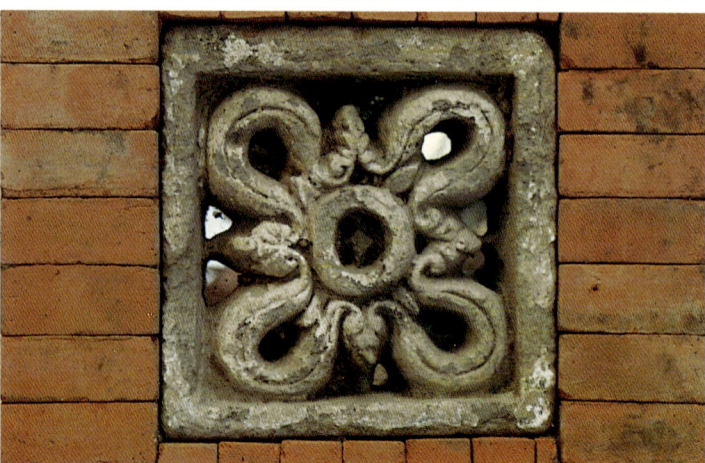

ORNAMENTATION → **STONE AIR VENTS 7.3**

177

7.4 Balustrades and Railings

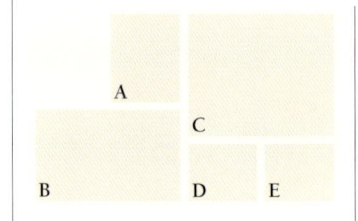

A. Painted bamboo temporary fence on the edge of a gamelan pavilion in a temple near Kintamani.

B. Limestone and paras balustrade trim on a batu pilah–faced terrace at the Amanusa. Batu pilah is a lower grade of paras ukir quarried in irregularly shaped lumps.

C. Traditional terrace balustrade constructed from paras ukir at the Villa Bebek, sitting beyond two bata bali screen walls.

D. A pleasant visual display of bamboo fences on pavilion bases at a temple complex near Nyalian, Klungkung.

E. The raja's reception hall at Taman Narmada water gardens in western Lombok (a Balinese colony since the 18th century). The building is a gem of Balinese chinoiserie, replete with wriggly blue railings in the Yunnanese style.

Balustrades are the broderie anglaise of Balinese architecture: the perforated trim which brings light and life to hard edges. Found both built-in, out of stone or brick, or temporary, as in the bamboo fences seen on temple buildings, the transparent trim helps soften building lines. Once a venue for great artistic expression of carving and colouring skills, the balustrade—where it now appears, on palace *loji* pavilions or hotel terraces—is often sanitized into architectonic abstraction.

The low garden wall in Balinese architecture is often perforated, allowing for a better passage of air and light and pretty patterns. Larger freestanding screen walls, such as *aling-aling* (see photo D, page 64), are often found, elaborately carved with all manner of ghouls and goblins, in *pura dalem* temples.

The long pavilions, *bale lantang*, in mountain villages often have ceremonial sections sealed off with fine timber railings (see photos D and F, page 107) to differentiate the profane from the sacred space.

ORNAMENTATION → **BALUSTRADES AND RAILINGS** 7.4

179

7.5 Woven Elements and Cloth

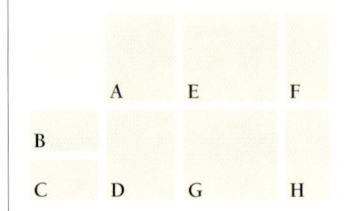

	A	E	F
B			
C	D	G	H

A. Woven sampiyan gantung decorations and lamak apron (with kasa undercloth) clothe a sanggah agung temporary shrine at a wedding ceremony in Sanur.

B. Welcome sign, made of kasa (holy white cloth), at the entrance to Banjar Sidakarya Kangin, in Sidakarya, a traditional village near Sanur.

C. An ancient turtle planter filled with dwarf water lilies, in the house temple of the Puri Nyalian, Klungkung. The poleng cloth wrapped around its base signifies that this is an empowered object.

D. Kasa temple sash around a guardian statue.

E. Detail from a lamak showing how the shaped banana leaf is applied to busung (young coconut fronds) using small "staples" made of slivers of bamboo, called semat.

F. A rich silk brocade underneath a palace-style Chinese-coin-and-mirror lamak on a temple shrine in Puri Nyalian, Klungkung.

G. Another lamak detail.

H. Dewi Sri, the rice goddess.

At ceremonial times, buildings as well as people are dressed up for the occasion. Colourful sashes are wrapped around columns and *ider-ider* bunting is hung from pavilion eaves. Woven coconut palm leaf, called *busung*, is shaped into drop earring-like "confectionery" called *sampiyan* and hung from pavilion or altar corners. Long "aprons" of woven palm and banana leaf, called *lamak*, are regular offering elements on the island's shrines. Then come the umbrellas, the coloured sashes on shrines and statues and the tall woven banners, called *penjor*, outside the main gate.

During the Galungan-Kuningan All Saints Season, all of Bali is a riot of decorativeness: woven *penjor* and tall cloth banners, called *umbul-umbul*, hang in front of house gates and temple gates respectively. Major corporations now sponsor the *umbul-umbul* on the roads to major festivals.

The colour of a banner, umbrella or shrine sash denotes the deity being honoured. Red is for Brahma, yellow or white is for Shiva and black is for Wisnu. The ubiquitous black-and-white chequered cloth, called *poleng*, is the standard of the spirit world.

ORNAMENTATION → **WOVEN ELEMENTS AND CLOTH** 7.5

181

7.6 Carved Wood

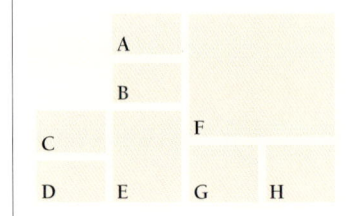

	A		
	B		
C		F	
D	E	G	H

A. *Detail of a timber door entablature, called* petitis, *on the main gate of the Jero Kubutambahan near Singaraja.*

B. *Timber air vent carved and painted in the Madurese-style on the courtyard wall of the Warung Mie at the Four Seasons Resort, Jimbaran.*

C. *An exquisite carved meten door in the Singaraja style (late 19th century).*

D. *Lacy carved* petitis *(patra cina-style) on a puri-style door painted in a classic Balinese colour scheme.*

E. *Copy of a northern Bali palace door at the Canggu Puri Mertha hotel.*

F. *Winged lion depicted on a 19th-century carved timber air vent window (puri style) in the Denpasar Museum Collection.*

G. *Twin doors from a timber window, fully carved in the* patra cina *style.*

H. *Unusual carved timber balustrade on a shrine building at Pura Pulaki, northern Bali.*

The Balinese are the most prodigious wood carvers in the history of mankind: whole forests have disappeared so that the world can have goldfish mobiles and other souvenirs. Carpenters and carvers have been busy on the architectural front too: there are carved doors on gates, richly carved shrine doors, *meten* pavilion doors and carved decorative columns and ridge plates on the *bale bali* or *bale payadnyan* ceremonial pavilions in almost every Balinese house. In certain temples, the pavilions are carved from top to toe: timber columns, *ulon* headboards, *pementang* tie beams and *tugeh* king posts are all richly carved and painted.

There are many carving styles: it is the ability of the Balinese artisans to break out of these standard patterns, called *patra*, however, that is their strength. This has led to many unique, dynamic carving traditions.

The tourism boom has spawned thousands of new directions for carved wood elements, both architectural and ornamental, often in styles borrowed from the decorative traditions of other Indonesian islands.

ORNAMENTATION → **CARVED WOOD** 7.6

183

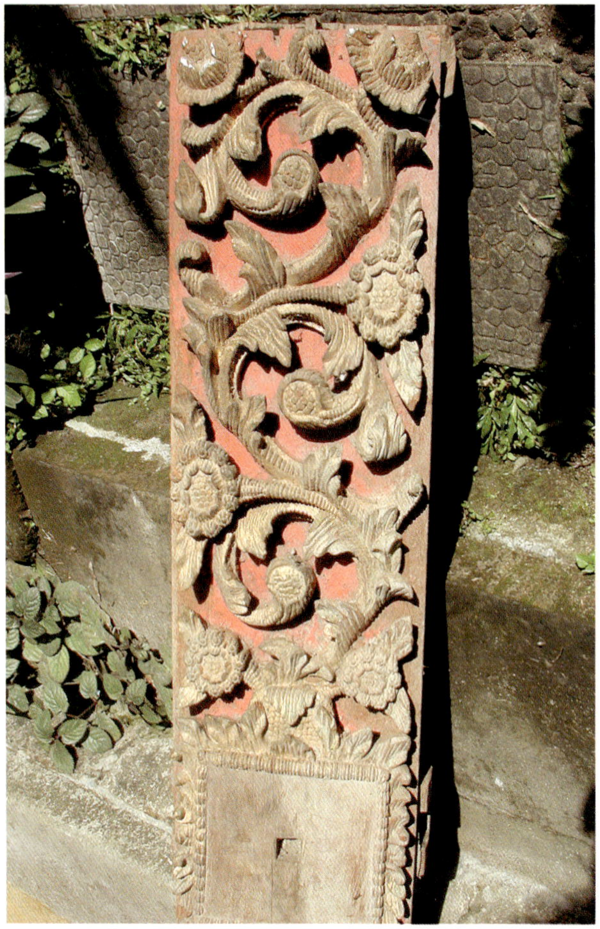

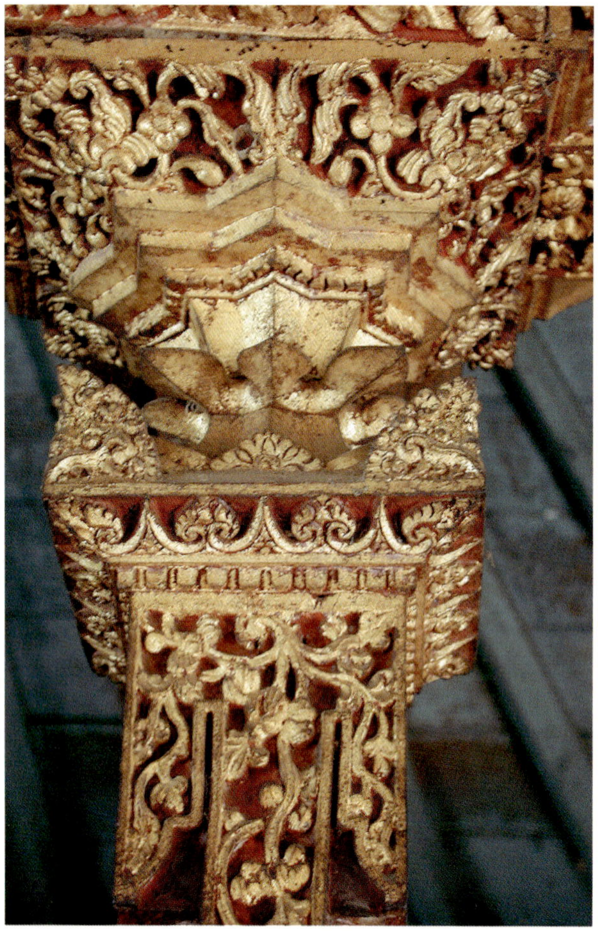

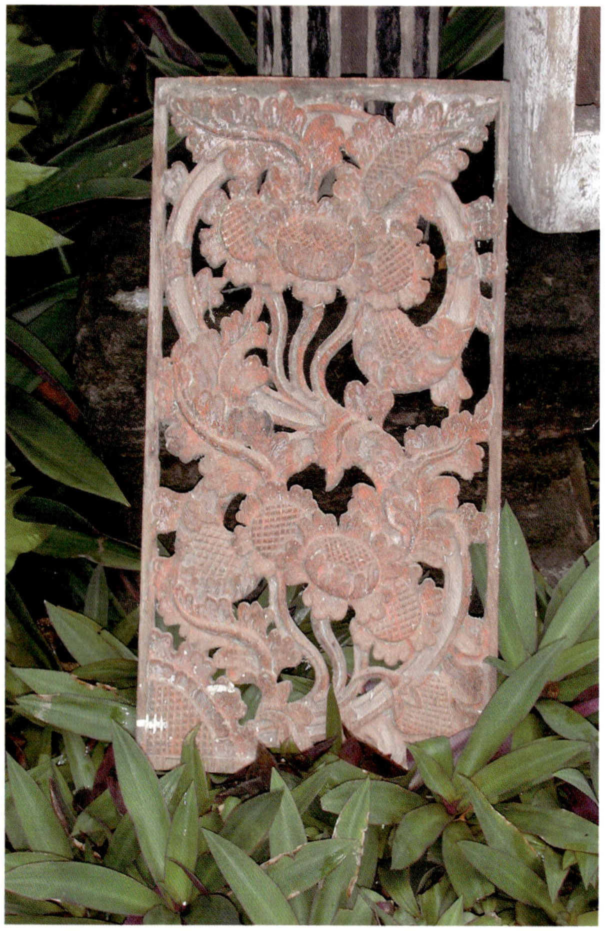

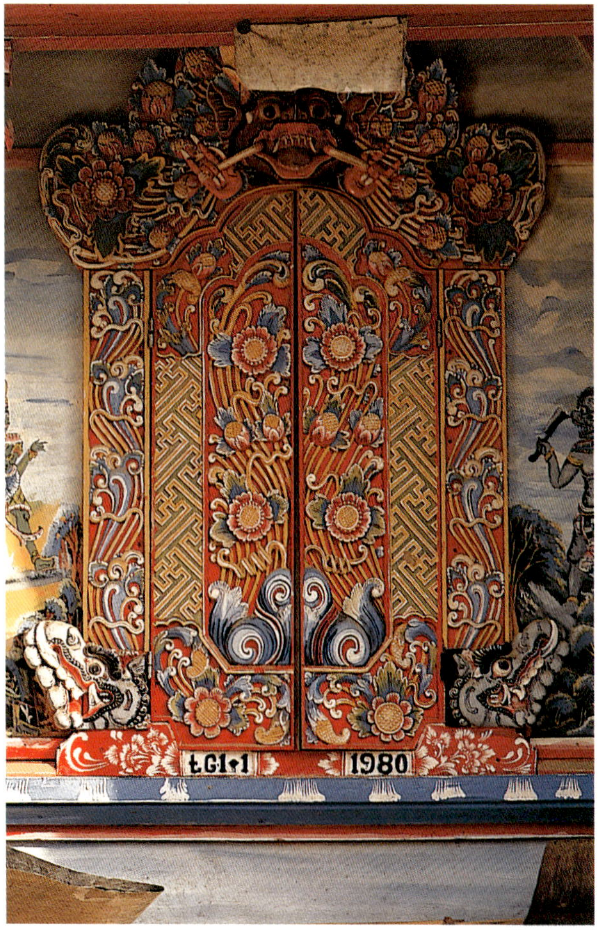
tG1.1
1980

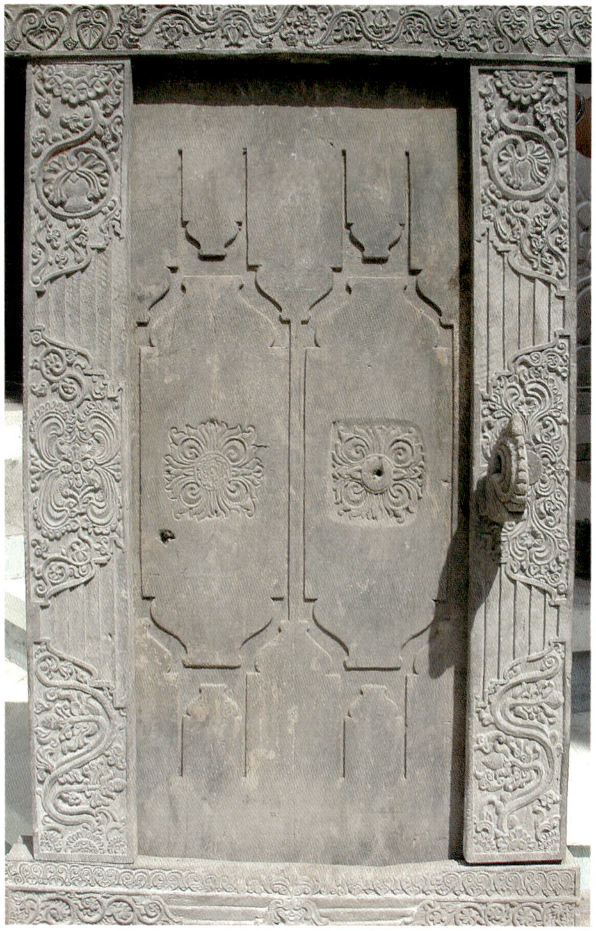

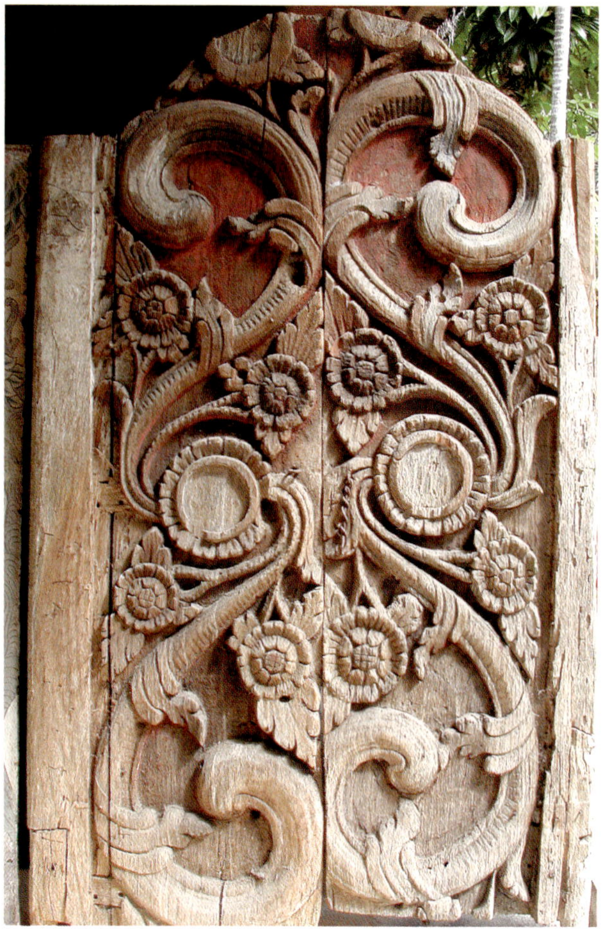

ORNAMENTATION → **CARVED WOOD 7.6**

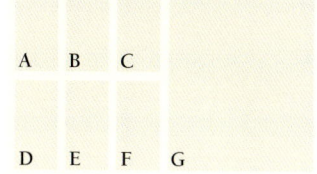

A	B	C	
D	E	F	G

A. Classic carved *dedeleg* roof plate. The carving is deep and beautifully composed: the gold *prada* and red *kinju* colouring suggests it came from a palace or ceremonial pavilion.

B. The king post, which generally rises from the back of a *singa* or a *garuda* statue, is itself a marvel of wood-carving technique. The pinched waist portion is called a *kincut*.

C. A carved timber panel from the side of a large northern Bali door.

D. Sebatu village near Tegalalang is famous for its technicolour carved shrines.

E. Classic single-leafed Majapahit-style door.

F. This surviving door fragment demonstrates that the looser, less intricate, Balinese carvings of old were often more beautiful.

G. Carved Majapahit-style 19th-century palace door, from the old Puri Denpasar palace, features a heraldic winged lion as its central motif. (Denpasar Museum Collection). The brother of this door is in the famous Volkenkunde Museum in Leiden, The Netherlands.

Following pages: A jero palace kori agung near Mengwi. From the 1960s, it was realized in brick and scored plaster with concrete ornamental coursework. Even the air vent rosettes are pre-fab concrete panels. The base of the gate is covered in terrazzo.

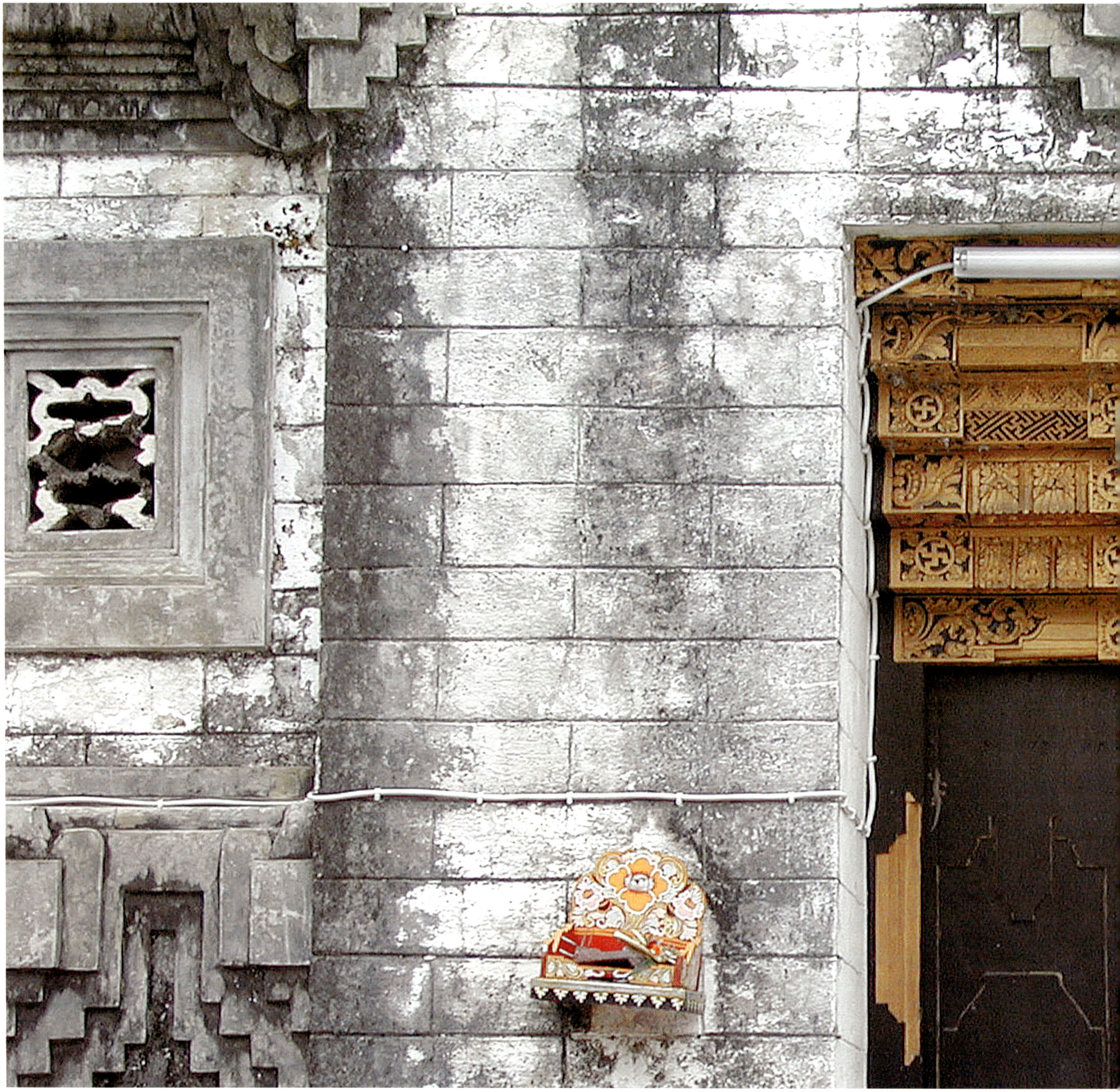

ORNAMENTATION

7.7 Colour

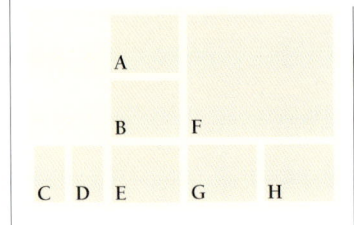

A				
B		F		
C	D	E	G	H

A. *Southern Chinese colour scheme on a temple shrine in Kedisan village on Lake Batur.*

B. *This northern Bali home has employed a wild Fauvist palette.*

C. *Unusual colouring and ornamentation on this house gate in Manggis village, eastern Bali.*

D. *Northern coast bungalow door in typical north coast colours.*

E. *This unusual gedong shrine in a mountain temple has sky blue decorative accents in the form of matching Balinese windows and doors.*

F. *The main gedong shrine of the very colourful and very Majapahit Pura Dalem Kepala, Kepawan.*

G. *Sai lion head carved and painted in an unusual yellow, black and white colour scheme over a shrine door in a temple near Mengwi.*

H. *Painted bedeg (woven bamboo) ceiling in a Chinese-style pavilion of the Puri Kanginan palace, Amlapura.*

Hindu cultures are always colourful: even the universe is explained in terms of colour, with the gods more colourful then the rest. In Bali, primary colours are generally associated with gods and demons—their statuary and their buildings—and the god-kings. Each palace has its house colours, too. Indian, Chinese and European colour schemes have all been adopted by Balinese architecture over the centuries, but they are always reinterpreted with Balinese flair. The use of paired colours in Javanese architectural decoration—the very Javanese green and yellow, or blue and white, for example—can be found in Bali, on gate doors in particular, as maroon and aqua, or black and gold. Chinese temple colours have been adopted too, often with two-tone purples or polychrome colour mixes replacing the classic Chinese *kinju* red and gold.

The natural colours of Balinese building materials—rich terracotta-coloured bricks, *paras* streaked with sulphur seams, the soft flannel grey of *paras ukir*, the straw colours of thatch—are colourful enough, set against the bright tropical greens of the landscape and the clear blue of the sky, without too much embellishment.

As mentioned previously, there is often an extra ornamental "edge" to ceremonial buildings. Black, red and white are the ancient colours for ornamentation on ceremonial or sacred structures and traces of this ancient ornamentation can still be found on temple buildings across the island.

ORNAMENTATION → **COLOUR 7.7**

7.8 Statuary

A		G	H	I		
B						
C	D	E	F	J	K	L

A. *Nineteenth-century gate guardians from the northern coast now guard this Sanur house fountain.*

B. *Primitive fertility figures carved from sandalwood, probably from a Bali Aga temple ornament.*

C. *Typical* singa *statue found supporting the king post in a bale bali pavilion.*

D. *Unusual* singa sendi *from a northern Bali temple.*

E. *Detail of a statue from a palace in northern Bali (relative of statue A).*

F. *Unusual anthropomorphic statue, possibly a monkey-man, by famed sculptor I Gusti Nyoman Lempad.*

G. *Wooden kul-kul drums from Bali Aga mountain villages.*

H. *Elephant railing on temple steps in Gianyar Regency.*

I. *Nineteenth-century* garuda *in a* pelinggih *shrine in the grounds of the Tanjung Sari hotel in Sanur. The shrine base has* garuda mungkur *ornamentation, a motif modelled on the* garuda's *crown.*

J. *Temple guardian statues are usually fully dressed for duty, complete with daily flower behind the ear.*

K. *Majapahit deer statues are found in the Majapahit shrines in many house temples on the island, commemorating the family's arrival from Hindu Java over 400 years ago.*

L. Pedanda *priest statues, male and female, guard this brick and* paras *shrine.*

Statues have various roles in Balinese architecture. The votive statues that sit in state in *piasan* pavilions and in *pelinggih* shrines in the island's temples have starring roles: they are the most important objects on the island. The winged lion statues that hold up king posts in *bale bali* pavilions, for example, have supporting roles. Many statues in house gardens and hotels are purely ornamental.

Shrine and temple gates are often flanked by guardian statues, called *sindu-wisindu*, as are the house gates to the palaces of the nobility. Statues also appear as bollards, or *sendi*, on important shrines and, occasionally, in Bali Style houses (see 5.4 Post Bases). Architect Geoffrey Bawa's famous museum building for Donald Friend had whimsical animal *sendi*, carved by Made Jojol and realized by local architect Ir. Robi Sularto.

Bali is really one big sculpture garden with tens of thousands of professional sculptors. Statues also appear protruding from bas-relief designs, as pilasters on larger temple walls and as spouts in water gardens such as Tirtagangga and the Puri Kanginan palace in Amlapura. Since the 1980s large more anatomically correct concrete statues of a distinctly municipal bent have been slowly replacing the stylized marvels once found at major intersections and at town centres.

Modern sculptors such as Wayan Cemul from Ubud, Nyoman Nuarta, Pintor Sirait from Bandung and Greek-born Phillipos of Sayan have recently enriched the Balinese sculpture scene which had been going through a period of Ramayanafication.

In 1995 the central government decided that Bali should have the tallest statue in the world—a statue of Lord Wisnu on his beast of burden, Garuda—and Nyoman Nuarta was commissioned to create the colossus.

ORNAMENTATION → **STATUARY 7.8**

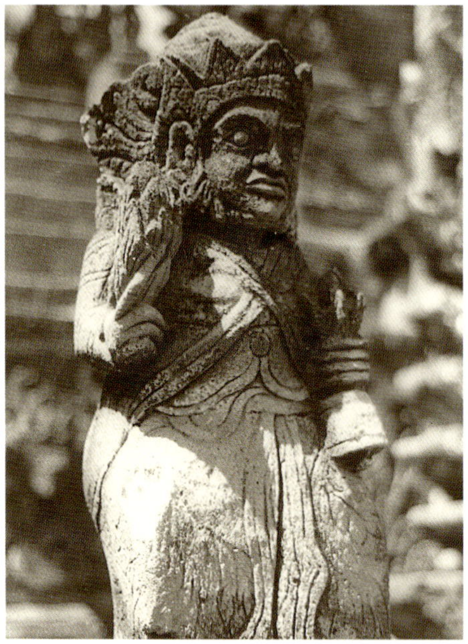
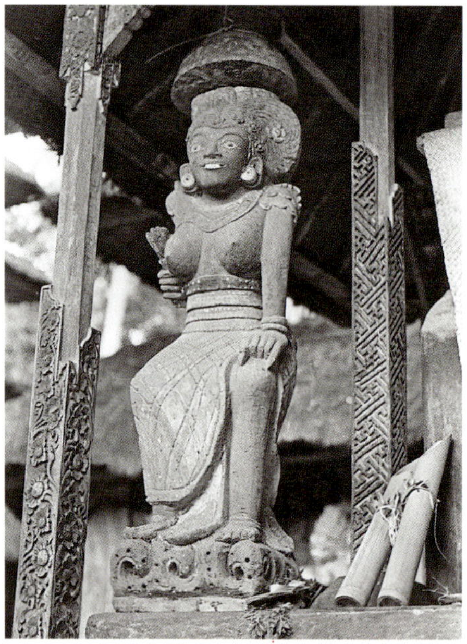
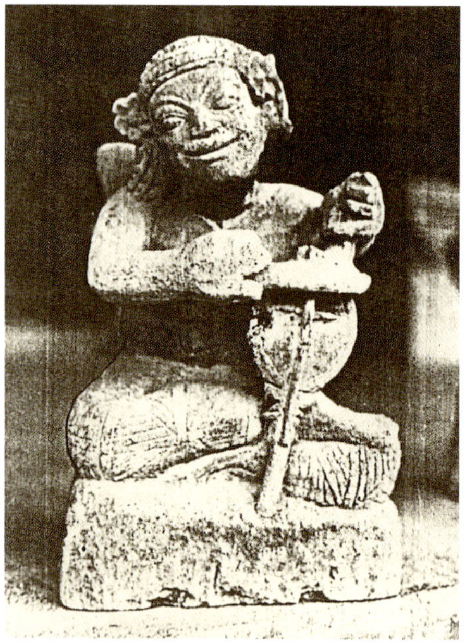
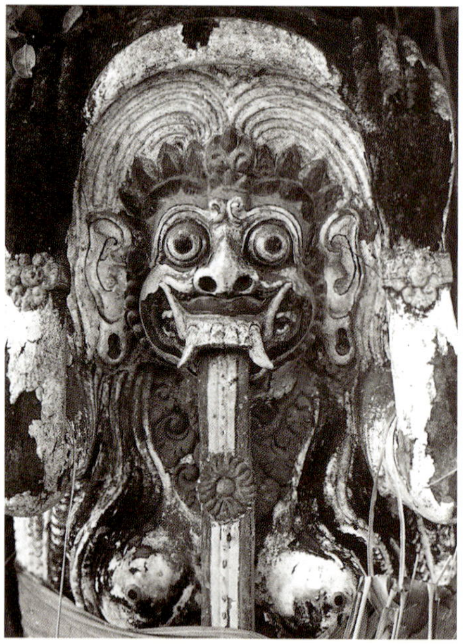
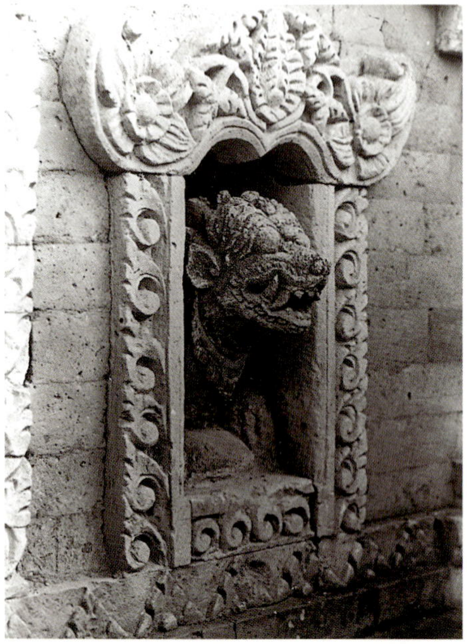
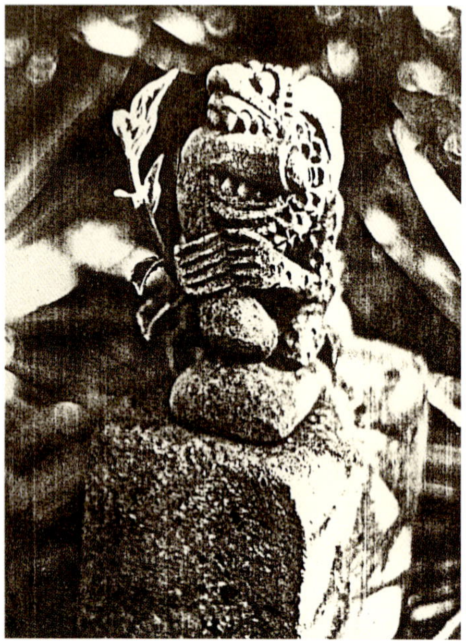
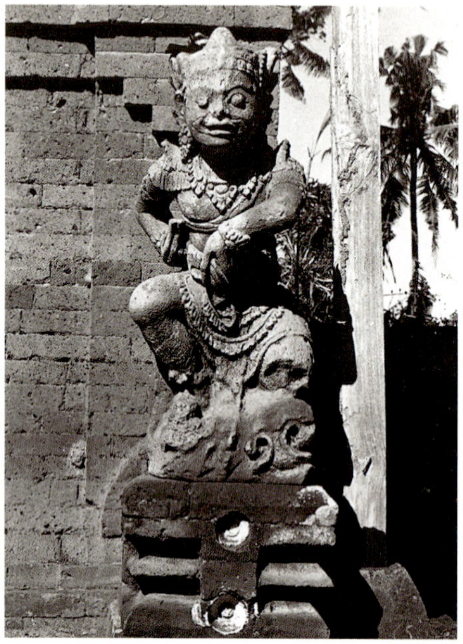
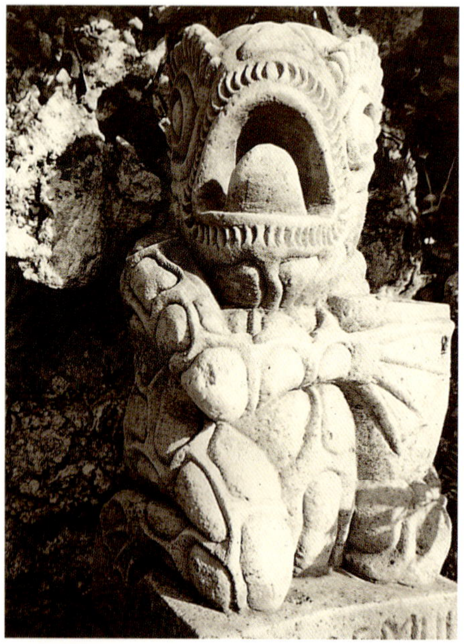
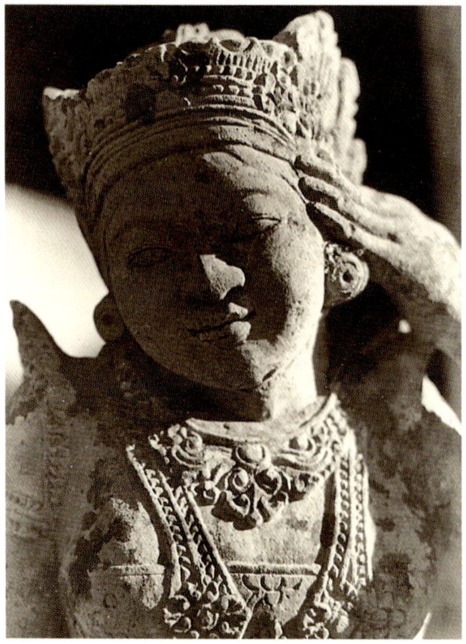
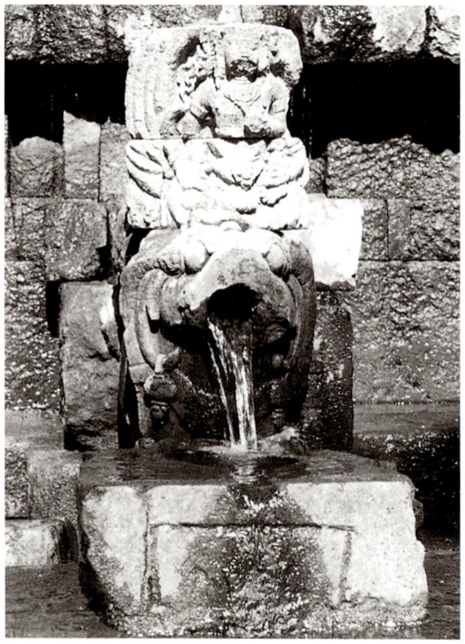
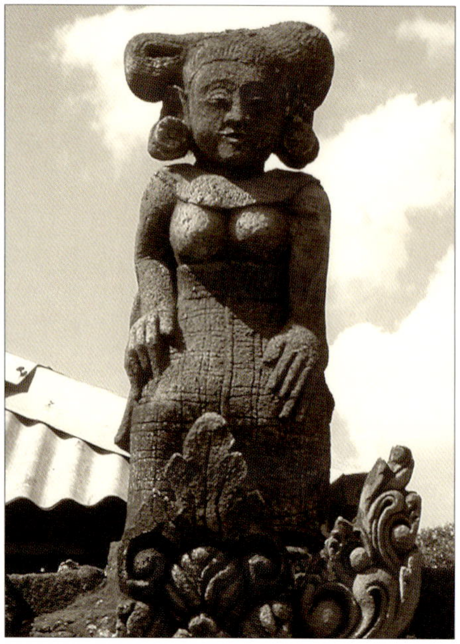
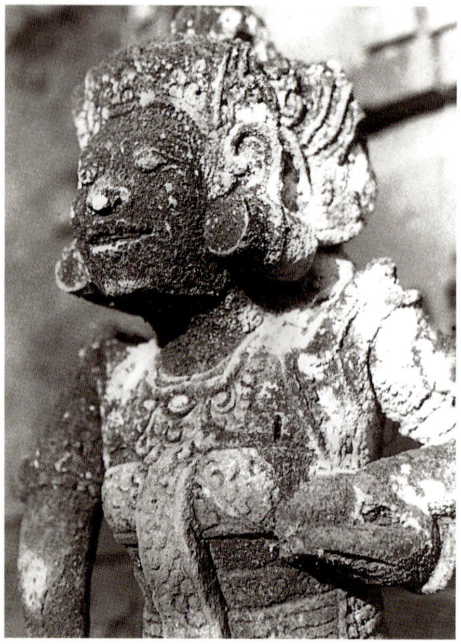

ORNAMENTATION → **STATUARY** 7.8

A	B	C	D		
				M	N
E	F	G	H		
				O	P
I	J	K	L	Q	R

A. The statue of the priest Dhang Hyang Nirartha at Pura Luhur, Uluwatu, depicted in this 1979 photo, has since been replaced.

B. A heavenly nymph carries the tirta holy water container on her head in this mountain temple.

C. Rebab-playing musician in the Denpasar Museum collection.

D. Effigies of Rangda, the demon witch, can be found in pura prajapati and pura dalem temples across the island.

E. Singa in a shrine niche.

F. Erotica by sculptor Cemul of Ubud.

G. Classic Denpasar Majapahit-style guardian statue.

H. Frog sendi by Cemul.

I. Saraswati by Lempad.

J. Unusual garuda-Wisnu spout.

K. Rare 19th-century stone statue of Saraswati, goddess of the arts, on a pilaster on the courtyard wall of Pura Beji, Sangsit temple.

L. Saraswati statue in Ubud.

M. Wisnu, the god of prosperity, and his divine consort, Dewi Sri, the rice goddess, carved out of paras ukir and painted white with eggshell paint. The statues are in the classic Klungkung style.

N. Majapahit-style guardian statues flank a shrine in the dalem court of the Pura Dalem Kepala, Kepawon, south Denpasar.

O. A rare brick Majapahit deer statue on the raised base of a shrine near Kuta. Many families descended from the Majapahit-era exodus from Hindu Java (13-16th centuries) have a deer effigy, the symbol of the Majapahit empire, on one shrine in their family or clan temple.

P. Mossy statues are everywhere in the dewy vales of Ubud. This photo was taken in sculptor Wayan Cemul's house.

Q. A grandstand of whimsical statues in an Ubud area shop.

R. Replica of the crouching tiger that guards the beji spring below the Amandari Hotel.

7.9 Boma and Sai

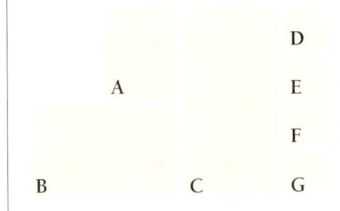

		D
A		E
		F
B	C	G

A. Boma-like kala head as a protector—note the curly beard and mane—on an 18th-century gateway at the Taman Sari Royal Baths, Hamengku Buwono Palace, Yogyakarta, central Java.

B. A classic Boma made from cotton threads on a balsa base decorate a cremation bier.

C. A classic Boma entablature, with tiers of Sai effigies above, on a temple gate at the Pura Dalem, Guwang, Ketewel.

D. Carved festoons meet in the jaws of the Kurthi Mukha "Face of Glory" on this south Indian temple door. The Kurthi Mukha is a terrifying creature born from the anger of Shiva that devoured itself up to its face. The Kurthi Mukha is the mask of time that destroys everything but is also believed by some to be associated with Rahu, the demon of the eclipse.

E. Simha Mukha (lion face) in India, a decorative motif popular in the Vijayanagara period.

F. The fanged face of glory (Kurthi Mukha) on the pinnacle of a famous gapuram gate (gapura in Javanese) at the Padmanabhaswamy temple in Trivandrum, Kerala, India.

G. Detail of a shrine pavilion showing a Boma carved in paras above the door.

The popular Hindu god Boma (the protector), son of Durga and Shiva (the destroyer), guards all important portals in Bali. Descended from the *kala* heads that guard the portals on many ancient Hindu Javanese *candi* temples, the Balinese Boma is often depicted with a full set of upper jaw teeth, long fingers and spooky fingernails and a frightening, yet curiously benevolent expression. A one-eyed Boma face is called a Karang Boma. Bomas are found carved into brick, shaped out of *paras* and, in some cases, just painted onto walls over doors.

The Sai, also found carved on temple gates and shrine bases, are often lion-like befanged faces. They are descended from the south Indian Kurthi Mukha—variously known as the face of fame, glory or time—seen in ancient Indian architecture and statuary. The name Sai probably comes from northern coastal Javanese villages, as a Chinese puppet effigy there is called Barong Sai. Many anthropologists believe that the Boma and Sai are Tibetan Tantric in origin.

ORNAMENTATION → **BOMA AND SAI** 7.9

195

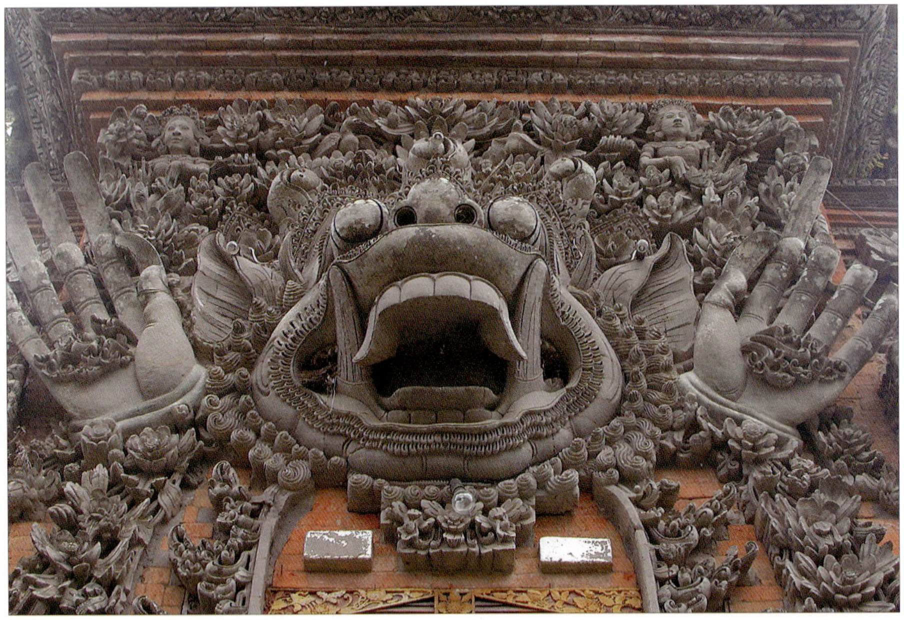
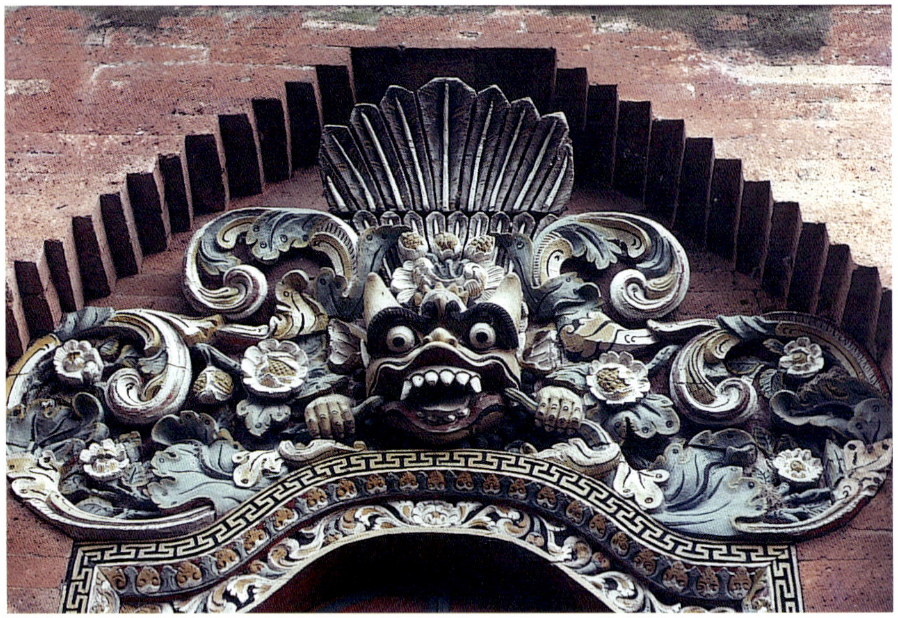

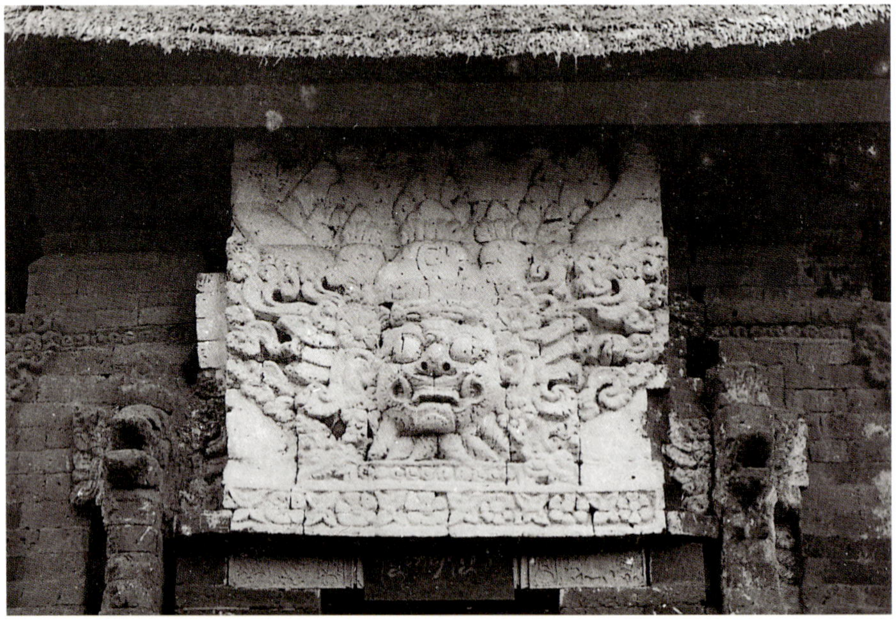
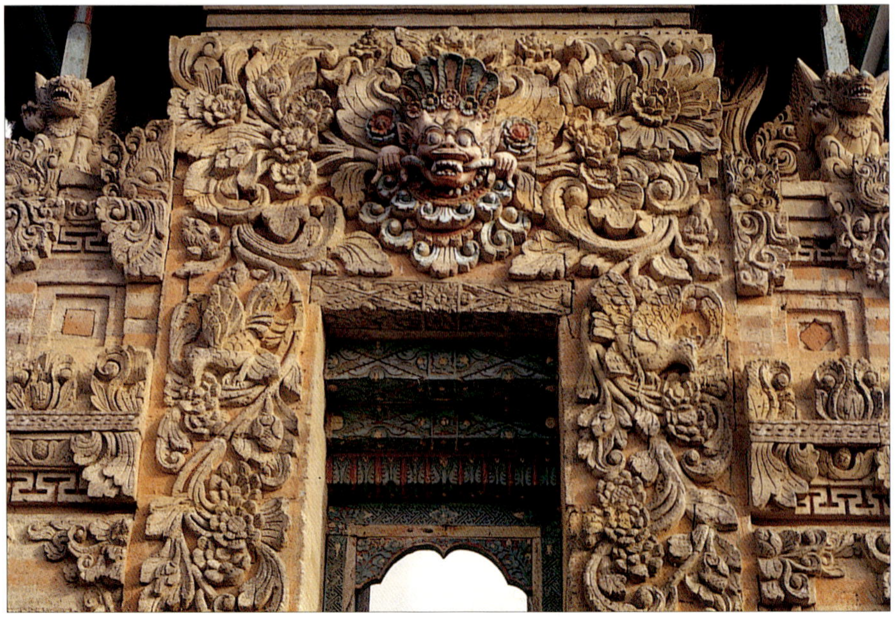

ORNAMENTATION → **BOMA AND SAI 7.9**

A	B	
		F
	D	
C	E	G

A. Giant Boma carved in paras ukir on a temple gate.

B. Sai over a house gate in Klungkung.

C. Boma effigy carved in paras on a palace pavilion base, Mengwi.

D. Majapahit Sai, flanked by brick naga dragons, on this tall gedong shrine outside Kuta.

E. Carved and coloured Sai on a mountain temple gate.

F. Weirdly anthropomorphic garuda on a temple base presents like a Boma protector.

G. Sai on the base of the bale bali in Puri Gede Karangasem palace, arguably the grandest extant traditional palace pavilion in Bali.

Following pages: The entrance gate to John and Cynthia Hardy's compound in Sayan. The door is from Java but the adobe gate and simple attendant shrine are pure old Sayan style.

197

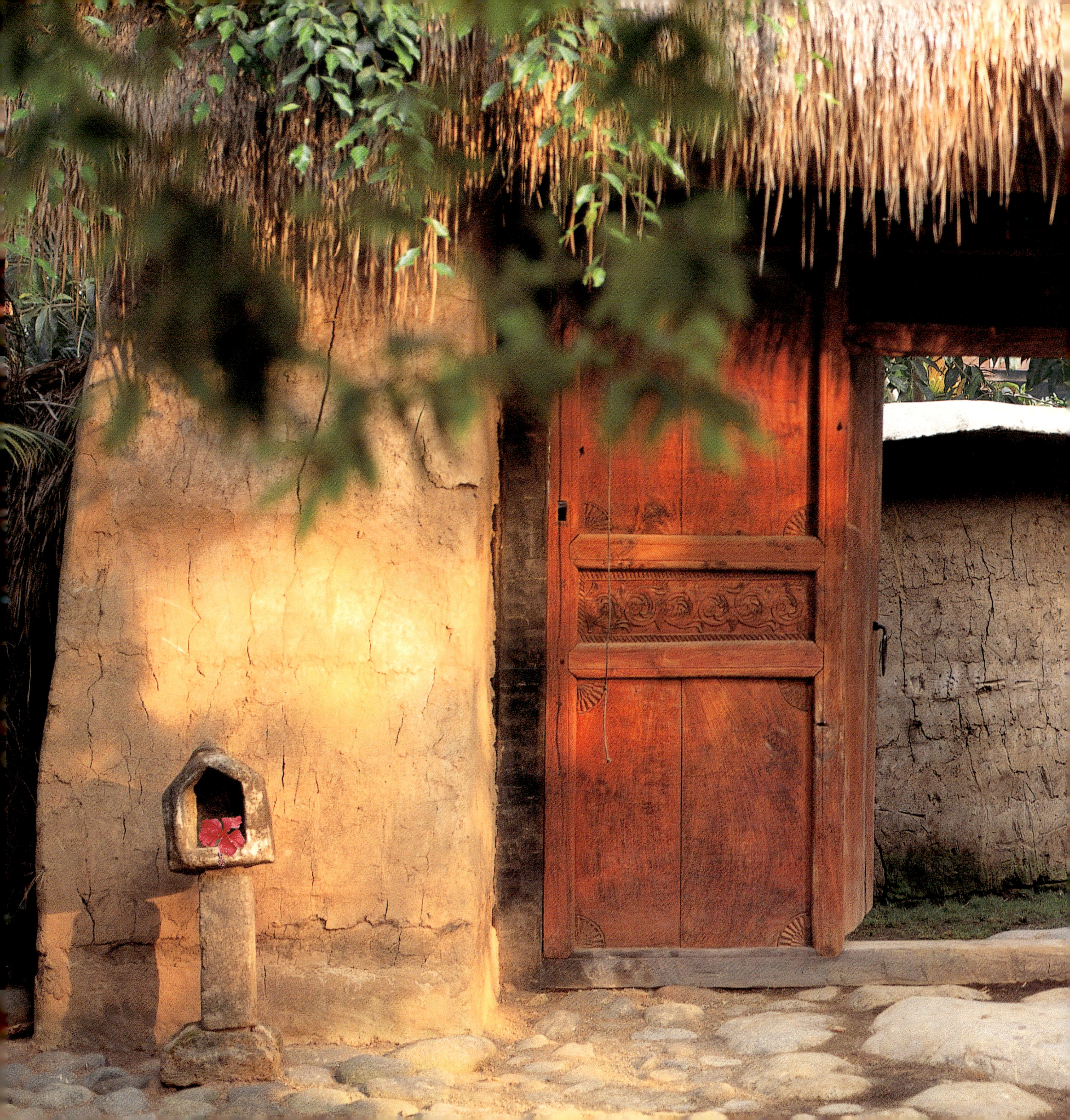

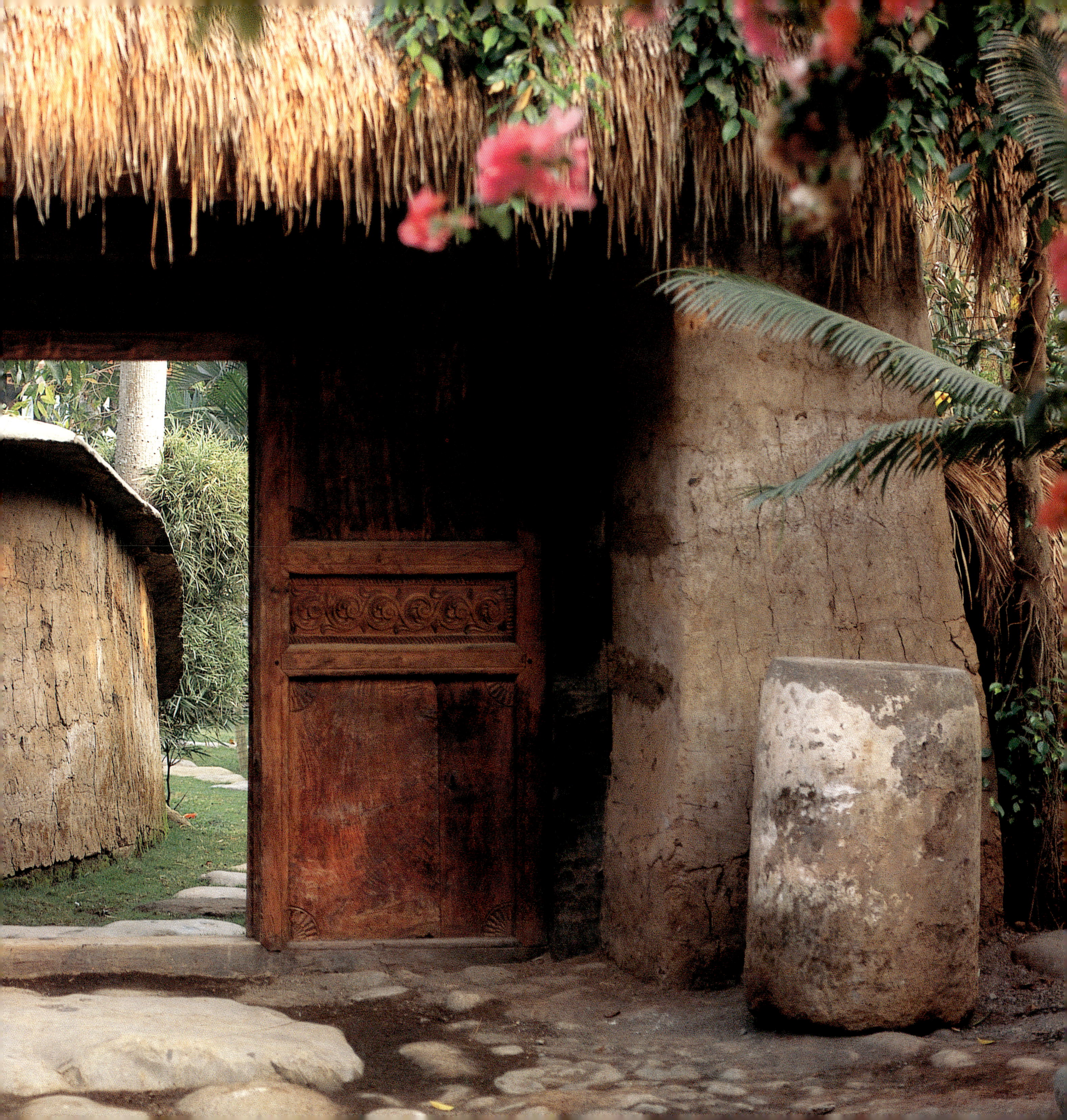

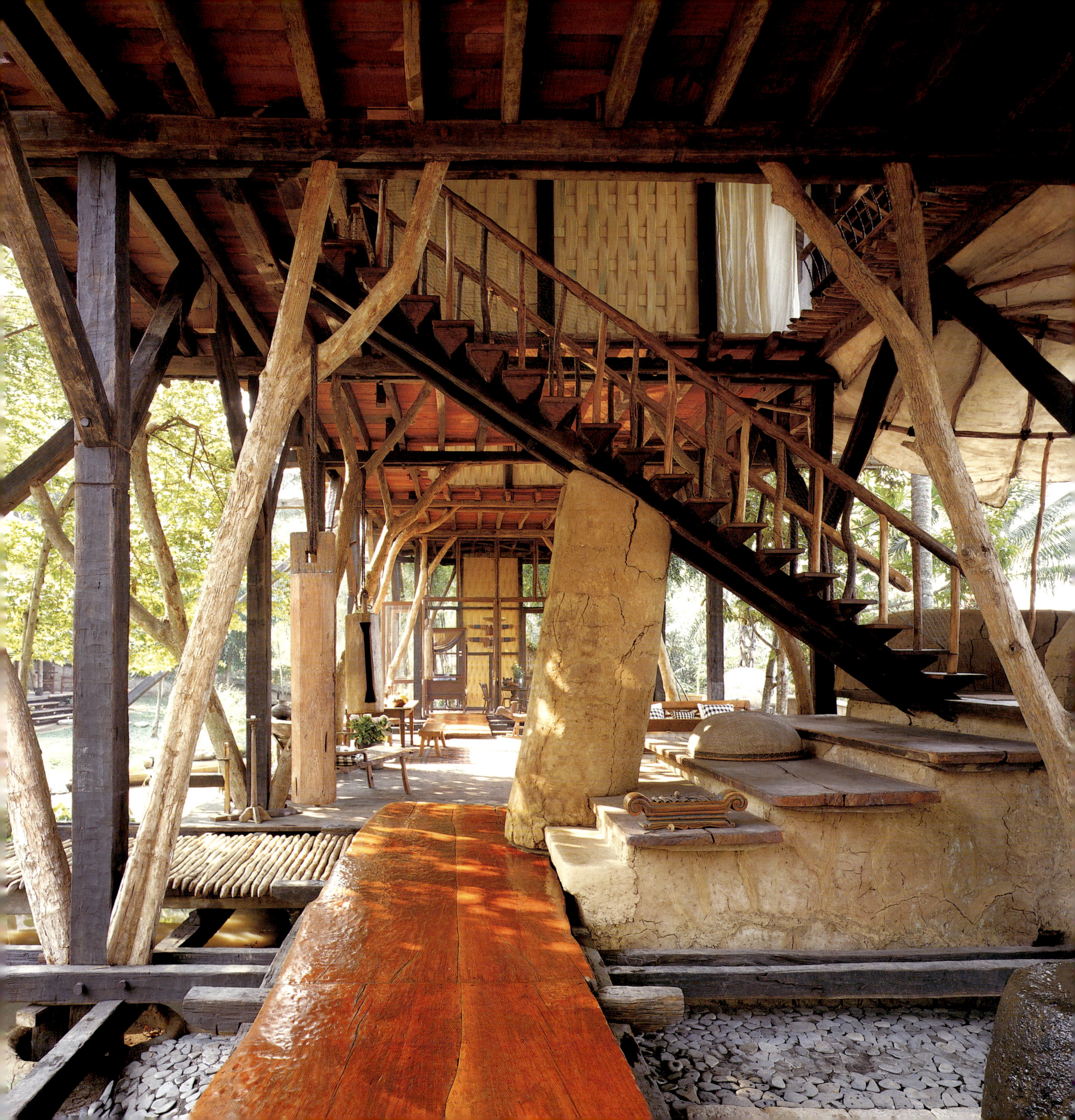

CHAPTER 8

Architectural Hybrids

8.1	Early Modern Hybrids	202
8.2	Chinese Influence	206
8.3	Javanese Influence	208
8.4	Late Modern Hybrids	210

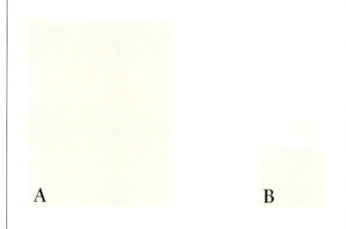

A. Many practitioners—local, national and foreign—have taken indigenous architectural styles and given them a twist to produce interesting hybrid forms. Architect Cheong Yew Kuan's main house for the John Hardys, in Sayan, featured some inspired architectural detailing. Rustic and traditional Balinese architectural elements were combined.

B. The island's first tourist hotel, the Bali Hotel was built in Dutch colonial Deco style in Denpasar (1928). Masonry walls, tiled roofs and glass windows were alien to south Bali before this building.

Bali is addicted to change. Ever since Walter Spies invented the modified *wantilan* in an attempt to get his baby grand between the columns, the island's architecture has been in a race car to architectural hell. The world's most gorgeous tropical architectural culture has over the past 50 years—since independence and the push for modernity—been stormed by the latest trends from overseas.

Early-20th-century hybrids include the Art Deco *kantor*-style bungalows (still visible on the north coast and in the mountains) and the Soekarno-sponsored Nippo-Balinese Ranch House movement evident in Bali in the presidential palace in Tampaksiring and the many *puri anyar* (new palace) wings in Gianyar built during the 1960s.

The 1970s saw a demand for ethnic flavour in government buildings. Following the example of Dutch architects in various world fairs and colonial expositions (see photo F, page 203), local architects created pavilion-style concrete buildings with a pseudo-Balinese decorative veneer. This trend continues in some areas to the present day.

The start of late modern hybrids can be attributed to Australian architect Peter Muller's seminal, pivotal Kayu Aya hotel (1971), now the Bali Oberoi. Muller adapted Balinese traditional architecture without abusing it: his work signalled a return to basics and inspired a generation of Bali lovers.

Sri Lankan architect Geoffrey Bawa's work for Wija Waworuntu and Donald Friend at Batujimbar Estates also produced some elegant traditional-modern hybrids, as did Kerry Hill's work on the public areas for the Palmer and Turner-designed Bali Hyatt (1972). Warwick and Lisa Purser's Rustic Charmer mini-palace in Campuhan, Ubud (1973) and Waworuntu's Tanjung Sari hotel (1968) in Sanur both had enormous influence on the fashion stakes too.

By the early 1990s, architectural arrogance had arrived with a vengeance as nouveau riche taste swamped the island's emerging middle class and tacky developments displaced noble ventures. The Balinese, with little concept of pollution—whether environmental, cultural, aural or physical—did little or nothing to save their beaches and streetscapes.

The Soeharto era's determination to develop at all costs, coupled with its appalling taste, plunged Bali into an architectural Dark Age from which it may never emerge.

8.1 Early Modern Hybrids

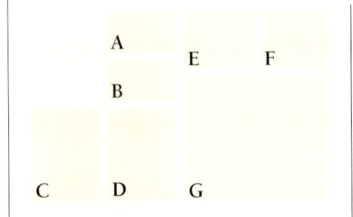

In the 1930s a dedicated group of confirmed bachelor aesthetes moved into Ubud and set up studio-homes. As was the fashion amongst European artists living in exotic locations, they utilized local architecture, modifying it to meet their recreational and work needs. The Balinese Rustic Charm movement was born at this time with the studio-homes of Walter Spies (now the Hotel Campuhan, and unrecognizable after a recent renovation) and Rudolf Bonnet (this early *puri kantor*-style bungalow still stands, north of Ubud's Puri Saren palace).

Belgian aristocrat Adrien Jean Le Mayeur de Merprès built a home on Sanur beach in the 1950s. Still standing north of the Grand Bali Beach hotel, it was an early modern hybrid in the Dream Home category. Coastal Dream Homes, inspired by this original, continued with collector Jimmy Pandhi's 1960s Sanur pleasure garden (now the Baruna Beach Hotel) and Judith and Wija Waworuntu's Tanjung Sari hotel.

These early hybrids were on a human scale, cottage-like and, generally, more Balinese courtyard garden than colonial-era house.

A. The northern Bali mountain retreat of Munduk was a Dutch hill station during the years 1910-45, when the Dutch had a permanent administrative capital in Singaraja. Some miniature mansions built in a Balinese-Dutch bungalow style still survive.

B. Belgian painter Adrien Jean Le Mayeur de Merprès shared his dream home, built in Sanur in the 1950s, with his model-wife-muse, Ni Pollok. The main salon of this legendary beachside compound of simple bamboo cottages and idyllic Balinese gardens was rich in Balinese palace-style decorations.

C. French Empire-style gates were popular in Bali at the turn of the century: Napoleon's eagle approximated the Balinese garuda. These early hybrids mixed third empire with third world.

D. The old Art Deco-style Balinese gate to the main market in Gianyar was pulled down in 1996 when the market was renovated.

E. Guestroom verandah at the Bali Hotel (1928), photograph circa 1984. The Batavia (Jakarta) colonial style would influence the island's architecture for the next 50 years.

F. Holland's pavilion at the 1931 Colonial Exposition in Paris featured hybrid Balinese-Batak (northern Sumatra) buildings.

G. Taman Ujung water palace was built in 1921 by the last raja of Karangasem. The central pavilion was an exotic hybrid of Dutch, Chinese, Balinese and Moorish elements. The last raja's uncle was a great patron of the arts, and patron of water follies on a grand scale, in west Lombok in particular. This photograph is pre-1963, when the eruption of Mt Agung, and the earthquakes of 1976, destroyed most of the buildings.

ARCHITECTURAL HYBRIDS → **EARLY MODERN HYBRIDS** 8.1

204

ARCHITECTURAL HYBRIDS → **EARLY MODERN HYBRIDS** 8.1

A		E
	B	
C	D	F

By the 1970s the Rustic Charm movement had dissolved. The flippancy of tourism and the hippie movement took over from the isolated romantic dedication of Bali's early expatriate pioneers. Gone were the gnome homes of the demi-indigenous, replaced by designer attempts at Ethnic Chic.

A. *A painting by Australian artist Donald Friend of Christopher Carlisle's Balinese house in the early 1970s. Friend's own house and garden in Batujimbar was once a temple to Rustic Charm. It has since been gentrified beyond recognition.*

B. *This powder room in a Bali Style garden in Singapore is modelled on Majapahit-era secular pavilions dotted around the famed Putri Champa Mausoleum in Trowulan, east Java.*

C. *The kori gate of the mock-up villa for the Four Seasons Resort, Sentul, west Java. The project was a late-blooming Rustic Charmer in the six-star hotel category. It was also an attempt at a Sundanese-Balinese-modern style (Designer: P.T. Wijaya Tribwana International).*

D. *The Jero Kubu where I wrote my first book on Balinese architecture in 1985. The garden was quintessentially Balinese in its blended overuse of ornamental elements. During the 1980s it was considered a landmark of Ethnic Chic.*

E. *Hill-tribe megastars John and Cynthia Hardy broke new Rustic-Chic ground in 1994 when they commissioned Malaysian architect Cheong Yew Kuan to build a family compound in Sayan.*

F. *Designer Putu Suarsa's influential bamboo Rustic Charmer in the Big Bamboo complex in Sidakarya, near Sanur.*

8.2 Chinese Influence

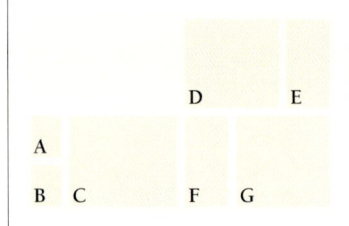

A. Bust of the leader of the Chinese artisans who were sent from Canton to Karangasem in the 1930s. A Chinese architect, Tan Hu Cin Jin, tax collector for the Raja of Mengwi in the 17th century, was the designer of the famous Taman Ayun temple.

B. Many of the island's shrines are distinctly Chinese in appearance.

C. The Chinese pavilion in the ceremonial court of the Puri Kanginan, Amlapura.

D. The Chinese shrine at Pura Batur, the second-most important temple in Bali. Since ancient times Balinese of Chinese descent have worshipped at this sanctuary.

E. Chinoiserie carvings on the backboard (ulon) of a shrine pavilion at Jero Kubutambahan, Buleleng.

F. Rich Chinese-style carving on a door at the haute chinoiserie Puri Kanginan, Amlapura.

G. The Soeharto Suite of the Intercontinental hotel, by Jakartan designer Hadiprana, is a showcase for the over-the-top Chinese-Balinese interior style so popular in Jakarta during the years 1985-97.

The earliest artefacts in Bali—the sacrificial adzes and kettle drums, both of which still play important parts in many ceremonies—came from the culture of Neolithic peoples who travelled down from what is today Yunnan province in China, around 1,000 BC. Chinese decorative and architectonic influences have been seeping into the island's architecture and its ceremonies, either directly or via Java, since the establishment of trade links with China in the 7th century AD.

Architecturally, Bali is part southern Chinese, part southern Indian. Vassal princes from the courts of Canton, traders who established ports such as Singaraja and Kuta, and warlords such as Kublai Khan, all brushed the north coast and left people and architectural ideas behind. The slight up-turn on gate, shrine and ceremonial building roofs; the decorative timber railing (after Chinese fretwork patterns) on pleasure pavilions; and the use of gold leaf on violent colour combinations are all evidence of Chinese influence. Even the symbol of the Balinese universe—two *naga* encircling a cosmic turtle, as depicted on many of the island's *padmasana* shrines—is pure Chinese.

The courts of Java and Bali had trade relations with China and Vietnam (Champa in particular) for hundreds of years up until the modern era: many Balinese palaces and ports benefited from these relations.

In 1920, for example, the king of Canton sent a team of Chinese carpenters and masons as a present to the raja of Karangasem in eastern Bali. They worked on a major Dutch-Balinese-Chinese palace called Puri Kanginan in Amlapura, which survives today fairly intact. Their hybrid style was quickly adopted by all palaces throughout Bali, thereby assuring that it would be all the rage for generations of nouveaux riches.

Today, descendants of this style can be found in concrete shophouses of palatial proportions along the island's thoroughfares, as Chinese Indonesians resettle in Bali after the political upheavals of 1998.

ARCHITECTURAL HYBRIDS → **CHINESE INFLUENCE 8.2**

8.3 Javanese Influence

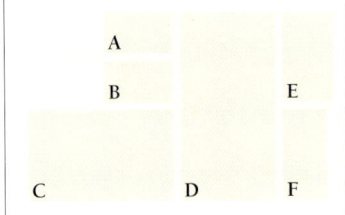

A	
B	E
C D	F

A. *The remains of the 16th-century Hindu temple of Candi Penataran in central Java show the detailed courtyard configurations of Javanese temples during the classic era. The towering prasada shrine, the stocky gedong shrine house and the elaborately styled and raised stylobate are Javanese architectural elements that found their way to Bali towards the end of the Majapahit period, when Islam was adopted by most Javanese.*

B. *The Javanese office- (kantor) style house was imported to Bali during the 1960s. This charming camouflaged version survives in an army camp in northern Bali. Javanese taste has spread throughout Indonesia through the military, just as Dutch taste was once disseminated through the colonial army and its wing, the women's choirs.*

C. *The Setinggil audience court at the Kraton Kasepuhan palace, Cirebon (West Java) built in the 16th century in the Javanese Hindu Majapahit style that also influenced Bali.*

D. *The Javanese terrace in the Villa Bebek, Sanur. Note the wall panels from Javanese houses used as fill-in between Balinese columns.*

E. *Ir. Bagus Suryadarma Wijana, brother of top sculptor Nyoman Nuarta—of Garuda-Wisnu Kencana monument fame—trained in architecture in Bandung. His Bali work features many interesting Javanese accents, such as this flying buttress.*

F. *The palaces of northern and eastern Bali often copied the neo-colonial-Javanese style found in the palaces of Solo. This gate, at the Jero Kubutambahan, feels very Solo-nese.*

Much of Balinese architecture grew out of Java during the classic Hindu era. Bali's palace families have never forgotten their links to Java: in the 19th century, some Balinese nobles even sent their children to Javanese noble houses to complete their education. The young Balinese would return with refined Javanese tastes in interior decoration, landscape design and courtly costume. European architectural trends crept into Bali via these Javanese palace connections during the early colonial era, when Bali was left uncolonized.

During the late colonial era, urban architectural trends travelled from Jakarta, Bandung and Surabaya to Balinese towns via government agencies and the military. Over the past 30 years, an increasing number of Javanese architects has made their base in Bali, most notably the late Ir. Robi Sularto whose early studies on Balinese architecture informed a generation of Jakartan architects. Many young Balinese architects return from architectural training in Java with enhanced mannerist decorating skills. The pas de deux continues.

ARCHITECTURAL HYBRIDS → **JAVANESE INFLUENCE** 8.3

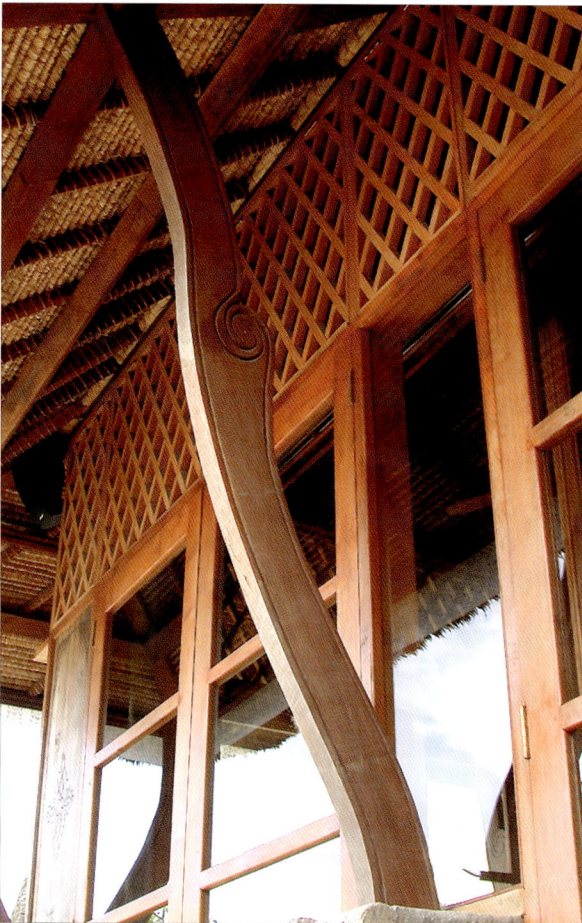

8.4 Late Modern Hybrids

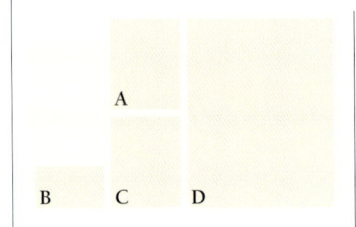

A. Architect Lek Bunnag of Bangkok was inspired by native Lombok building traditions and Bali Style glamour in the Lombok Novotel hotel on Kuta beach, Lombok.

B. Bali's first duty-free colosseum, at Kuta roundabout.

C. Bright ox-blood red roof-tile paint used on a wall of a Bali Style house, the Villa Kirana, in Sayan.

D. The private quarters of fashion designer Milo's octagonal pavilion, fondly called Octopussy Galore by local buffs.

By the year 2000, the world's most gorgeous island had become the tourism world's messiest (if most fascinating). It had taken just 30 years.

One could rake through the muck and define strains of urbanism—the Going for Baroque, Ghost Train Gothic, Bali Style Babylon, Cappuccino Rococo—but they are all excessive and mannerist and worth but scant attention.

As I write, developers from Surabaya and Jakarta on neighbouring Java and from Perth and Singapore, swarm over Bali throwing up shophouses, Korean BBQ restaurants and duty-free malls, all cheaply realized with a smattering of Balinese detail. Carved panels are applied gratuitously, like decals. A style book documenting these horrors (and some gems) wins medals in the U.S. and becomes the bible for emerging New Asian architects and New Bali Style practitioners around the globe. Where have you gone, my lovely?

Meanwhile two of this year's World's Top Ten Hotels (any category) are in Bali—the Four Seasons Resort, Jimbaran and the Amandari—mostly due to their architecture and gardens. The pages of *Architectural Digest* regularly brandish exotic images of Bali Style dream homes, designed by young regional architects such as Cheong Yew Kuan, Ernesto Bedmar and Lek Bunnag. In landscape design, the island has been a great training ground, too, for regional stars such as Bill Bensley, Carl Prinsic and Nyoman Miyoga. Trends in tropical garden design seem to start in Bali—the Balinese gardeners, pavilion builders and stone carvers have certainly become the tropical garden world's brightest stars.

The "force" is still with the island's architectural and landscape design—but is it fighting a losing battle against gloBALIzation?

ARCHITECTURAL HYBRIDS → **LATE MODERN HYBRIDS** 8.4

212

ARCHITECTURAL HYBRIDS → **LATE MODERN HYBRIDS 8.4**

A. Bali-based architect Guy Morgan's Star Trek special for Batavia Connection, a homewares showroom on the Nusa Dua by-pass.

B. The entrance tower of the Villa Kirana, with porte-cochere by Indonesian sculptor Pintor Sirait.

C. The winner of the Terry Stanton Memorial Gems of Modern Balinese Architecture Award—Petrol Station Category. The magnificent split-level, split-personality Pertamina Padang Galak. The building was noted for its hovercraft quality and the broad pink stone feature surrounds on its portal and windows.

D. The pool in the luxury villa of the Amankila in eastern Bali, designed by Ed Tuttle. Part cabana, part bale, the poolside pavilion is a true gem.

Following pages: The very photogenic twin pagodas of the Hindu-Buddhist Candi Kuning on Lake Bratan in Bangli Regency, arguably the crowning achievement of Balinese temple architecture's late classic era (18th–20th centuries).

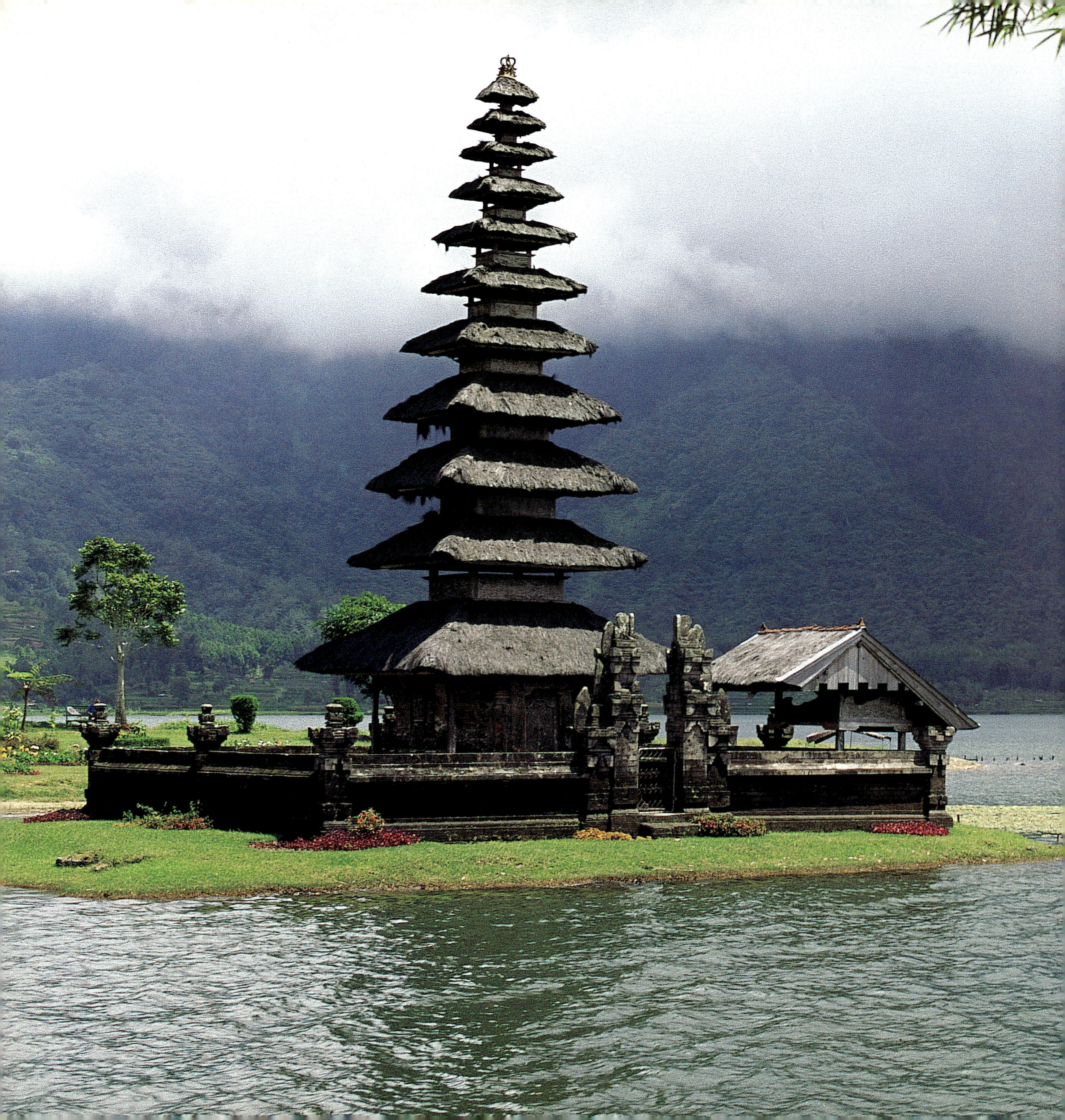

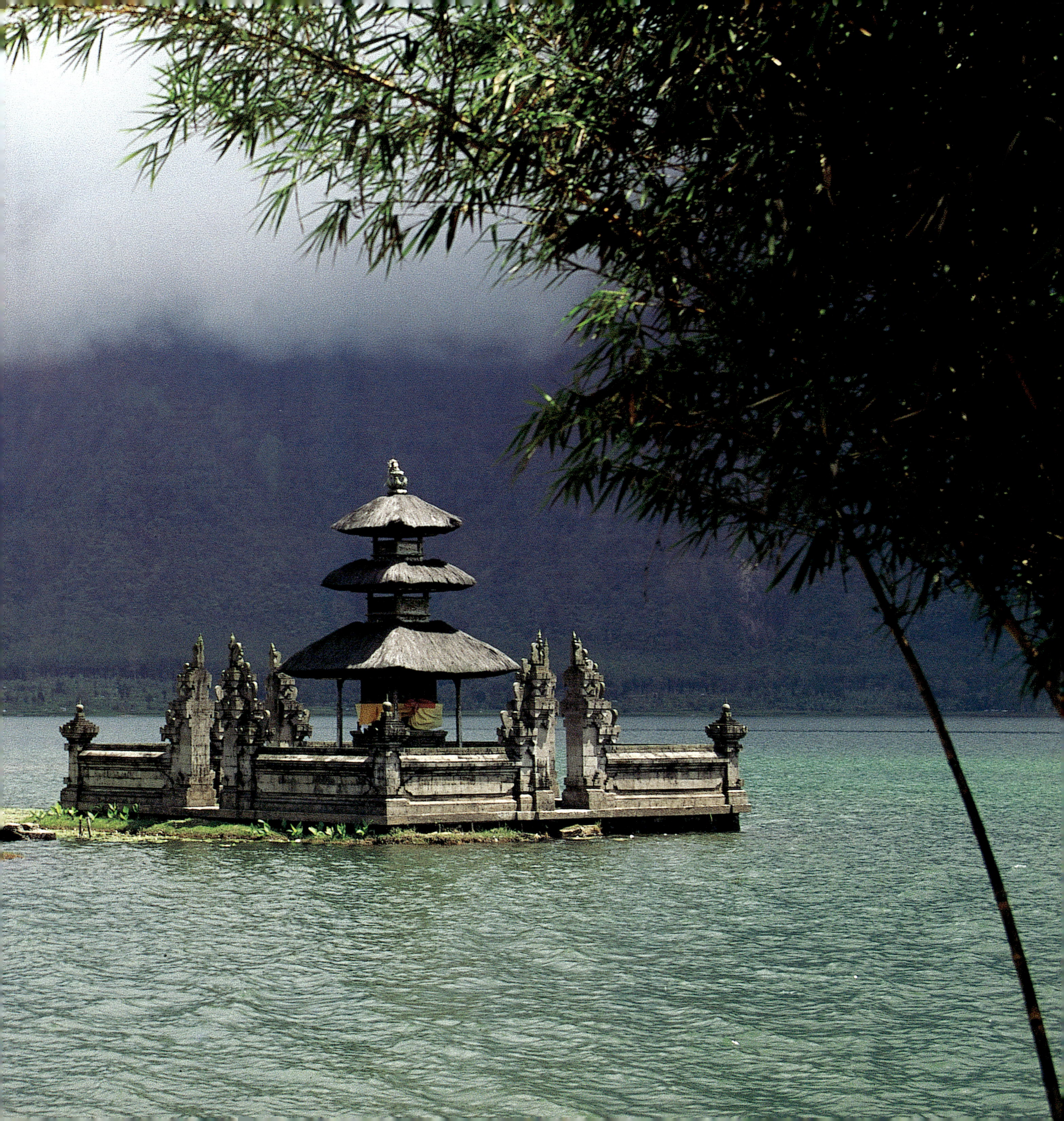

Map of Bali

Places where architectural treats can be found

Air Sanih **F1**	Ketewel **F5**	Sampalan **H6**
Amlapura **I4**	Kintamani **G2**	Sanggingan **F4**
Bangli **G4**	Klungkung **G5**	Sangsit **E1**
Banua **F3**	Krambitan **E5**	Sanur **F6**
Batubulan **F5**	Kubutambahan **F1**	Sawangan **F7**
Batujimbar **F6**	Kuda **G3**	Sayan **F4**
Batukau **E3**	Kuta **F6**	Sebatu **F4**
Batur **G2**	Lake Batur **G2**	Selat **H4**
Bayunggede **G3**	Lake Bratan **F2/3**	Seminyak **F6**
Bedugul **F3**	Lake Buyan **E2**	Sempidi **F5**
Bedulu **F5**	Lake Tamblingan **E2**	Seririt **D2**
Belantih **F2**	Legian **F6**	Sibanggede **F5**
Berawa **E6**	Manggis **H4**	Sidakarya **F6**
Besakih **H3**	Marga **F4**	Sidemen **H4**
Bongkasa **F4**	Mendaya **B3**	Silakarang **F5**
Bugbug **I4**	Mengwi **F5**	Singapadu **F5**
Bukian **F4**	Munduk **E2**	Singaraja **E1**
Campuhan **F4**	Munggu **E5**	Songan **G2**
Canggu **E6**	Negara **B3**	Sukasada **E1**
Cau **F4**	Nusa Dua **F7**	Sukawati **F5**
Denpasar **F6**	Nyalian **G4**	Suter **G3**
Gaji **F5**	Nyuhkuning **F5**	Suwung **F6**
Gianyar **G5**	Padang Galak **F6**	Tabanan **E5**
Gilimanuk **A2**	Padangkerta **I4**	Tampaksiring **G4**
Gobleg **E2**	Payangan **F4**	Tanah Lot **E5**
Guwang **F5**	Pecatu **E7**	Taro **F3**
Iseh **H4**	Peliatan **F5**	Tegalalang **F4**
Jimbaran **F7**	Pemuteran **B1**	Tejakula **G1**
Jungutbatu **H6**	Penelokan **G3**	Tenganan **H4**
Kapal **F5**	Pengastulan **D2**	Tirtagangga **I4**
Kedewatan **F4**	Penulisan **G2**	Toyapakeh **H6**
Kedisan **G3**	Petang **F4**	Trunyan **G2**
Kepawon **F6**	Pulaki **B1**	Ubud **F4**
Kerobokan **F6**	Renon **F6**	Ujung **I4**
Kesiman **F6**	Saba **G5**	Uluwatu **E7**

D
E
F
G
H
I
1
2
3
4
5
6
7
B A L I S E A
B A L I S E A
I N D I A N
O C E A N
BULELENG
BULELENG
BANGLI
KARANGASEM
TABANAN
GIANYAR
KLUNGKUNG
KLUNGKUNG
BADUNG
Kubutambahan
Air
Sanih
Sangsit
Singaraja
Sukasada
Tejakula
Seririt
Pengastulan
Gobleg
Lake
Buyan
Lake
Tamblingan
Munduk
GUNUNG
LESONG
GUNUNG
CATUR
Lake
Bratan
Bedugul
GUNUNG
SANGIYANG
TAMAN NASIONAL
BALI BARAT
GUNUNG
BATUKAU
Penulisan
Belantih
GUNUNG
BATUR
Songan
Lake
Batur
Kintamani
Batur
Trunyan
Penelokan
Kedisan
GUNUNG
ABANG
Bayunggede
Suter
Banua
Kuda
Telaga Waja
GUNUNG
AGUNG
Besakih
GUNUNG
LEMPUYANG
GUNUNG
SERAYA
Batukau
Petanu
Pakrisan
Taro
Petang
Sebatu
Cau
Bukian
Tampaksiring
Tirtagangga
Payangan
Selat
Padangkerta
Tegalalang
Ayung
Bangli
Unda
Amlapura
(Karangasem)
Iseh
Ujung
Marga
Bongkasa
Tenganan
Sidemen
Manggis
Kedewatan
Sanggingan
Sayan
Campuhan
Ubud
Bugbug
Yehempas
Nyalian
Amuk
Bay
Peliatan
Nyuhkuning
Bedulu
Krambitan
Tabanan
Klungkung
Gianyar
Mengwi
Silakarang
Kapal
Sibanggede
Singapadu
Sukawati
Munggu
Sempidi
Saba
Batubulan
Guwang
Tanah Lot
Gaji
Ketewel
Lombok
Kesiman
Kerobokan
Canggu
Berawa
DENPASAR
Padang Galak
Sanur
Renon
Badung Strait
NUSA
LEMBONGAN
Jungutbatu
Sampalan
Toyapakeh
NUSA
CENINGAN
Seminyak
Legian
Batujimbar
Sidakarya
Kepawon
Suwung
Kuta
NUSA
PENIDA
PULAU
SERANGAN
Jimbaran
Bukit
Peninsula
Nusa
Dua
Sawangan
Uluwatu
Pecatu
Lombok
KEY
Major road
Minor road
Track
Regency boundary
0 kilometres
10
0 miles
10

Glossary of Terms

adat
  tribal law
adegan
  column post
adegan beton
  concrete pillar
ajeng pura
  temple forecourt
alang-alang
  elephant grass thatch
aling-aling
  screen wall, often inside temple gates
alun-alun
  Javanese term for village square
ancak saji
  reception court in a palace
angkul-angkul
  simple form of Balinese gate
apit-apit
  purlins, which tie roof rafters together
arca
  votive statue
bade
  funeral bier
bale agung
  ceremonial long pavilion/audience hall of the gods
bale bali
  ceremonial pavilion
bale bandung
  eight-post pavilion with a porch
bale bengong
  corner pavilion/belvedere
bale bundar
  eight- or ten-post square pavilion
bale kambang
  "floating" pavilion, on an island in an ornamental lake or formal water garden
bale lantang
  long pavilion
bale loji
  corner pavilion for entertaining, often found on palaces, with an exaggerated (high) stylobate
bale patok
  similar to *bale bengong*
bale pawedan
  temporary pavilion erected for the high priest during major ceremonies
bale payadnyan
  open pavilion for offering rituals in a temple
bale pemegat sot
  special "oath breaking" pavilion found just inside the gate of many of the island's *pura agung* (grand temples)
bale piasan
  grandstand for the gods

bale sakenam
  six-post pavilion often used as a kitchen
bale sakepat
  four-post pavilion at the corner of palaces
bale sakutus
  a workhouse pavilion
Bali Aga
  ancient Balinese culture of the mountains
balok
  column length of coconut wood
bancingah
  open square or common near a *puri* (see also *alun-alun*); enclosure built on "virgin" land for important ceremonies
banjar
  sub-village community unit
baris
  warrior dance
barong
  village mascot/lion effigy
bata bali
  roman brick
bata citakan
  unbaked clay brick
bata matah
  unbaked clay brick
bata pasang
  brick coursework
bata pripihan
  shaved brick coursework
bataran
  stylobate
batu bukit
  coarse limestone
batu candi
  andesite
batu galang
  stone air vent
batu palimanan
  fine limestone (from Palimanan village in west Java)
batu pilah
  coarse volcanic tuff
batu teplek
  slate
bedeg
  woven slits of bamboo
beji
  holy spring
betaka
  decorative carved apex panel inside a square roof ridge plate
Boma
  benevolent demon/protector figure, often carved above Balinese gates
Brahma
  god of fire and creativity

bubuk
  mite that infests bamboo
busung
  young coconut palm leaves
candi
  Buddhist stupa or Hindu-era Javanese temple
candi bentar
  split-gate, found in temples
canggahwang
  timber brace/buttress found on pavilion posts
Cili
  ancient fertility symbol, found carved on temples
dalem
  the innermost court of a temple
dedeleg
  decorative apex plate covering a rectangular ridge plate
Dewi Sri
  the rice goddess
dolken
  timber column, often of coconut wood
dore
  terracotta roof ridge tiles
dulang
  raised tray fashioned from wood, used in ceremonies as a table for offerings
emper
  awning
gamelan
  metallaphone orchestra
gandengan
  carried or supported by, for example the flanking wall of a gate
garuda
  mythological bird of prey
gedong
  vault-like enclosed building
gedong persimpanan
  gedong for keeping holy *arca* statues
gerantang
  extra portion of roof, giving rise to a double bargeboard/extended eave
griya
  Brahman house
gunung rata
  stepped or tiered stylobate on a pavilion
ider-ider
  bunting, tied onto pavilion eaves
iga-iga
  rafters
ijuk
  string made from sugar palm fibre
ikatan
  tied material; or measure of tied objects

jaba
  area outside a house or temple
jaba tengah
  larger temple's first courtyard
jaro-jaro
  grilles on a Balinese window
jempana
  palanquin
jero
  a palace house, or palace wife (from Sudra caste)
jeroan
  courtyard inside a palace or temple
jineng
  four-post rice loft
joglo
  four-post traditional Javanese house
jongkok asu
  foundation for pavilion post
kahyangan tiga
  three main temples of a Balinese village
kala
  demon
kantor
  office (from the Dutch)
kasa
  white cloth used in ceremonies
kayu nangka
  jackfruit wood
kayu seseh
  coconut wood
keben
  woven basket for offerings or storage
kelod
  south
ketan
  glutinous rice
kincut
  carved element on king post
kinju
  Chinese red paint
klangsah
  woven fronds of coconut palm
kolong
  eaves
kori
  house gate
kori agung
  palace gate
krupuk
  prawn crackers
Ksatriya
  princely caste
kul-kul
  slit-drum
lamak
  apron on shrine boxes woven from banana and palm leaf

GLOSSARY OF TERMS

lambang
  roof plate

legong
  classical dance

leneng
  low walls (for sitting) found outside gates

limasan
  eight-post, Javanese-style, hipped roof construction

lumbung
  six-post rice loft

maligia
  highest level of ceremony for soul purification

malimas
  pyramid roof

mandi
  traditional bath house

melis
  procession of gods (*arca* statues) to the sea

menjangan majapahit
  the golden deer symbol of the Majapahit empire

merajan
  house temple of a noble family

merajan agung
  house temple in a *puri agung* palace

meru
  tiered, pagoda-like shrine pavilion

meten
  the main sleeping pavilion in a courtyard home

moksa
  achieving oneness with the godhead through spontaneous combustion

mukur
  purification ceremony for departed soul

mulas
  to whitewash

naga
  dragon

naga banda
  ceremony of the dragon effigy used in royal cremation rites

odalan
  temple festival/anniversary rites

padma
  water lily shape; spirit effigy

padmasana
  altar to the sun god, Surya, found in most temples and many house shrines

padmasari
  elaborate version of *padmasana*

paduraksa
  roofed temple gate; also name of wall pilasters

paku pipet
  hanging woven coconut palm decorations

palimanan
  limestone from Palimanan village, Java

panggung agung
  temporary shrine pavilion usually made from bamboo

paon
  kitchen

papalihan
  brick coursework

paras
  volcanic tuff

paras batik
  spotted volcanic tuff

paras batu
  pitted volcanic tuff

paras taro
  soft camel-coloured volcanic tuff from Taro village

paras tempelan
  applied veneer of volcanic tuff

paras ukir
  fine, carvable volcanic tuff

parekan
  palace servant

paruman
  shrine pavilion in temple

patih
  princely warrior

patra
  ornamental style

patra cina
  Chinese decorative motif

patra mesir
  Egyptian (Mesir) decorative motif

payadnyan
  holy enclosure; or temple pavilion as in *bale payadnyan*

payogan
  an auxiliary shrine building

pedanda
  Hindu (Brahman) priest

pelinggih
  shrine

pemade
  king rafter in roof frame

pemelaspasan
  consecration ceremony

pementang
  tie beam

pemucu
  hip rafter in roof frame

pemugbug bucu
  ridge of thatch ("bucu" meaning the very corner bit)

Pengerebongan
  mass trance festival held annually in East Denpasar

penjor
  tall woven banner, which signifies a ceremonial period in a house or village

pesisir
  coastal

petitis
  carved lintel on door or window

pewedan
  pavilion for incanting the holy Vedas

piasan
  shrine pavilion in a temple

plangkiran
  shrine box in northeastern corner of most rooms/pavilions

plangkiran gantung
  hanging *plangkiran*

poleng
  black-and-white cloth representing the spirit world

pondok
  hut in the rice fields

popolan
  adobe

praba
  altar box portion of a *pelinggih* shrine

prada
  gold leaf

prasada
  stone pagoda

pripihan
  shaved and rubbed brick coursework

pura dalem
  temple to Lord Shiva

pura desa
  temple of origins

pura penataran agung
  state temple, often attached to *puri agung* palaces

pura prajapati
  graveyard temple (to Bhatari Uma)

pura puseh
  temple of origins, or to the founding spirits

puri
  palace

puri agung
  grand palace

rab
  roof or thatch

rab alang-alang
  thatched roof

rab ijuk
  sugar palm fibre (black) thatch

rab klangsah
  woven coconut leaf thatch

rab sumi
  glutinous rice stalk thatch

Rangda
  evil witch consort of the *barong*

rebab
  stringed instrument, of Middle Eastern origins

Sai
  decorative element resembling the face of a winged lion

saka
  column

sakenam
  six-post pavilion, often used for kitchens

sakti
  holy/empowered

sampiyan gantung
  hanging woven offering

sanggah
  commoner's house temple

Saraswati
  goddess of knowledge and the arts (and architecture)

semat
  fasteners, made from slivers of bamboo, used in making offerings

sendi
  bollard, plinth that supports pavilion columns

Shiva
  Hindu god of cyclical reincarnation

simbar
  carved corner decoration, usually on a shrine base

sindu-wisindu
  guardian statue pair, most often found guarding temple gates

singa
  winged lion

sirap
  teak roof shingles

stylobate
  raised pavilion base

sumi
  rice straw used for thatching

Surya
  the Hindu sun god

taban
  platform between pavilion columns

tali ijuk
  twine made from *ijuk* (sugar palm fibre)

Tantri
  Balinese version of Aesops fables

taring
  temporary shade structure, made from bamboo

tatakan tugeh
  carved element at base of king post

teba
  backyard area behind house compound

tiang
  column

tingklik
  bamboo xylophone

tirta
  holy water

tiying
  bamboo

tugeh
  king post

ulon
  head board on platform in ceremonial pavilion

umah
  house of commoner

umbul-umbul
  coloured banners (part of temple gods' arcadia)

undagi
  traditional architect-priest

wantilan
  large community pavilion, often with tiered roof

warung
  food stall

Wisnu
  the Hindu god of prosperity

Picture Credits

ILLUSTRATIONS

Anak Agung Cakranegara: 53B,C, 87D,E, 126A.

Chang Huai-Yan: 1, 127H, 128B.

Deni Chung: 20A, 32D, 36A, 54A,B,C, 58B, 88A, 92B, 216.

Donald Friend, reproduced with permission of the Arnott Estate: 36C, 204A.

Bruce Granquist: 8, 18D, 30B, 46A,B,C,E, 85G, 86B, 89G, 174B, 209C.

Adrien Jean Le Mayeur de Merprès, reproduced with permission of Christie's Singapore: 36B.

Stephen Little: 57D.

W.O.J. Nieuwenkamp, reproduced with permission of Bruce Carpenter: 17D,F, 27D, 31D.

Ida Bagus Nyoman Rai, reproduced with permission of Albert Beaucourt: 100–101.

I Nyoman Sudana: 13E.

I Nyoman Tjakra: 26B.

PHOTOGRAPHS

Amandari: 21C, 49H, 128A, 129E.

Bali Oberoi: 21D, 34C.

Luc Bouchage: 96A.

Deni Chung: 108B, 110D, 154B, 160B, 161E,F,G,H, 164B, 165F,G, 176A,D, 177H, 180C, 182C, 184E, 196A, 206A, 209E.

Editions Didier Millet archives: 29D, 73J, 76C, 84C, 77G, 98A, 114A.

Isabella Ginanneschi: 38A.

Reto Guntli: 157E.

Jerry Harpur: 127F, 204B.

Rio Helmi: 4B, 15D, 18A, 32E, 40B, 44D, 49I, 60-61, 65F,H, 68A, 69E, 75F, 82–83, 84E, 92C, 108A, 111G,L,O, 112B, 114E, 115N, 116A, 117K, 118A, 121E,H, 132A,B, 133E, 135F, 136A,C, 138A, 139D, 142E, 145E,G, 148A, 149G, 153E, 158A, 159D, 168B, 173D, 184D, 196B, 206C, 207F, 214-15.

Brent Hesselyn: 76A.

Courtesy of *House and Garden*, Thailand: 113M, 122C.

Don Jensen: 37D,F.

Made Kader: 30A, 92D, 114C,D, 148C, 162D, 180B, 186–87, 212A.

Annie Kelly: 42–43, 44A, 176B.

Guido Alberto Rossi: 16A.

Tim Street-Porter: 4A, 5A, 6, 12A, 14B, 15E, 19H, 21E, 22–23, 24E, 27E, 28C, 33F, 35, 37E, 38B, 40C,E, 41F, 44C, 51G, 52A, 57E,H, 58C, 59D, 66C, 75G, 79B,C, 81F, 91I, 93E, 99D, 103B, 105D,E,F, 109D, 110A, 111M, 112A, 115I, 118B, 123D,E, 129F, 132D, 134A,D, 137E, 138C, 145D, 145F, 146A, 147E, 150–51, 155E, 156A,B,C, 157D,F, 166–67, 168A,C,D,E, 178B, 188B,E, 190F, 191H,I, 193P,Q, 195C, 198–99, 200A, 205E,F, 211D, 213D.

Tan Hock Beng: 129C,D,G, 207G.

Luca Invernizzi Tettoni: 123G, 124A.

Claude Vanheye: 124C, 210C.

Richard Watson: 120C, 122A,B, 161I.

Thilly Weissenborn, reproduced with permission of Yu-Chee Chong: 10–11, 165C.

Made Wijaya: 5B, 7, 12B,C, 14A,B, 15C, 16B,C, 18B,C, 19F,G,I,J, 20B, 24A,B,C,D,F, 25G, 26A, 27F,G, 28A, 29E, 31C,E, 32C, 33H,I, 34A,B, 40A,D, 44B,E,G, 45I, 46D, 47F,G,H, 48A,B,C,D,E,F,G, 50B, 51D,E,F,H,I, 53D, 55D,E,F,G, 56A,C, 57F,G, 58A, 62A, 63B, 64A,B,C, 65E,G, 66A,B, 68B,C,D, 69F,G,H,I,J, 70A,B,C,D,E,F,G, 71H,I,J,K, 72A,B,C,D,E,F, 73H,I, 74A,B,C,D, 75F, 76B, 77D,E,F, 78A, 79D, 80A,B,C, 81D, 84A,B,D,F, 86A,C, 87F,G, 88B,C,D, 89E,F, 90A,B,C,D,E,F, 91G,H, 92A, 94A,B,D,E, 95F,G,H,I,J,K,L,M,N,O,P,Q, 96B, 97C,D,E,F,G, 99B,C,E, 103C,D, 104A,B,C, 106A,B,C, 107D,E,F,G,H, 108C, 110B,C, 111E,F,H,I,J,K,N,P, 112C,D, 113E,F,G,H,I,J,K,L, 114B,F, 115G,H,J,K,L,M, 116B,C,D,E,F,G,H, 117I,J,L, 118B, 119C,D, 120A,B,D, 121F,G, 123F, 124B, 126C,D,E, 130–31, 132B, 132E, 134B,E, 136B,D, 138B, 140A,B, 141C,D,E, 142A,B,C, 144A,B,C, 146B,C, 147D,F, 148B, 149D,F,H, 152B,C,D, 153F,G,H,I, 154A,C,D,E, 158B,C, 159E,F, 160A,C,D, 162B,C, 163E,F,G,H, 164A, 165D,E, 169G,H, 170A,B,C, 171D,E,F,G,H,I, 172A,B,C, 173E, 174A,C, 175D,E,F,G,H, 176C, 177E,F,G,I,J, 178A,B,C,F, 179C,D,E, 180A,D, 181E,F,G,H, 182A,B,D,E, 183F,G,H, 184A,B,C,F, 188A,C,D, 189F,G,H, 190A,B,C,D,E, 191G,J,K,L, 192A,B,C,D,E,F,G,H,I,J,K,L, 193M,N,O,R, 194A,B, 195D,E,F,G, 196C,D,E, 197F,G, 202A,B,C,D, 203E, 204C,D, 206B, 207D,E, 208A,B, 209D,F, 210B, 212B,C.

Made Wijaya's collection: 12D, 19E, 26C, 28B, 32A, 44F,H, 50A, 56B, 64D, 73G, 81E, 102A, 134C, 141F, 152A, 168F, 185G, 201B, 203F,G, 210A.

Caroline Younger: 32B, 33G, 50C, 127G, 149E, 162A, 163I.

Every effort has been made to trace the copyright holders and we apologize for any unintentional omissions. We would be pleased to insert the appropriate acknowledgements in any subsequent edition of this publication.

Projects designed by Made Wijaya, and realized by Ir. I Gusti Ngurah Sarjana, P.T. Indosekar and P.T. Wijaya Tribwana International, illustrated in this book:

ARCHITECTURE, LANDSCAPE, & INTERIOR

Jero Kubu, Sanur, Bali
69F, 77G, 80A, 86C, 90A, 94E, 104C, 117J, 204D.

Villa Bebek, Sanur, Bali
24B, 31E, 37E, 40D,E, 79C,D, 108B, 110B,C, 111J, 113I, 116D, 120D, 123D, 152D, 176A, 179C, 209D.

Villa Angsa, Sanur, Bali
68D, 80C, 107E, 190A.

Taman Bebek, Sayan, Bali
40C, 52A, 111P, 113M, 122F, 125C.

Villa Kirana (Alexander House), Sayan, Bali
37D,F, 40A, 58A, 134A, 210C, 212B.

Canggu Puri Mertha, Canggu, Bali
20B, 34B, 124C, 182E.

Dar Al-Ariq, Canggu, Bali
58B, 92D.

Jocki House, Berawa, Bali
51E.

Warung Mie, Four Seasons Resorts, Jimbaran, Bali
36A, 182B.

LANDSCAPE DESIGN

Gemini House, Batujimbar, Sanur, Bali
110A.

Four Seasons Resort, Jimbaran, Bali
49I, 53D, 111O, 157E,F.

Bali Oberoi, Seminyak, Bali
21D.

Amandari, Sayan, Bali
21C, 49H, 128A, 129C,D,E,F,G.

Nusa Dua Beach Hotel, Nusa Dua, Bali
44H.

Four Seasons Resorts, Sentul, West Java [unfinished]
204C.

Sentul Culture Centre, Sentul, West Java
95I,J.

Ngo House, Singapore
173E.

References

Albanese, Marilia, *Ancient India – from the Origins to the XIII Century AD*, White Star, Italy, 2001.

Bali: A Traveller's Companion, Achipelago Press, Singapore, 1995.

Brown, Percy, *Indian Architecture (Buddhist and Hindu)*, Taraporevala, Bombay, 1959.

Bruhl, Odette, *Indian Temples*, Oxford University Press, London, 1937.

Budaya Indonesia Arts and Crafts in Indonesia, Royal Tropical Institute, Amsterdam, 1987.

Carpenter, Bruce, *Willem Hofker – Painter of Bali (1902–1981)*, Picture Publishers, The Netherlands, 1993.

Carpenter, Bruce, *W.O.J. Nieuwenkamp – First European Artist in Bali*, Uitgeverij Uniepers Abcoude, The Netherlands, 1997.

Champakalakshmi, R. and Kris, Usha, *The Hindu Temple*, Roli Books, India, 2001.

Covarrubias, Miguel, *Island of Bali*, Alfred A. Knopf, New York, 1937.

Cooper, Ilay and Dawson, Barry, *Traditional Buildings of India*, Thames & Hudson, London, 1998.

Eiseman, Fred B., *Bali Sekala and Niskala*, Periplus Editions, Hong Kong, 1990.

Falconer, John, *Photographs of Java, Bali, Sumatra 1860s – 1920s*, Les Editions du Pacifique, Paris, 2000.

Fontein, Jan, *The Sculpture of Indonesia*, National Gallery of Art, Washington, 1990.

Goad, Philip and Bingham-Hall, Patrick, *Architecture Bali: Architecture of Welcome*, Pesaro Publishing, 2000.

Hamzuri, Drs., *Rumah Tradisional Jawa*, Proyek Pengembangan Permuseuman D.K.I. Jakarta, Departemen Pendidikan & Kebudayaan.

Helmi, Rio and Walker, Barbara, *Bali Style*, Times Editions, Singapore, 1995.

Hoefer, Hans, *Insight Guide Bali*, Apa Publications, Singapore, 1995.

Indonesian Heritage, Vol. 6, Architecture, Archipelago Press, Singapore, 1998.

Kempers, A.J. Bernet, *Ancient Indonesian Art*, C.P.J. Van Der Peet, Amsterdam, 1959.

Lueras, Leonard and Helmi, Rio, *Bali High: Paradise From the Air*, Times Editions, Singapore, 1990.

Michell, George, *Hindu Art and Architecture*, Thames & Hudson, London, 2000.

Michell, George and Mertinelli, Antonio, *The Royal Palaces of India*, Thames & Hudson, London, 1994.

Moojen, P.A.J., *Bali*, Adi Pustaka, The Hague, 1926.

Pearce, Barry, *Donald Friend 1915–1989*, Art Gallery of New South Wales, 1990.

Perez, Rodrigo, Encarnacion, Rosario and Dacanay, Julian, *Folk Architecture*, GCF Books, 1989.

Powell, Robert, *The Tropical Asian House*, Select Books Pte Ltd, 1996.

Pre-War Balinese Modernists: 1928–1942, from a private European collection (including works selected by Gregory Bateson and Margaret Mead), Christie's International Singapore Pte Ltd, 2001.

Pucci, Idanna, *The Epic of Bali*, Alfred Van Der Marck Editions, New York, 1985.

Rhodius, Hans and Darling, John, *Walter Spies and Balinese Art*, Terra, Zutphen, Amsterdam, 1980.

Rowland, Benjamin, *The Art and Architecture of India*, Penguin Books, London, 1953.

Stuart-Fox, David J., *Once a Century: Pura Besakih and the Eka Dasa Rudra Festival*, Sinar Harapan, Jakarta, 1982.

Tan Hock Beng, *Tropical Architecture and Interiors*, Page One Publishing, Singapore, 1994.

Tan Hock Beng, *Tropical Resorts*, Page One Publishing, Singapore, 1995.

Tan Hock Beng, *Tropical Retreats: The Poetic of Place*, Page One Publishing, Singapore, 1996.

Taylor, Brian Brace, and Sansoni, Barbara, *Geoffrey Bawa*, Concept Media, Singapore, 1986.

Tettoni, Luca Invernizzi and Francione, Gianni, *Bali Modern: The Art of Living*, Periplus, Hong Kong, 2000.

Tuong Vo Van, *Vietnam's Famous Ancient Pagodas*, Nha Xuat Ban Khoa Hoc Xa Hoi, Hanoi, 1993.

Waterson, Roxana, *The Living House. An Anthropology of Architecture in South-East Asia*, Oxford University Press, Singapore, 1990.

Wijaya, Made and Ginanneschi, Isabella, *At Home in Bali*, Abbeville Press Publishers, New York, 2000.

Wijaya, Made, *Balinese Architecture* (photocopy), Wijaya Press, 1984.

Wijaya, Made, *Statues of Bali* (photocopy), Wijaya Press, 1984.

Wijaya, Made, *Stranger in Paradise – the Diary of an Expatriate in Bali 1979–80*, Wijaya Words, Bali, 1995.

Wijaya, Made, *Tropical Garden Design*, Archipelago Press and Wijaya Words, Singapore, 1999.

Wijaya, Made, www.strangerinparadise.com

Index

A
adegan 96, *96–9*
adegan beton 96
adobe 65, *66*, *73*, *133*, *137*, *141*, 144, 158
air vents 112, *112–13*, *169*; ceramic *165*; stone 176, *176–77*; timber *134*, *182*, *183*
ajeng pura 80
alang-alang 97, 114, *115*, *117*, 140, *141*, *142*
aling-aling 68, *68*, *170*, 178
alun-alun 18
Amalou, Reda 114
Amandari 20, *20*, 34, 45, 58, 128, *128–29*, 156, 210; bath *128*; doors 112; pool pavilion *49*; village lanes *21*, *129*
Amankila 34; bar *118*; lobby *123*; pillars *150–51*; pool *213*; steps *93*
Amanusa 34; lobby *35*, *118–19*; swimming pool *168*; terrace *178*
ancak saji 32
andesite *see batu candi*
angkul-angkul 69, *71*
apex plates *see dedeleg*
apit-apit 86
artisans *130–31*
audience hall of the gods *see bale agung*

B
backyard *see teba*
bade 144, *146*
bale 44, 45, *45*; *bataran* 90, *90–91*; construction 86, *87–89*; elements 85; enclosed 50, *50–53*; roofs, 54, *54–58*; steps 92, *92–93*; types 46, *46*, *47*
bale agung 18, *18*, 25, 46, *46*, 87, 118; *bataran* 90; *taban* 102
bale bali 30, *30*, 44, 46, 47, 56; annexe *161*; roof 54; storage 118, *121*; *taban* 102
bale bandung 33, 46, *189*
bale banjar 118
bale bengong *10–11*, 63
bale bundar 45, 46, *46*, 47, 48
bale kambang 32
bale kul-kul see kul-kul tower
bale lantang 13, 14, 18, *27*, 46; Pura Batu Karo *19*; Pura Batur *135*; Pura Besakih 78; roof *115*; storage 118, *119*; *taban* 102
bale patok *21*, 32, 34
bale pawedan 80
bale payadnyan 80, 103
bale pemegat sot: Pura Besakih 78; *taban* 102, *103*
bale piasan 56, 87; *taban* *104*, *105*
bale sakenam 30, 46, *46*, 54, *84*
bale sakepat 46
bale sakutus 46
Bali Aga villages *12*, 13, 14, *16*, *17*, 148, 170; temples 56
Bali Hotel *201*, *203*
Bali Hyatt 38, 58, 201; gardens 78
Bali Oberoi 20, *21*, *34*, 36, 58, 66, 74, 102, 122, 201
Bali Sani Suites 20
Bali stone 148
Bali Style: gardens 38; homes 36, 50, *51*, *80*, 85, 90, 122, *122–25*, 176, 190, 210
balok 134
balustrades 178, *178–79*, *183*
bamboo *132*, 136, *136–39*; bargeboards *115*; fences 65, 107, *136*, 178, *179*; house *139*; kitchen door 110; rafters 86, 97, 114; screens *106*, *107*, *108*; shingles *12*, 56, 65, 116, *117*, *132*, *136*, *138*; storage shed *132*; truss work *18*; wall panels *109*, *121*, 136
bancingah 13, 144
banjar 13
Banjar Singgi: temple gate *70*
banners 180
Banua: temple shrine *86*
banyan trees 13, 18
Baruna Beach Hotel 78, 202
bata bali 158, 168
bata citakan 158
bata matah 158
bata pasang 158
bata pripihan 158
bataran 56, 85, 86, 90, *90–91*, 118
Batavia Connection *212*
bathrooms 36
batu bukit 156
batu candi 148
batu galang 176
Batu Karo: *jineng* *121*
batu pilah 178
batu teplek 148
Batubulan 170
Batujimbar Estate 20, 36, 201; doors *110*; gate *156*
Bawa, Geoffrey 20, 36, 41, 50, 66, 122, 156, 162, 190, 201
Bayunggede 13, *15*, 158; houses *132*; *meten* *117*; *pura puseh gedong* *55*; roofs 116
beams *see lambang*
bedeg 106, *109*, *136*, *138*, *189*
Bedmar, Ernesto 36, 210
Bedugul: *wantilan* *42–43*

Begawan Giri *22–23*
Belantih 13, 53, 110
belvedere *see bale bengong*
Bensley, Bill 152, 210
betaka 114, *114*, 115
Big Bamboo Villas *38–39*, 109, 136, *205*
bollards *see sendi*
Boma 194, *194–97*
Bonnet, Rudolf 58, 202
Bouchage, Luc 96
Brahma 13, 180
brick 158, *158–59*
brick and *paras* 174, *174–75*
bubuk 136
Bugbug village *16*
building materials *132*, 133, *133*
Bukian 152, 158; house gate 71, *153*; temple gate *73*, *141*; temple compound *24*
bungalows *134*, 201
Bunnag, Lek 210
bunting *see ider-ider*
buttresses *see canggahwang*

C
candi bentar 26, 56, 63, 68, *70*, *73*
Candi Penataran *50*, 208
Candi Sukuh *45*, 102
Canggu Puri Mertha hotel 20, *34*, *124*; door *182*
canggahwang 85, 96, *96–99*
Carlisle house *204*
Cekog, Pak 156
cement 162, *162–63*
Cemul, Wayan 94, 173, 176, 190, 193
ceramic 164, *164–65*
Chan Soo Chian 36
Cheadle House 58
Cheong Yew Kuan 20, 36, 91, 201, 205, 210
Chinese influence 26, 99, *111*, *116*, 140, 164, *165*, 169, 176, 188, 206, *206–7*
Cirebon: palace gate *70*
clan temples 13
cloth 180, *180–81*
cockfighting *12*, 18, 25, 45
coconut frond screens *106*
coconut thatch *see klangsah*
coconut wood *see seseh*
Colonial Exposition, Paris, 193, *203*
colour 180, 188, *188–89*
column foundations *see jongkok asu*
columns *see adegan*; *tiang*
communal baths 13
community hall *see wantilan*
coral 156, *156–57*

corrugated iron roofs *116*, *117*, *132*
courtyard elements, 63; gates 63, *63*, 68, *68–73*; ground surfaces 78, *78–79*; organization of space 80; walls 64, *64–67*, *132*
courtyard gardens 38, *38–41*
courtyards 25; hotel 34, *34–35*; house, 25, 30, *30–31*, 36, *36–37*, 79, 80; palace 32, *32–33*, 64, 80; temple 26, *26–29*; village *12*, *15*
Cranach, Diana von 126
cremation grounds 13

D
dalem 27, 28
Dali: village square *25*
Darling, John: house *24*, *105*
dedeleg 85, 114, *114*, 184
deer statues *191*, *193*
Denpasar Art Centre *169*
Dewi Sri 17, *57*, *181*, *193*
dolken 96
Dong S'on 13
doors 110, *110–11*, *134*, *168*; carved *182*, *183*, *184*, *185*
dore 85
Dream Homes *51*, 54, 58, 162, 164, 202, *208*, 210
drum towers *see kul-kul* towers
dulang 120
duty-free emporium *210*
Dwijendra, Dhang Hyang 73

E
earth 158, *158–59*
Eka Dasa Rudra ceremonies 76
Elephant Cave *see* Goa Gajah
elephant grass thatch *see alang-alang*
emper 54, *54*, 102, *105*
Environmental Bamboo Foundation 136

F
forecourt *see jaba*
Four Seasons Resort, west Java: gate *204*
Four Seasons Resort, Jimbaran 20, 45, 210; doors *111*; limestone path 78; pavilions *49*; pergola *157*; PJ's restaurant kitchen *53*; spa *164*; swimming pool *157*; Warung Mie restaurant *36*, *182*
Friend, Donald 36, 99, 201; house, *41*, 94, 95, 156, *157*; museum *40*, *51*, 122, 190; painting *36*, *204*
Fripp, Terry 122
funeral biers *see bade*

INDEX

G
gandengan 69
Gandha, Emily 78
Gardener, Bradley 20
Garland, Linda 136, 162; estate 59, 138, *139*
garuda 171, *172*, 190, *191*, 192
gate steps 74, *74–77*, *161*
gates: courtyard 63, *63*, 68, *68–73*; house 68, *72*, *149*, *156*; hybrid style *202*; temple *134*, *141*, *174*, *175*, *195*
gedong 47, 50, 55, *158*, *159*
gedong persimpanan 50
gerantang 140
Geria Guang: gate *68*, 69
Geria Ketewel: gate *72*
Gianyar 201; market gate *202*; palace square *10–11*; *wantilan agung 10–11*
Goa Gajah 32
government buildings 48, 58, 174, 201
Griya Ketewel: *sendi* 94
ground surfaces 78, *78–79*
Grounds Kent Architects 20
Gunung Penanggungan 64
Guwang: *bale agung* 87; door *134*; *meten* 50

H
Hadiprana 206
Hardy, Cynthia 199, 205
Hardy, John 199, 205
Hardy house *67*, *91*, *200*, 205
Helmi, Ela 152
Helmi, Rio 152
Hill, Kerry 36, 118, 168, 201
Hotel Campuhan 202
Hotel Chedi 148
hotels: palace-style 34, *34–35*; village-style 20, *20–23*
houses: hybrids *200*, *202*, 205; modern 36, *36–37*, 38, 50, *51*, 54, 58, *58–61*, 80, 92, 162, 164, 201, 202, *204*, 205, *205*, *208*, 210; traditional 25, 30, *30–31*, *81*
hybrid architecture *200*, 201, *201*, 202, *202–5*, 210, *210–13*

I
ider-ider 180
iga-iga 85, 86, 114, 136
ijuk 55, 56, 57, *115*, 116, 140, *140*, *141*
ikatan 114
Indian influence 26, 99, 110, 114, *116*, 176, 188, 194
Intercontinental hotel: Soeharto Suite *207*
ironwood shingles see *sirap*
Iseh: gate *72*

J
jaba 25, 26, 28, 30, 63, 64, 80
jaba tengah 26
Japa, Dewa 94
Javanese influence 32, 38, *56*, 64, 68, 188, 208, *208–9*

jero 25
Jero Kubu 80, *90*, 204
Jero Kubutambahan: *bale bali 160*; carving *207*; gate *33*, *209*; *petitis 182*; shrine pavilion *97*
jeroan 26, 27, 32, 74
jineng see *lumbung*
Jojol, Made 95, 190
jongkok asu 86

K
kahyangan tiga 25
kantor-style houses 122, 164, 202, *208*
Karang Boma 194
kasa 180
Kayu Aya hotel 36, 58, 102, 112, 122, 152, 201
keben 120
Kedisan: temple shrine *188*
Kent, Jack 162
Kerry Hill Architects 20
Kesepuhan Palace, Cirebon *48*
Ketewel 170
kincut 184
king posts see *tugeh*
kitchen see *paon*
klangsah 116, 117, 140, *140*, 142, 145, 147
Klungkung: doors *111*
kolong 86
kolong tiying 52
kori agung 68, 70, 154, *186–87*
Kubutambahan: house temple *48*
Kuda: temple gate *69*
kul-kul 12, *19*,*191*; tower *13*, *18*, *19*, 32, 45, 46, 78, *91*, *149*,*173*
Kurthi Mukha 194, *195*

L
La Taverna hotel: garden courts *78*
Lake Batur *14*, *15*
Lake Bratan *42–43*, *214–215*
Lakeman, Philip 122, 164
lamak 180, *180*, *181*
lambang 85, 86, 96, *96–99*
lava rock 17, *24*, 148, *148*
Legian-Seminyak 14
Le Mayeur de Merprès, Adrien Jean 36, 202
Lempad, I Gusti Nyoman 32, 154, 190, 192
leneng 64, 74, *74–77*
limestone 148, *149*, *150–51*, 156, *156–57*
Little, Stephen 56, 110, 112, 176
Lombok Novotel hotel *210*
long-houses see *bale lantang*
lumbung 12, *14*, 30, *30*, *44*, 46, *82–83*, 84, 86, 120, *121*; *bataran* 90; roof 54, 55, *81*, 114, *117*; storage 118

M
Majapahit influence 32, 48, 64, 71, 99, 110, *111*, 158, 170, *189*

Majapahit Museum, Trowulan: shrine *56*
malimas 54
mandi 36
Mengwi Palace see Puri Mengwi
merajan 30
merajan agung 81
meru 27; roof 54, *55*
Mesjid Agung, Yogyakarta 68
meten 30, *30*, 36, 46, *46*, 50, 51, 117, *138*, *149*, 176; door *182*; wall *107*
Milo: house 125, *211*
Miyoga, Nyoman 210; villa *40*
Morgan, Guy 122, 213
mulas 156
Muller, Carole 20, 36, 127, 128
Muller, Peter 20, 36, 49, 58, 66, 102, 109, 112, 122, 128, 152, 201
Munduk 202; shrines *57*

N
Nieuwenkamp, W.O.J. 17, 26, 30, 38
Nippo-Balinese Ranch House movement 201
Nirartha, Dhang Hyang 73, *192*
Nuarta, Nyoman 190, 208
Nusa Dua Beach hotel 34, *44*

O
offering niche *171*
office-style see *kantor*-style
Oldroyd, Graham 122, 164
ornamentation 168, *169*, 169

P
Padangkerta *13*, *16*, 148; house gate *149*; *meten 149*; shrine *56*; temple *149*; wall *24*, *64*
padma 171
padmasari 56
paduraksa 26, 64, 68, *68*, 70, 76, *158*, 175
pagoda see *meru*
palaces see *puri*
palimanan 148
Palmer and Turner 201
Pandhi, Jimmy 78, 202
panggung agung 80
paon 30, *30*, 36, 90, 144
papalihan 152
paras 152, *152–55*; carving 170, *170–73*
paras batik 152
paras batu 148, 152, *153*, 154
paras bukit 156
paras sanggingan 152
paras taro 152, *155*
paras tempelan 152
paras ukir 152, *152*, *153*, 174
Parker, Glen 122
paruman 56
patra 182; *cina 182*; *mesir* 171
pavilion courtyards 25, 38
pavilion elements 85; air vents 112,

112–13; base 90, *90–91*; beams 96, *96–99*; buttresses 96, *96–99*; columns 96, *96–99*; construction 86, *87–89*; doors 110, *110–11*; king posts 114, *114–17*; platforms 102, *102–5*; post bases 94, *94–95*; roofs 54, *54–55*, 114, *114–17*; screens 106, *106–9*; steps 92, *92–93*; space division 122, *122–25*; space organization 118, *118–19*; steps 92, *92–93*; storage 120, *120–21*; walls 106, *106–9*; windows 112, *112–13*
pavilions 45; enclosed 50, *50–53*; hotel 34, *44*; house 30, *30–31*, 36, *47*; palace *44*; shrine *44*, 45, 47, 56, *56–57*; temple 24, 26, *26*, 28, *44*, 45, 47, 48; types, 46, *46*; village 18, *18*, *19*
payadnyan 56, 144, *170*
Payangan: palace gate *70*
payogan 56
pedanda 102; statues *191*
Peliatan: *bale bundar* 48
pelinggih 56, *56*, *57*
pemade 86
pementang 86, 114
pemucu 86
pemugbug bucu 116
Pengerebongan temple festival 74, *74*
penjor 180
Pertamina Padang Galak *212*
Pesamuan Ceramics 164
Petang village: bungalow *134*
Petanu River 152
petitis 110, *182*
pewedan 56, 80, 145
Phillipos 190
PJ's restaurant kitchen *53*
plangkiran 96; *gantung* 114
plaster 162, *162–63*
platforms see *taban*
pleasure gardens 32, *32*, 62
poleng 180, *180*
Pollok, Ni 202
pondok 144
Pont, Henri Maclaine 56
popolan see adobe
post bases 94, *94–95*
praba 56
Prinsic, Carl 210
procreation pavilion see *meten*
PT Wijaya Tribwana 20
public buildings (traditional) 18, *18–19*
Pura Batu Karo, Tabanan *19*, *28*; *taban* 102
Pura Batur 74; *bale lantang* 135, *138*; Chinese shrine *207*; gate 77, *134*; *taban* 102
Pura Beji, Sangsit 27, 90; carvings *152*, *153*; *sendi* 170; statue *192*; steps *92*
Pura Besakih 74, 76: courtyard 78; *kul-kul* tower *28*, *149*
pura dalem 25
Pura Dalem, Guwang: gate *195*

Pura Dalem, Kesiman: steps *74*
Pura Dalem, Pengerebongan: carving *174*, *175*
Pura Dalem Kepala, Kepawon: *gedong 189*; statue *193*
pura desa 25
Pura Desa, Guwang 26, *119*; gate *70*, *73*; pavilion *99*; shrine base *91*
Pura Desa, Ubud: *kori agung 154*
Pura Gunung Kawi bathing springs *27*; shrine *57*
Pura Jagatnata, Ketewel *27*; garden *38*; gate *27*; *meru 55*; shrines *147*
Pura Jati: wall *148*
Pura Kehen, Bangli 74, *76*
Pura Lingsar, Lombok: doors *111*; gate *69*
Pura Luhur, Uluwatu courtyard *81*; festival *29*; statue *192*
Pura Maospahit, Denpasar: *gedong 159*
Pura Mengwi: house temple *105*
Pura Pengerebongan, Kesiman *63*
Pura Peyogan Agung Ketewel *44*
pura prajapati 13
Pura Pulaki *104*, *149*; *bale payadnyan 104*; balustrade *183*; shrine *170*
Pura Puncak Penulisan: coursework *154*; *gedong 103*
pura puseh 25
Pura Puseh, Bayunggede *68*, *142*; *gedong 55*
Pura Puseh, Gaji *68*
Pura Puseh, Guwang *65*; gate *175*
Pura Puseh, Tenganan *12*, *28*, *44*, *56*, *77*
Pura Ratu Agung, Suwung Gede *156*
Pura Sakenan 156
Pura Tirta Empul, Tampaksiring *26*
Pura Ulun Swi *see* Pura Batur
Pura Uluwatu 156
puri 13, 18, 25; courtyards *10–11*, *25*, *32*, *32–33*, *64*, *80*, *90*
puri agung 25, 32
Puri Agung Jero Kuta 32
Puri Agung Kesiman: *merajan agung 81*
Puri Agung Klungkung 32
puri anyar 201
Puri Anyar, Gianyar: prince's verandah *32*
Puri Batubulan: gate *69*
Puri Denpasar: door *185*
Puri Ganesha *48*, *126*, *126*; *wantilan 96*
Puri Gede Karangasem 32, *32*, *162*, *163*; Boma *197*; courtyard *90*; gate *72*, *73*
Puri Gianyar 32
Puri Kanginan 32, *33*, *162*, *162*, *164*, *206*; carving *207*; ceiling *189*; Chinese pavilion *206*; statuary *190*
Puri Kesiman 32
Puri Mayura, Cakranegara *62*
Puri Mengwi *146*; air vents *165*
Puri Nyalian: carving *174*, *175*; shrine *115*
Puri Saraswati *33*

Puri Saren, Ubud *33*
Purser, Lisa 201
Purser, Warwick 201
Putri Champa Mausoleum 205

R

rab 85, 140
Rabik, Amir: house *59*
rafters *see* iga-iga
Rai, Ida Bagus 9
railings *178*, *178–79*
Rangda *192*
rice goddess, 17
rice lofts *see* lumbung
rice straw thatch *see* sumi
ridge covers *see* dore
roof plates *see* lambang
roofed gate *see* paduraksa
roofs 114, *114–17*; bamboo *138*, *139*; pavilion 45, 54, *54*, *55*
Rustic Charm movement *38*, *92*, 201, 202, 204, 205

S

Sai *172*, *189*, *194*, *194–97*
sakti 94
sampiyan gantung 180
Samuan Tiga temple, Bedulu: ceremonial pavilion *48*; gate *70*; *gedong 47*
sanggah 30, *30*; *agung* 180
Sanggingan 152
Sanur: temple compound *24*
Saraswati *192*
sashes 180
Sayan: house compound *31*; *wantilan 19*
screens 52, 106, *106–9*
Sebatu 158, 169, 184; *gedong 158*
Sempidi: shrine *170*
Sendangduwur: mosques 110
sendi 52, *84*, 85, 94, *94–95*, *135*; carved *170*, *171*, *190*, *190*, *192*
Serai hotel 20, *21*, *123*
seseh *59*, 134; pillars *52*; rafters 114
Shiva 13, 63, 180
shrine pavilions *see* gedong, pelinggih
shrines 63, *84*, 85, 86, *149*, *163*, *206*; carved *184*; hanging *114*; house *80*; temporary *145*
Sidemen, Pedanda 175
Silakarang 170
simbar 152
sindu-wisindu 190
singa 171, *172*, *183*, *185*, *190*, *192*
Singapadu: *bale agung* 18
Singaraja: house compound *31*
Sirait, Pintor 190, 213
sirap 134
slate 148, *149*
sleeping pavilion *see* meten
slit-drum *see* kul-kul

Songan 14, *17*, 148; gate *70*; *meru 55*
Spies, Walter 36, 58, 168, 201, 202
spirit house 45
split gate *see* candi bentar
stairs *see* steps
statuary *168*, 190, *190–93*
steps: gate 74, *74–77*, 161; pavilion 92, *92–93*; temples *149*
stone 148, *148–51*
storage *115*, 118
stylobate *see* bataran
Suarsa, Putu 41, 136, 205; bamboo house *109*
subak 17
subak temples 16
sugar palm fibre *see* ijuk
Sularto, Robi 190, 208
sumi 140, *141*
sun god 30
Surya 30
swastika *171*
Symon *127*, *128*

T

taban 68, 85, 102, *102–5*, 118
Tabanan: *bale loji 172*
tali ijuk 114
Taman Ayun Cultural Complex 158
Taman Ayun temple 206
Taman Bebek *122*; pavilion *52*; Presidential Suite *124–25*; window *113*
Taman Narmada: Fountain of Youth shrine *111*; *meten* 51; reception hall *179*
Taman Ujung water palace 32, *96*, 203
Tampaksiring: presidential palace 201; temple 18
Tan Hu Cin Jin 205
Tanjung Sari hotel 34, *34*, 36, 201, 202; statue *191*
Tantri *173*
taring 80
Taro 152, 158
tatakan tugeh 114
teba 30, 63, 80, *81*
temple: courtyards *24*, *25*, *26*, *26–27*; gardens 14; gates 14, 26, 64, 68, *68–73*, *111*, *134*, *141*, *158*, *172*, *174*, *175*, *195*; offerings *166–67*; steps *75*, *149*
temple of the dead *see* pura prajapati
temples 13, 14, 18; house 25, 30
temporary architecture 144, *144–47*
Tenganan 148, *148*; *bale agung* 18; house gate *77*; *lumbung 12*, *90*; offering niche *171*; pavilion-temple *51*; shrine *175*
terracing 74, *74–77*
terracotta 160, *160–61*
terrazzo 160, *160–61*
thatch 140, *140–43*
tiang 85
tiles 164, *165*

timber 134, *134–35*
Tirta Gunung Kawi, Sebatu *24*
Tirtagangga *190*; water palace *32*
tiying see bamboo
tourist village *14*
tradesmen *130–31*
Trowulan 158
Trunyan *15*, 110, 148; gate *76*
tugeh 85, 114, *114–17*, *184*
Turner 201
Tuttle, Ed 41, 122, 156, 213

U

Ubud village square *15*
Udayana, King 32
Uluwatu temple: gate *73*; steps *74*
umah 25
umbul-umbul 180
undagi 25, 32

V

Villa Angsa *80*; bamboo screen *107*
Villa Bebek *123*; air vent *176*; balustrade *179*; cottage *108*; courtyards *24*, *31*, *37*, *79*; doors *111*; garden *40*; gate decoration *152*; Javanese terrace *209*
Villa Kirana *37*, *40*; entrance tower *212*; painted wall *210*; staff house *58*; walkways *134*
Villa Tirta Ayu *127*, *127*
villages *12*, 13–14, *15–16*; lane *12*, 14; square 13, *15*, *17*, 18; temples 25
volcanic tuff *see* paras

W

walls 106, *106–9*; courtyard 64, *64–67*
wantilan 13, 18, *18*, *19*, 36, *42–43*, 45, 46, *46*, 118, 201; *bataran 90*; columns *96*, *97*; floor 118; roof 54, *117*; steps *92*
wantilan agung 10–11
warung 17, 30, 45, 144, *144*
Warung Mie restaurant *36*, *182*
Waworuntu, Judith 34, 36, 202
Waworuntu, Wija 34, 36, 201, 202
Wijana, Bagus Suryadarma 208
Wijaya, Made: projects 220
windows 112, *112–13*
winged lion *see* singa
Wisnu 13, 180, 190, *192*, *193*
wood carving 182, *182–87*
Wos River 152
woven elements 180, *180–81*

Y

Yokasara, Anak Agung 20, 152

Z

Zecha, Adrian 34, 41
Zieck, Hinke 164